SINS OF MY FATHER

Also by Lily Dunn

Shadowing the Sun

A Wild and Precious Life: A Recovery Anthology
(co-editor Zoe Gilbert)

SINS OF MY FATHER

A Daughter, a Cult, a Wild Unravelling

LILY DUNN

WEIDENFELD & NICOLSON

First published in Great Britain in 2022 by Weidenfeld & Nicolson,
an imprint of The Orion Publishing Group Ltd
Carmelite House, 50 Victoria Embankment
London EC4Y 0DZ

An Hachette UK Company

1 3 5 7 9 10 8 6 4 2

Some parts of this book were previously published as the following essays
Aeon: 'The Lost Children', 'The Joy of Intimacy'
Granta: 'The Fog and the Sea', 'It's Only Skin'
Hinterland: 'Waiting for God'

A CIP catalogue record for this book is
available from the British Library.

ISBN (Hardback) 978 1 4746 2327 8
ISBN (Export Trade Paperback) 978 1 4746 2328 5
ISBN (eBook) 978 1 4746 2330 8
ISBN (Audio) 978 1 4746 2339 1

Typeset by Input Data Services Ltd, Somerset

Printed and bound in Great Britain by Clays Ltd, Elcograf, S.p.A.

MIX
Paper from
responsible sources
FSC® C104740

www.weidenfeldandnicolson.co.uk
www.orionbooks.co.uk

For Jane and Ben

Time present and time past
Are both perhaps present in time future,
And time future contained in time past.

T.S. Eliot, 'Burnt Norton', *Four Quartets*

Contents

Prologue

I imagine that the fog had lifted, that it was a bright morning when my father finally dragged himself from his bed. He found his dressing gown on the chair, but didn't bother with slippers, despite the broken cassette cases jagged across the floor. His cat Hope was circling the room, meowing for food and flicking her tail at his inertia, but he had become bad at listening. He might have blamed it on his new girlfriend, the groggy mornings and his disrupted routine. Late at night she would pour him another drink, or disappear to her mum's hilltop house, Nirvana blasting to hell. She only had to fall out of bed and pull on her coat five minutes before her shift at the People Store at ten. How lucky she must have felt to have caught my father that first day he shuffled into the store to buy himself a single steak; an English writer and publisher with money and a pretty house on Bolinas's main drag. He still found it peculiar to see her and not his wife in his bed and despised her for it. 'You're back,' he muttered, thick-tongued and crabby, uncertain in that moment who he saw.

For most of the night, from the cassette player by the bed, he would cling to his guru's songs of synthetic wisdom as if he were grasping at the last threads of his life '. . . *like a house which is in darkness, and many spiders are living, their nests, and its scorpions are living and the snakes are enjoying and suddenly you bring light there* . . .' But he so rarely saw the light these days, just as he would not have heard the storm, so quick and unexpected; how the skies snapped open and dumped a sea of rain onto the dry streets, and the collarless dogs barked a thunderclap when it suddenly stopped. Just as he failed to see the glass antique shade that was broken from that fight he would rather forget, the photos of his not yet ex-wife face down, her fine Swiss crockery pushed to the back of the kitchen shelf; everything dusty and out of place. He did not recognise the power of the sun as it cut through the curtain, insistent here in California, so bright and relentless, despite the recent sadness of the house. Did he feel its warmth on his back? He did not want to.

I was not there that portentous day in 2003, when he tripped so spectacularly into his final freefall, but I had visited the year before. It was his first Christmas in the house and without his wife. He had chosen this place and she had not liked it, and after twenty years of marriage she had left. It was too bohemian with its wayward souls hanging about. The man outside the community centre who when greeted with 'How are you?' tells you, 'I don't know', bemused. A woman with stripes of chocolate cake like tribal marks across her cheeks, strings of oranges around her neck, clothes made of silver foil. The legendary Tree House John, a Vietnam veteran who had drowned his trauma in alcohol and later meth, who earned his name from spending years living in a treehouse with a group of Bolinas flower people. My father had been drawn back to a community, a theme in his life since boarding school, only this one was full of crazies, drop-outs, drug addicts and drunks.

Yet he was proud of his house. It was the first he had owned since he left us in our Islington home, my mother, with my brother and me aged eight and six. He had been on a crusade since then, from Pune, in India, where he'd met his guru, to Rajneeshpuram in Oregon, to Italy, where he ran a community, to various apartments in Hampstead during brief returns to London, and then to Marin County, when he was awarded a Green Card for his publishing and packaging company that produced books that were popular with West Coast hippies,

The Art of Peace and *Illustrated Rumi*. Despite the sweat on his brow and his restless fingers, he had finally settled: a two-storey, wood-panelled and white house, tucked away behind eucalyptus and willow, with a wooden porch and gauze door, a big white fence, which, for a time, protected him from what lay outside. A refuge where he could finally stop, withdraw from the world and write.

Like his wife, I found Bolinas oppressive and suffocating. Just twenty miles north of San Francisco, it was a town in hiding, with one way in, one way out, at the end of an estuary, bounded by seawater on all sides. A community of industrious and indignant locals, hostile to outsiders, its motto was: 'Live and let live – just leave us alone'. The residents tore down street signs as they were put up and blacked out road markings: artists, musicians and writers lived in their clapboard houses in the hills; financial crisis fallouts escaped here to camp in their cars. Part of its culture was the acceptance of those who were not welcome elsewhere. Once embedded in this town, it was difficult to leave. So apposite, it seems now, that the first house my father committed to buying after all those years was right next door to Smiley's, the town's only bar.

On that bright morning once the fog had lifted, I imagine him drifting from room to room, unaware of the empty wine bottles stacked up by the sink, and last night's attempt at dinner crusted on saucepans and plates. He did not see Hope as she curled around his legs and urged him towards the food larder. Blindly, he searched for one of his cordless phones, in their various states of charge, buried in the sofa, flashing with a message: perhaps his wife had rung again, late, after everyone slept, or that morning before he was awake. She phoned him still, so many times each day; he could rely on her to wish him goodnight.

Then he sat down in his Harrods bathrobe, now worn and stained, settled at his computer, its wink of bright light his link to the living world – the world that was awake – hoping, always, for recognition. His eyes were puffy and tired; he rubbed his coarse white- and ginger-flecked beard. There was a time when he would receive gushy emails from his agent in response to various proposals, but not anymore. He was trying to sell a book on war, another on sex, and the beginnings of a more personal idea – *Dousing the Flame*, a memoir about his alcoholism. He had recently finished a novel, a love letter to his wife who returns as a ghost to watch over him, but the publishers didn't get it – *arseholes*. Faced with rejection, he rose up, pushed back, sent stroppy emails. Those big-shot editors he had brought in favours for – the guys at Knopf and HarperCollins – could *fuck off*.

Did my father see the heaps of papers that will have piled up on his desk by now? Bills left unopened, demands for payments on the house, which was mortgaged to the hilt, HP on the big SUV that sat like a bully in the drive; credit-card bills for his expensive new teeth and pricy restaurants when his new girlfriend dined out with her friends on my father's dime; the rent of his wife's apartment in New York – thousands of dollars a month – which he still paid for, despite her going to bed each night with a new man, a scion of American aristocracy. Did he taste the stale booze on his morning breath, see the age spots on his hands? Could he hear the chattering tourists, fat on hash browns and maple syrup pancakes from Coast Café across the way, meandering along Wharf Road? Bolinas Beach had been a draw when he first arrived, but on foggy days the long flat stretch of muddy sand reminded him of his parents in misery in their last years, bitten by the cold and concrete of Felpham Beach, in Bognor Regis. Did he see the glass balanced precariously on top of his unopened mail, its base sticky with that last regretful dribble of wine? He will itch with his need to fill it again.

This particular morning he chose instead to rest his eyes on an email. His guru's words still bubbling up from his dreams: '*Suddenly you bring light there,*' his honey-warm lisp. '*The light does not clear the spiders and the scorpions and the snakes but it makes you aware of them and it is good to be aware . . . Because then the house can be cleaned.*' Perhaps these words made Dad laugh, with a wafty memory of all those orange-clad devotees nodding and smiling into the sun, hanging everything, their families, their homes, their entire lives, on words that were simply plucked from the sky. The power of miracles. Or did he suddenly feel irritated? 'Arrogant twit' he might have said, the ridiculousness of his guru's gilded ride.

I imagine him squinting and then putting on his glasses. How a shaft of light struck the blinds so hard that it painted lines through the room stabbing pain through his eyes, dust motes hanging like warnings, abandoned manuscripts, torn paper, crossed-out words. He heard a hard thump from the ceiling above, and a crying out for his attention, followed by a curdling laugh, and felt a stab of irritation at the woman's coarseness, so extremely different from his beautiful wife, who *was* still his wife despite being thousands of miles away. He was suddenly exhausted, abandoned. *How am I going to get out of this hellhole?* Turning towards the comfort of his computer screen, my dad clicked on the email:

I am Abram Ivanov, Barrister to a Late Engineer S Dunn who bears your last name and came from your country. On 22nd January 2003, our late client, his wife and their only daughter were involved in a car accident and it was a pity that our late client and his family all lost their lives.

After much search, I have traced you as his next of kin and need you to help me repatriate the property and fund that belongs to my client above, which is valued at 8.5 million USD, before it is turned back, unclaimed, to the state. Do please contact me directly on my private email address below.

What did he do then? Did he stand up and take the empty glass to the kitchen, his cat Hope, still not fed? Did he feed her, or himself first? I know he was drinking then, but I don't know if the morning drinking had started yet. Judging by the speed of his decline over the following years, let's imagine it had. He walked to the fridge and took out a bottle of chilled white wine he had bought at the Coast Café the previous night, paying restaurant prices without a second thought. He never dined there but waved his credit card over the counter after the People Store had closed. He expanded with the first sip; he literally grew; it helped him feel stronger, bigger, a Messiah, his previous incarnation as Attila the Hun.

Back at his desk he was pumped up when he read the email again. *Next of Kin. Property that must not go back to the state.* The fucking state. *S. Dunn.* Ha! *8.5 million dollars.* At fucking last. 'About time,' he said out loud and took another swig.

Like a child in a sweetshop, my dad had eyes only for sugar-coated wealth, the fantasy of becoming a millionaire. A desire that had become increasingly ridiculous to everyone but himself. My father had spent his entire life dodging debt, moving money between buried bank accounts, selling off cars before he had paid for them, putting my mother's name on rental agreements after their divorce so that final demands arrived on *our* doorstep. He understood the scammer mentality, but remained the scammer's ideal victim, since his whole existence relied on the delusion that he was special, more cultivated, planetary, cosmic than anyone else. So, when my brother and I would later confront him, laughing with disbelief that he had fallen for this scam, he would bat us away. Of course he had a long-lost relative that no one knew about; of course this idiot relative had died with no known next of kin. These things happen to me. I am the Master, the enlightened. I am telepathic. I can walk through walls. He was not normal like everyone else; he had supernatural powers. The usual rules did not apply. Goddam it. He deserved this!

My father fixed his eyes on the email. He refused to come down from such elevated heights. He would not glance at his hands as he moved the mouse to hit the cursor on reply, nor see the small hook of want – of greed or desperation – that had buried itself in his shoulder move down his arm to his knuckles, playing his fingers like strings, tapping out his response. Was it really in the morning? Had there been a storm? Was he drunk, or simply a lonely, deluded fool?

It has been thirteen years since my father died. I measure it by my daughter's age, and she is almost fourteen. He died six months after she was born. So much has happened in between, and yet I still hear the echoes, pulling me to return, to try to understand the raging disaster – how it could have gone so catastrophically wrong. The scam, my father's wilful misreading of a situation that appeared so clear to everyone else; and my passivity in the aftermath, letting him stumble towards his death. The tragic irony of just the five of us at Dad's cremation: me, my brother, my mother, her sister and my brother's wife, standing in a circle on the concrete in that desolate place in Devon, which meant nothing to any of us. I use the past tense now, because it was a brief hiatus, between the end of his life and the urgent persistence of his afterlife. My brother had been forced to cut off all contact from our dad in the months before he died. But that day we had laughed – the frantic, suffocating, shameful laugh that bursts through the nose and spasms the throat. We laughed for Dad, his disbelief that somehow when he wasn't looking this calamity had happened. He would have been flabbergasted. *That's me, in this Godforsaken place? In that coffin? You have got to be kidding.* His overblown swagger and grandiose self-belief protected him right to the end.

The funeral director had a sympathetic nobility despite her appearance. Her matt of brown hair stuck with sweat to her forehead, her exaggerated features resembling Tubbs from *The League of Gentlemen*. She stood, short and stout, at the centre of the circle we five made, in her A-line black skirt and shiny shoes, calves the size of melons, solemn and apologetic: 'He was a big man–' She paused, and my brother's face went ashen. 'We had to wheel him in on a trolley.' I felt sick with hysteria. But we were grateful to her when she spoke so gently: 'How many of us can know that there will be five people who love us so much that they would be there at the very end?' With those words she took away the desperate surrealism of this, so ridiculously subdued after such a momentous life.

But Dad was with me the entire time. His spectre, the dream of the person I had hoped he might grow old to be, wealthy still in his cashmere coat, expensive slippers, and the bulk of his strong back, hovering there beside me with his long beard and luxuriant hair, like a mythological god. I was always so romantic about him. His eyes were pleading as he listened intently to my reading of the poem he had penned, I don't remember it now – *something about wings; blackened wings* – and the song we chose for when they wheeled the trolley out, Lou Reed, perhaps, and an easy tone of a life led to the full, by his own lights, burned out now, snuffed like a candle blown out. I leaned towards him, comforted by what I believed to be benign, and he whispered to me again, as he had that night in Italy: *You understand me, my daughter. The only person who knows me.* Aged twelve with my scabbed-up knee from losing control of my scooter, left alone on that lonely road. I didn't know what he meant then – was I special? Did I see all of him? More than anyone else? But this was Devon, not Italy, and he was no longer alive. It was cold and damp, and the circle of us was so small, so sad in the blank and grey.

Of course my husband wasn't there. He had stayed in London with our baby daughter because she had a cold, but the truth is that I didn't want him to bring her; I didn't want my precious daughter anywhere near him. Not even when he was still alive. My mother's husband wasn't there either. He was unwell, a rare thing. We joked, the five of us, of how Dad must have made this happen: drifting up above on his puffy cloud, a bolt of lightning in his hand, striking down any male competition, or spearing the front door at the last minute to prevent it from opening.

I was determined in the following years that he should not touch our lives, that my children would be free of him. But I had no idea when I walked from the crematorium that day, turning my back to the smoke that curled from the furnace, that he had followed me; and when I got into the car, he got in with me. He visited my dreams, lying beside me in the dark, such tender sweetness as he reached out and touched my arm. He was so vividly there, and I drowned in tears often waking myself in the dead of night from sobbing, my husband unable to offer comfort. He followed me in those many nights that refused to end, when I wandered through London streets sodden with booze, spilling and splitting, buttons popping, my skin bursting; everything flooding out on a midnight wall beside the dustbins at Shoreditch Church; those strangers I hugged in the dark. I was determined that my children would not be touched by this.

But then they were.

Aged six and eight, the same ages that my brother and I were when our father walked out, my marriage broke down. It was impossible, after years of trying. Such unfathomable silence. I had retreated, until he had only a sliver of me, and then I slipped away.

Now here I stand in my brand-new kitchen, in a new city, with a new man, and children who are settled and happy, and I at times let myself imagine that I am healed. But in the simple moments, making supper for my family, listening to music and drinking a glass of wine, my dad has slipped into its syrupy poison, threatening ruin. I want to see clearly and yet I am compelled still to smudge the edges, to wipe grease over the surfaces.

But something has changed: the wine is beginning to make me heavy, and its blurriness, once enjoyable, now brings a headache, a feeling that I have done wrong; that *I* am wrong. When my partner and I talk into the evening my laughter is tainted by this feeling; when I kiss my son goodnight my breath is heavy with it. Sometimes, I tighten my lips, so the acid of my shame won't burn him; so he won't be touched by this contaminant that I can still consume despite it having killed my father. I am so aware of it now, of the glass set on the counter and how much is left, as I put it to my lips, of each and every sip, of how readily the liquid slips down. I deliberate over another glass. Despite it taking me a week to drink a bottle, I bury it in the recycling bin, the glint of it winking like a warning fire. Shame, 'the swampland of the soul' as Jung describes it, has escaped from my depths, and on its hands and knees it has determinedly crawled towards standing. It grips hold of my heart now and it squeezes.

One evening, I am on the phone to my brother: 'I will not read your book about Dad,' he tells me. He does not understand why I keep bringing our father right back into the centre of the lives we have so carefully curated despite him.

'That's okay,' I say, over and over. 'I understand.' I keep saying it, even though I can feel upset flapping about inside me like an injured bird.

'It is your story, not mine,' he says calmly. 'I don't want to go back into it again.'

'Honestly, it's fine.' But my voice is shaking. I am causing trouble again.

'It's not okay, Lil. What he did.'

'I know,' I say. Of course, I know. But I also know that we tell ourselves the same stories, those necessary fictions, in order to survive, and sometimes the stories become old and stale, and sometimes they were never right in the first place. 'But—' I want to say, what if we misunderstood him? What if my going back will be better for everyone, not just me, but for you as well, and Mum? – What if? *The only person who knows me.* My father said this to me. He gave me that gift to try. Time present and time past, both present now.

His ghost rises within me again, and I grip the kitchen counter to stay upright. I hold my breath against my tears, those demanding tears, and feel suddenly so small. I glance around at the kitchen and its shiny counters, at my partner there beside me, but it is all too grown up. I am too young to live here, to have this man by my side.

Into the evening, we slowly go. We wipe the dirt from the counters and sweep the dust from the floor, and I touch the surfaces of my new life. I stand at the centre of the room and remind myself of how far we have come, how broken we were when we arrived.

'Is it right?' I ask him. 'Am I doing the right thing?'

He smiles down at me and pulls me to him. 'How could you not?' he says.

Exile

Where did it begin? my father wrote in a scrappy notebook. He was then in the last months of his life, having lost his wife, his girl-friend, his home, his computer, his desk, his books, his cat, his right to be a US citizen. Three years had elapsed since the email, the scam, then his fleecing by Russians who took his money and gave him nothing in return, but a stripping bare of his soul that prefigured his fall into destitution.

I picture him alone on that bench on the seafront in Ilfra-combe, Devon, the last place he ever lived. His hair is limp and tired, clothes soiled, and the salt wind in his face causes his eyes to stream. My father had no teeth in his final years, all extracted by an expensive dentist in San Francisco who persuaded him to have a bridge, before the money ran out and his mouth turned in on itself, a perpetual downward curve of misery. I imagine the shopfronts behind him were worn and rusted, their canopies tattered from the wind, seagull shit on everything. *The town is full of people, doing,* he wrote. *Wish I was doing rather than waiting.*

He was always waiting, for the postman to arrive with a care package from his now ex-wife – Swiss chocolate wrapped up beautifully in tissue paper and ribbon, silk hankies from SAKS for his streaming nose, slips of money. For Dean from the local cab firm who bought him bottles of Jack Daniels from the off-licence with money that was supposed to be spent on food. A phone call from 'one of my two ex-wives' – the other is my mother. A phone call from me, or from my brother, when he will ask for money which we wire over, until we finally refuse. He waits for his life to come good again. For the agents to reply to his emails, the publishers to say yes to his proposals. Always, for money to arrive.

Or he may have been in the dry house, or one of the B&Bs he moved between when the dry house threw him out for drinking. He sits on the edge of the pink polyester-frilled bed and writes these unfocused words:

> *Where and when did it begin?*
> *Some might utter sentences of despair –*
> *Can't say myself! Was it when I was born?*
> *Maybe at conception? Go the other way – I'm 60 now.*
> *Maybe it started at 50? Or, or, or?*
> *In California, London, in my heart, in hers?*

My brother and I knew that he asked himself this question in his lucid moments: How did it happen? How did such a rich and good life end up here? My father staring out at the blank of the seaside town out of season, numb to the rain that winter, and the fierce lonely wind.

Where and when did it begin?

My aunt, his sister, herself a sober alcoholic with the help of Alcoholics Anonymous, always used to say he was born that way, that his self-destruct trigger boiled down to a simple malfunctioning gene. But he was born many things, and there were many doors leading to many different corridors, to many different rooms. Perhaps it was the narcissist in him that led him this way, setting fire to everything in his wild impatience to transcend the ordinary, to be special. But what a fall, to end up here, a derelict drunk with nothing. Still making up stories to avoid the reality of what was happening.

In those last months, he kept fiddling with the proposal for his memoir, *Dousing the Flame, Journals of Alcoholism*. The opening line: 'This is the personal story of a man who once struggled with alcoholism and fought back to return his life to normal again, having faced the destruction of his emotional and professional existence.' I see him drinking while typing, so far gone in his denial, revelling in the drama and placing himself as the hero at its centre. This document is so full of lies I can barely bring myself to read it. He cannot even be honest in his memoir. On one of the final pages, he writes about how he lives alone now with his adorable Abyssinian cat, both back in the UK. His great return, to his country of origin, his family, to all that matters to him in this particular fantasy. But Hope had not made it back with him. She had stayed too long, been too loyal, and it had killed her. He failed to feed her just as he barely fed himself, and she had eventually curled up beneath a tree and died.

One rainy day, in 2013, when I was still married but wild in my grief, I returned to Ilfracombe. I wanted to see where my father had lived during those desperate last months of his life, after being deported back from the US in a wheelchair, and with nothing to his name but his Mulberry shoulder bag and Panerai watch. The Benevolent Society had settled his $100,000+ medical bill, run up with no insurance, and had put him on a flight back home, and my brother, mother and her sister had met him off the plane. We had been told he was very ill, and it had been my aunt's idea to take my dad to Devon to be nursed back to health in the cottage hospital where she worked. But on arrival Dad appeared to have made a speedy recovery and quickly discharged himself to set off on his last careening run. My aunt was also trying to protect my brother and me: I was nine months pregnant at the time, with my first child; and he had two children aged under six. We were scared of Dad turning up on our doorstep, and still had nightmares about our rescue trip to California the year before, when, out of his head, he had prowled through the night, thumping into furniture and slamming doors, and we stared into the dark, the two of us sharing the spare bed. 'We have no room for him,' my brother and I repeated, as if trying to convince ourselves.

But with a brand-new baby, I had not seen my dad during those last months of his life and so I wanted to return. My aunt invited me to stay with her in South Molton, so I left my husband and our two children back in London and took the car. I drove wildly along the motorway, the windscreen wipers slapping streams of water from my vision, the sky darkening the closer I got to Devon. I wanted to search out the gay couple who owned the B&B where Dad eventually died, and delivered orders of boiled eggs whenever he demanded it; vodka, scones and jam, more vodka. When my dad had blacked out in the shower, drunk, and the house shook with the weight of him falling, they went up to his room to help. I wanted to say thank you for caring; but also, I wanted to stand close enough to share the same breath with those people who were the last to see my father alive. Did he still have a glint in his eye in those final weeks, convincing them of his impending wealth, flashing that silver tongue, hundreds of thousands of dollars owed by Chronicle Books and St Martin's Press for manuscripts that he would never write? My aunt still tells the story of how he demanded she take him to the local bank on that first day she met him at the airport, and she wheeled him in. How, despite his dereliction, he managed to demand an appointment with the manager, a decent country man who had never seen his like and was bamboozled into giving him a loan of £1,000 set on the promise of an American contract about to be signed. I wanted to understand how he could still have that magic, even when his shoes were so broken they let the rain in.

The last time I had seen my dad was the morning of our flight home from California in October 2005, a few months after my wedding, when, recently showered, his shaking hand had moved a strand of wet hair from his forehead and he had promised he would go to AA. I only half believed him. I had taken his hands in mine and said: 'Make sure this isn't the last time I see you,' knowing in my heart that it was.

'But you're pregnant,' my brother had said each time I expressed my anguish during the following year at not helping him. I held the mound of my stomach with both hands and made promises to my unborn baby: *I will protect you whatever happens.* But I still had his daily calls coming in at odd hours, his quiet laughter at the absurdity of it all, his pleading for money, and my desperate piecing together of the silences in between. *Keep it simple: wash hair; body clean* were the words he repeated in that scrappy notebook. Perhaps the owners of the B&B did see through the lies, glimpsed the wretched man beneath. I find this more painful to admit to. Their caring of him came from a deep sense of humanity.

From the list of B&Bs where Dad had been, I headed first to Stumbles Inn, the last place he stayed, but there was nothing but boarded-up houses, damp from sea spray. No sign of the gay couple when I asked a local newsagent. They were long gone. Another business failed after a harsh winter; another dream thwarted.

Disappointed, I moved to the next on the list, the Pack o'Cards, a grand Georgian folly that sits on the road to Combe Martin, triangular with multiple chimneys to literally resemble a house of cards. Built in the seventeenth century by local squire George Ley to celebrate his huge winnings in a card game, there were four floors to represent the four suits, thirteen doors and fireplaces on each floor (representing the number of cards in each suit) and fifty-two stairs (the number of cards in a pack). Our father would have found this place absurd and thrilling. I sat in the cavernous bar, its walls covered in memorabilia, and watched a group of locals, rowdy in the afternoon, finding refuge from the dark waves of autumn rain. Quietly, when reception was empty, I snuck up the stairs to a long corridor of shadow and white where doors were left open to rooms plump from their recent spruce and vacuum. A four-poster bed with peachy eiderdown and fluffed-up pillows, nylon lace curtains diaphanous and ghostly. It was dim in the rain-soaked afternoon light. There was another room, further down the corridor, not yet cleaned, its duvet half on and half off the bed. An empty glass on the bedside table, the smudge of a fingerprint. The room smelled sour, of sleeping strangers.

Standing in the doorway, I conjured an image of my dad propped up on pillows, drink in one hand and remote control in the other; his socks rolled into a ball, thrown into the corner. I grasp at this image now to imagine where he was in those last hours, and I have summoned it so many times that it has solidified as memory: how he lies awkwardly on the floor, still holding the TV remote control, only his cheek is resting on the acrylic carpet, one trouser leg bunched up to reveal milk-white skin pocked with scabs. He is dead.

His story ended in a room like this, alone in a B&B in Ilfracombe in April, on the week of his sixty-first birthday, when my daughter's life had just begun.

But in that moment on my return, he stirs. He comes alive, and I am able to be with him one last time. I hear words from a T.S. Eliot poem, '. . . *be still and wait without hope/For hope would be hope for the wrong thing . . . But the faith and the love and the hope are all in the waiting . . .*' and walk over to him. 'Do you mind?' I ask politely kneeling on the bed. When he turns to me, he smiles, his rheumy eyes full of regret, and I become a daughter again, lying beside him with my head on his chest. I can hear his heartbeat, slow and juddering like a much-loved car hanging on. He puts his hand on my shoulder and it is heavy and warm. I allow myself to hope: what if he turns it all around and gets better again? '*So the darkness shall be the light, and the stillness the dancing.*'

I feel so close to him. 'Dad,' I say, with the first of the tears stinging my eyes. 'What happened?'

Let's imagine, as psychoanalysts have explored, that we as infants are 'born into trauma'. That our birth causes the first of many deep anguishes, separated as we are from our mother and the lulling liquid warmth of her womb. According to both Otto Rank and Freud, birth is the earliest anxiety that a person experiences, and a kind of blueprint for all that follows. The psychoanalyst Wilfred Bion takes this idea further by suggesting that pain is also experienced in the rough sea of sensations that the baby feels, the undifferentiated feeling states he calls 'unthought thoughts' and sense impressions before actual thinking comes into being. The infant, according to Bion, is consumed by a maelstrom of chaos which resembles death, and relief is found only in the mother's arms; a mother strong enough to take these bursts of turmoil into herself in order to define them and give her child the language and understanding to overcome them. Without this, according to Bion, the child risks growing to hate the emotions that run through him or her, such madness, such mayhem, and sets out to live life rid of such chaos, and to not think at all.

I have often observed people in a drunk or drugged-up state, at illegal raves, all-night clubs, in friends' living rooms, and been struck by how like a baby they become; how they regress to that neonate state of no thought, numb of emotion; losing control of speech, all sense, even their limbs, as if regressing back to that safe paradisal place before the violence began, when anything was possible.

In those last years of drinking, my dad shrunk on a diet of vodka and scones, became incontinent, his shit everywhere, eventually so disconnected from himself that he would vomit in the morning only to start drinking again. In the end, he turned in on himself like a helpless embryo, and returned to the hazy watery world from where he began.

My father was born in 1946, in Cranford, Hounslow, on the outskirts of west London, landing into a world of net curtains and wall-to-wall carpets, the hush of the mundane, where neighbours competed for the latest model washing machine. Material status was important to his parents, as if their self-conscious display of wealth and order might smother the shame they were trying to shake off. His father was from an aspirational middle-class family and had saved his mother from her working-class roots and the stain of adultery. As a teenager and beauty queen, she was first married to her agent, who then repeatedly cheated on her, and gave her VD; but in a moment of vulnerability she had turned to his cousin for comfort, and it was her adultery on the divorce certificate that was the cause of the irretrievable break-up.

Shame came knocking again when my grandfather got her pregnant on their first weekend away, and my dad was conceived. They covered it up by quickly getting engaged. He was her ticket to redemption, and this young woman jumped at the chance of a second marriage. He was happy to oblige, as he was smitten with her, the beautiful telephonist on the switchboard at Sperry Gyroscope in Bracknell, where he worked as a senior engineer, her soft and big-eyed face, neat calves and curved ankles in stockings, his very own Betty Grable. But his mother did not approve of her son marrying a divorcee and refused to attend their wedding. He had suffered his own trauma when aged eight his young father had suddenly died in the influenza epidemic, leaving behind his mother and five children. She never got over it, and when my dad and aunt visited their grandmother she always seemed to be in bed, cursed with the depression of grief.

My dad's mum had a difficult pregnancy with him, morning sickness so terrible she had to be hospitalised and put on a drip; it was as if she were vomiting her baby away. She shrank, reduced to a slip of a thing, with a magnificent mountain protruding from her tiny waist. When he was finally born, she was astounded that she had managed to give birth to this huge baby, over nine pounds in weight. He was beautiful, with bright blue eyes and a wisp of blonde hair, and a quality that made the nurses stop and sigh. In a letter to her husband from hospital she is full of passion and gratitude. 'You gave me a boy!' Finally old wounds could heal. She was accepted even by her mother-in-law who was thrilled to have been presented with a grandchild.

A natural extrovert who was made for the stage with her film-star looks, my dad's mother loved the attention her son brought her. She would push him in his pram down the street like a prince in his carriage, his own striking beauty sending passing women into raptures. 'Isn't he adorable,' they would croon, and she would smile as if the compliment belonged to her. He learned quickly that pleasure could be gained from these strangers with their lipsticked smiles, and that he had a certain power to make women soften. But it was an ambivalent pleasure, one he sought out but also reviled. He was shy and fragile in temperament and must have felt exposed in his pram with the admiring faces peering in, as he often pulled his blanket up and over his head.

I am reminded of Ted Hughes's *Tales from Ovid* and his version of Echo and Narcissus:

> Gossips
> Came to Tiresias: 'Can her boy live long
> With such perfect beauty?'
> The seer replied: 'Yes, unless he learns to know himself.'
> All regarded these words as a riddle –
> Till time solved them with a strange madness.

Was my father's fate written in his childhood beauty and the adoration he received from others?

My grandmother was house proud. She meticulously cleaned her home, but also had a lady visit three times a week. In the last years of my grandparents' life when they had grown nasty to each other, she turned mad by the wind in their seaside cul-de-sac, and he frustrated and blind, my granny told my mum that one of her main regrets was that she had spent so much time plumping up cushions, so many hours she could have enjoyed with friends and family. She was a powerful character who needed to feel wanted, and because she had worked from girlhood, she took on her role of mother and housewife with the same efficiency. For the four years before her second child was born, my grandmother's focus was on my dad, who she dressed up in rompers and frills and paraded along the Sussex coastline. She loved to tell a story about how he was surprisingly empathetic for a child so young. When they took him to meet one of his father's uncles who had a growth on his face, they were concerned about how he might react to the deformity, that he might be scared or say something hurtful. Instead he reached up to the man and touched the growth and said: 'Does it hurt?' Such a wonderful boy, her golden child, her prodigal son. He who was good and obedient, lived by the house rules and never got his feet dirty. Such a long drop from such vaulted heights. He would do anything to avoid conflict, whereas his sister stood up to her mother and fought back.

My granny's happiest years were after her return to work, once her two children had grown up, selling Hotpoint washing machines at Debenhams and then on the shop floor at Bobby's in Bognor Regis, beautifully dressed and perfumed, her hair set in perfect waves. When we visited my grandparents on a Sunday with our mother even after my father had left, she would serve us small pots of trifle and fruit salad in jelly and, standing in her immaculately fitted dress, would act out stories from her week at work, or relay gossip, while I imagined the bustling shop floor, the *cha-ching* of the cash register, the canned applause of *Are You Being Served?*

My father never spoke of any of these things, of his parents, of his childhood, so there is much that I have to piece together from what I knew of them and from what his sister now tells me. I do know that throughout his life he felt ambivalent about his mother's love, which was intense, adoring but also critical. My aunt remembers terrible fights in the house when they were growing up – their dad fleeing and their mum slamming cupboard doors and sulking, withdrawing her love when she didn't get her way. 'Like a four-year-old,' she recalls. Sometimes the sulking went on for days. When their dad returned home after one of these rows, their mum would ignore him until he grovelled in regret, terrified of upsetting her again, and this is how the pattern continued. She would turn to her son for reassurance, my father being just a child. With her head hung low, she went mournfully to his room and interrupted his play to sit on his bed and re-enact her grievances and ask for his love. He was young and innocent in his adoration still and would wrap his arms around her neck.

'I don't want to hear about it!' My grandmother would hold up her palm when faced with anything she didn't agree with or found distasteful. She also couldn't face pain. When my brother and I went to visit them once around the time our parents separated, I could not stop crying. I don't know why. Maybe I missed my mum; or maybe staying with my grandparents reminded me too much of my dad who had recently run away to a faraway place called India. My granny, impatient with me, or perhaps finding my crying unbearable, banished me to the garden. I remember facing the hedge on the front drive and crying and heaving, trying to repress the tears and catch my breath, too confused by her response to knock on the front door to ask to go back in. Was it her nervous disposition? Her husband soon learned that it was easier always to keep certain truths from her. Years later, he never told her that he had discovered that his son, my dad, had forged his signature on a bank loan he had previously refused to help him with. This was in the years after my dad left us and was scrabbling for money to spend more time at the ashram with his guru. His father was furious and it was confirmation that his son couldn't be trusted, so much so that he took him off his will as sole executor. He told his wife none of this. When we played board games with our grandparents as children, around their brown-tinted glass coffee table with its *Woman's Weekly* and *Radio Times* on the shelf beneath, my granddad would cheat to let my granny win and she would be delighted as if the achievement was legitimately her own.

When my father was just seven, he was sent away to a prep boarding school, Long Close in Slough, absurdly only ten miles away from where they lived. It was 1953. My aunt wonders if this removal came about because their dad was worried about the intensity of their mum's love of her son, bordering on possessiveness: perhaps he wanted to separate them, jealous and wanting his wife back? But most likely boarding school was the ultimate statement that they had clambered up a social rung, never mind that they could barely afford it. My father's gender came at a cost: denied the comfort of home and a day school which his sister could enjoy simply because she was a girl. He was the boy and had the power to assure the family's place in the middle class by going to the right school and getting the right job. There were high expectations for my father to become a doctor or a lawyer, and his mum was desperate still to erase her own working-class roots.

If we imagine, then, that birth is the first touch of trauma, the first piercing of what was previously whole, and the loving arms of a mother might then cushion the small disillusionments that follow, reminding us of the primal unity that we associate with pleasure, then this was my father's first fall. He was cast out. His expectation of family and home was suddenly violated. The golden dawn of his childhood was over.

My dad rarely spoke of his time at boarding school, and so I barely thought of it before I had children of my own. But my son, now aged eleven, regularly expresses his horror at the idea. 'Would you ever make me go?' searching my eyes for some hidden secret plan. 'I would kill myself if I had to leave you.' The thought is so far from my mind, it is difficult to even imagine it. Mainly, because I know it would cause him harm. I would go as far as to say that his sudden exile from what is rightfully his, a family's protection and unconditional love, would feel to him like a death. But my dad was not eleven when he was first sent away, he was seven.

A sensitive and empathetic child, up until this point my father had drifted in the river of his life, his home his anchor. He could take this for granted; he knew nothing else. I have photographs of a long-limbed, bony boy with huge blue eyes, flowery lips, and a blonde sweep of hair. While his sister grins with spirit, my father has a more forlorn expression, caught in the liminal space of his dreams. This was my father, free to be himself because he was surrounded by people who loved him.

Like so many other boys sent to prep school for the first time, my dad had no idea what was coming to him when he sat on the edge of his bed and watched his mother pack his trunk. His parents probably told him: 'You're going to be a big boy and live in a school from now on. You will make many new friends and will soon get used to it. Boarding school will make you self-reliant, prepare you for life and a proper job, help you to grow up to be strong and capable.' These words are meaningless to a child so young. Later, my dad told my mum he had felt deeply anxious at the thought of this looming unknown, but anxiety can easily be interpreted as excitement. What did he think of the school as they drove up to it? I see his face so small against the glass, his eyes glinting with a liquid sky before they cloud in shade. Long Close was in a modern 1930s building with tall gables and bay windows, a jolly gingerbread suburban folly, but it must have loomed large.

My dad did once tell me though that he cried when he was left on the school step for the first time. He cried so much that he started to hyperventilate. He called out to his mum and when she did not turn back to him he screamed. His parents continued to walk, stiff-backed, with their toddler daughter in their arms, towards the car. His sister gave a puzzled glance from over their father's shoulder. In her mind she asked, 'Why is he not coming home?'

This was his first flight, only it was forced, and totally unlike all the starry-eyed, red-caped flights to follow. It was an eviction from the heart of his family, from all he knew and all that was familiar. Some psychoanalysts would suggest this marked the death of his soul. Was it here that he learned to be a runaway? Despite his rarely speaking of this experience, I know it shaped him. I can imagine what he felt by my aunt's reports of how he acted out on his visits home. The seizures, the waking nightmares, the lying, his secret and inappropriate fondling of her. Years later, when she confronted him about his sexual abuse of her, he confessed to having been brutally raped at school.

On that day, on that step, my father vowed to stop loving his parents for leaving him there and not responding to his cries, and he kept his word. Their attachment was severed, and the wound never healed.

I imagine my dad on his first night at Long Close. His bed is cold to the touch, and the sheets are scratchy. It smells metallic, vaguely antiseptic, nothing like the warm smells of home. He is startled, wide eyed, as he tries to find familiar shapes in the dark, too shocked to cry. How horrifying to think of his mother, father and sister back at home, clearing up after supper in the dark dining room. The awkward void left by his absence filled by a conviviality of activity perhaps; his chair pushed so hard against the table it is barely visible. Their family reduced to an unequal number, lopsided, askew.

There are so many first-hand accounts of how these young boys felt when they were first taken from home and left in these institutions. But how could they know that this feeling would grow like a poison tree within their body? How it would push against their heart, and its branches would tear at the lining of their stomach. They might be given a word – homesick. But they could never know this first night that the term would define them for years to come. What these boys are feeling is a deeply visceral sense of bereavement at just seven years old.

They should not be in this foreign place in the care of people who do not love them, and they do not have the tools yet to look after themselves.

Over the last few decades there has been a growing discussion, particularly within psychotherapeutic circles, of the damage that boarding school for children so young has inflicted on generations of adults, predominantly men, and predominantly those who have gone on to work in areas of executive power, as lawyers, political leaders and corporate CEOs – the backbone of the British establishment. Boarding-school survivors might represent a tiny elite, but as journalist George Monbiot, himself sent away at eight, points out, 'many of these people possesses a disastrous set of traits: dishonesty, class loyalty and an absence of principle'. This, Monbiot and many others believe, is the result of being sent to boarding school at a young age, severing the child's bond with home, love, trust and security. Added to that were the devastating effects of emotional and physical abuse that many of these schools, at times quite consciously, promoted. The traditional hierarchies of class, status or sporting prowess and the tribalism of the House system were upheld not by loving adults, but by schoolmasters wanting to enforce control, together with their surrogates, the vengeful prefects, themselves damaged by the same torturous mill. If trauma was not experienced directly, there were multiple traumas happening around these children, mostly designed to humiliate and ensure conformity in a government of fear.

More damaging perhaps was a child's harsh and immediate realisation on arriving in this alien place that he should not express any feelings. The older boys, vulnerable themselves, knew exactly where to find the younger boys' weakness; part of their survival strategy was to make others scared and inadequate in the same way as they had been made to feel some years previously. 'If there are two things that being sent to boarding school teaches you,' writes Monbiot, 'they are that love cannot be trusted and that you should never admit to needing help.'

It was only really in the 1990s that the psychological legacy of boarding-school survivors was even considered. Parents paid large sums of money to send their children away because they believed it was for the best. Any admission of cruelty, experienced or witnessed, by the children was complicated by their natural respect for the adults: schoolmasters and their parents who had sent them there. Guilt kept children quiet. If a child complained they were considered ungrateful for their parents' sacrifices, or they were weak and pathetic, 'a girl' for not bearing it like a man.

Psychoanalyst Joy Schaverien recognised a pattern of behaviours in her clients who had attended boarding school and, together with psychoanalyst Nick Duffell, coined the term boarding-school syndrome – 'a combination of opinions, emotions or behaviours' that manifest themselves in many different ways, the linking thread being problems around forming and sustaining intimate relationships. The 'transitional moment' of the kind my dad experienced on the steps of his school is what Schaverien considers the genesis of the syndrome – the point when everything that came before is lost. The child's primary attachment is ruined, and it will never be the same again. Even home, when they finally visit, will not feel the same to the child who is defended against it. Once when my children and I returned from a three-week holiday, my son ran around the house exclaiming 'everything looks different. It's bigger. I never noticed this before.' But we were all in it together: the kids could throw themselves on the sofa and settle back with a movie while I cooked pizza. The dislocation was temporary and only served to highlight the joy of my son's everyday existence at home.

During the school holidays or on occasional weekends, my dad and his sister played together in the garden, among the plum trees and roses. They would set up a pretend grocery store with packets of cereal, sugar and paper bags of potatoes. My dad was the shopkeeper, his sister the housewife coming to buy her groceries. Sometimes they swapped places and Dad dressed up in his mother's hat, coat and handbag. My father enjoyed replicating the simplicities of domestic life. On the last Sunday of the holidays, before his return to school, the two of them listened to *The Goon Show* on Dad's tape recorder.

Children will go to great lengths to keep their parents happy; they will also aspire to live up to the image that their parents have created for them. My grandmother had always believed my father to be the good child. During his absence at school, she felt her guilt and longing and, because she was afraid of pain, these feelings were uncomfortable for her. She was anxious to defend herself from blame or criticism. When her son returned, I imagine her sweeping him off to the local shops, waving to her neighbours that he was back, her grown-up boy, on his way to becoming a gentleman. My father liked to please and was frightened of his mother's flammable moods: even before he had left for school, he'd learned to bury his needs in the shade of hers.

His sister is convinced that this is when he began to lie. It started with small fibs, speaking fondly of the lessons he in truth despised, the many friends he had, or simply that he liked it at school, that he was doing well in his tests, that he was good at rugby or athletics. None of this was true. Those who were not academic threw themselves into playing team sports at these kinds of schools, but my father was uninterested in either study or sport. There was nothing for the artistic, imaginative and dreamy child. In fact, this kind of child was in particular danger.

I have a photograph of my dad dressed up for school. He is older, almost as tall as his mum beside him. They are both dressed immaculately. She wears a quality wool coat, buttoned up and tucked at the waist, with a velvet trim around her collar. A neat handbag hangs from her wrist and, with the same hand, she grips her leather gloves. My father wears a long coat, a duffel, double-breasted and held tight at the waist with a belt. His socks go up to his knees and his shoes are shined. In his school cap, he engages the camera but his smile is not natural; while his mother's face is open and bright, my father's is in shadow, and his eyes are uncertain. In fact when I look closer, I see that his face is reduced, creased and folded, scrunched up, as if he is a snail clinging hold of his shell. This was later; he is aged twelve or thirteen. He must have moved on from prep school at Long Close to senior school at Berkhamsted, where he stayed until he was seventeen.

My father left school with just four O Levels and no A Levels; he failed them all. What a terrible waste of money to a family who was not well off and would have struggled to meet the fees. What a dereliction of my father's youth. It makes me heavy-hearted to think of all that suffering for nothing. What if he had learned from ages seven to seventeen only to lie, to hate authority, to suppress his tender feelings and pervert his natural longing to love and be loved? It was a cruelty to send him there. I imagine it caused him irreparable damage. The damage rippled out to everyone he touched.

Aged eleven, one Saturday evening on a weekend break from school, my father and his sister watched *Three Thousand Leagues Under the Sea*. My aunt has since told me of how unexpectedly Dad left the room. At the time she wondered if he had become scared by the sea monster, but it seems that something else came over him. Was it a deep visceral anxiety about returning to school the next day, so bad that he was unable to engage with the simple treat of watching a film with his family?

Later that night, his sister woke to her brother yelling from the landing outside her bedroom. She opened the door to see him on the floor, his body rigid, repeatedly banging his head on the bannisters, as their mother tried to stop him and to comfort him. This was his first seizure, and I can't help thinking that it was his body's way of acknowledging all that he was unable to articulate. His voice was already lost to him.

I don't know for sure whether my father was raped at boarding school, but he did admit to my mum in the early days of their marriage that he was bullied, and that he hated the enforced sex games organised by the bigger boys. Fagging, where an older boy uses a younger boy as a servant, was still common practice in the 1950s – and pretty boys like my dad would have been singled out. In his notebooks, reflecting on his life, he wrote of being someone else's slave: *Fag! was the cry, from the mouth of one who had been there himself. Clean my boots, bend over and take the cane, stand still with your arms outstretched for an hour – Go to hell, too . . . I was such a small child*, he wrote, and the words are drenched with sadness for that boy. He *was* a small child. He was completely unprotected, too.

But he also would have learned to keep quiet. Expressions of emotion were seen as weakness, and were dangerous, and so my father and all those other little boys quickly pushed away their feelings until they did not feel at all. George Monbiot states that this leads to the deepest form of dishonesty. 'This duplicity becomes a habit of mind,' he says. 'If every day you lie to yourself, lying to other people becomes second nature.'

But where do these feelings of being undermined, bullied, intimidated go? Dr Bessel van der Kolk writes in his brilliant book, *The Body Keeps the Score*, of how traumatic events have a lasting effect on the body's immune system, the muscular system and the brain. An imprint that embeds itself in your nervous system. It is not simply the event itself that haunts you; its effects are played out again and again in the years that follow. They determine your behaviour, become part of who you are.

As a child, my aunt adored her brother. Four years his junior, she looked up to him, and because he was absent for much of her childhood, he shimmered with the mystique of the missed, an aura that was reinforced because he was the favoured child. She recalls being excited every time she went with her father to pick Dad up from school, and they were thrown together in the quiet holidays back at home, which were hermetic and uneventful. Dad was deprived of genuine affection, so he turned to his sister for comfort, and she enjoyed his attention. Perhaps in the absence of everyday sibling familiarity, their feelings for each other became confused. Together they shared an intimacy that she was too young to understand: she was jealous when my dad had friends over and was convinced that they would marry when they were older. In a family that never talked about sex, my aunt discovered too late that this was not possible.

But with four years between them what might have been innocent exploration between two children becomes more complicated. My dad's sister has three distinct memories, when she was aged five, ten and twelve, but is sure that there were other occasions that she has blocked out. In the first, she and Dad were caught in bed by their aunt. She was naked and they were in an embrace. 'We'd been playing a kind of doctor and patient scenario and he was inspecting my body', but it was enough to shock their aunt who was furious.

The memory from when she was aged ten is more vivid. She is not wearing underpants and is in her bedroom or his, and his face is between her legs. She recalls this as an 'awakening memory' because she pushed his head away and told him to stop. My dad was fourteen.

Her last memory is when they were all four in France on a family holiday. It was April 1962. A month before her twelfth birthday. My dad would have just turned sixteen. The four of them went to see a film and my grandfather – always the prude – was shocked at the sexual scenes, insisting they all leave. 'It created a big embarrassing fuss in the movie theatre,' she recalls. Dad had wanted to stay and was angry at their father, and so his sister comforted him back at the hotel. It was his turn to push her away. 'We mustn't do that anymore,' he said. 'It's wrong.'

'What about when I have breasts?' she asked. 'Will you want to do it then?'

'When you have breasts you won't want to be with me,' he said.

This was taken as a devastating rejection. My aunt was mortified. This and the sexual abuse that came before it, both remembered and buried, has, to her own admission, affected her relationships with men and her own capacity for intimacy.

How bewildering to her that he should stop when she reached puberty. Perhaps because as a child she had no agency? Perhaps he was beginning to feel his power over her threatened? I struggle over this still now. When she was a child was she simply an object for his exploration, not his sister, not even truly human? Or was she his one source of love and comfort, distorted by the unnatural dislocation of being sent away before his own sense of self and sexuality had been allowed to evolve, sent far away to a hostile sexualised environment.

By the time my dad decided to stop, he had already hooked her emotionally, and the damage was done. He would have been totally unaware of his effect on her because his emotional life was already a wreckage. He treated her like he had been treated himself. He brought the pandemonium of his school experience into his family home and tainted his sister's innocence. To what extent did this early experience map out my father's sexual transgressions that were to come?

There were other incidences like this. My aunt recalls one of Dad's boarding-school friends visiting during the holidays, the sounds of a kerfuffle from his bedroom, a sudden thump and something broken, after which the boy ran down the stairs and out through the front door. My dad blamed it on him. 'He tried it on with me,' he said dismissively.

My father was not a rebellious teenager. He preferred to hide in his home-made darkroom to develop photographs, rather than get drunk with his sister and her friends. Alan, his uncle on his mother's side, introduced him to photography, and the passion stayed with him throughout his life. But Dad's role model was sleazy. Alan was a roguish smooth-talking character, handsome with striking blue eyes against black hair. My aunt describes him as oozing sexuality. He drank openly, drove fancy cars, and gave my dad erotic photographs he had taken of his wife, my father's aunt, who was curvaceous and pretty. My dad, thrilled by their sauciness, showed these to his sister, who recalls how Dad was both attracted to Alan and repelled by him. When Alan died, his death certificate stated 'alcoholism'. Their mum was horrified that his alcoholism could be made public like that. It was a strange repressive generation when shame was in speaking rather than doing.

When they were adults, my aunt tried to talk to my father about the abuse a number of times. She wanted validation more than anything else, and acknowledgement from him that it had happened. She sent him letters which he ignored and when she asked him face to face, he turned angry and contemptuous, called her crazy. It was nothing compared to what had happened to him, he said. This is when he told her he had been raped.

In the last months of his life my father tormented himself with where and how it had all begun to go so terribly wrong. Alone in Devon in a hostel he wrote fragmented thoughts in his notebooks, unformed poems and ideas for his non-fiction books, cut through with cries for help, muted and made foggy by the drink and his inability even in the last moments of his life to grasp the magnitude of the mess he had made. But he was grasping at something – from way back perhaps – some primal incident or knot in time, on which he could pin this catastrophe. What would he have done if he had found it? Would he have navigated his way back?

But there are moments of clarity: *My God, My Dad! Where was he?* he wrote as if an image had just come to him. *A picture of my dad carrying me off to the sanctuary of hell and damnation.* It is part of a note to himself to include a chapter on his boarding-school experience in his memoir. It is interesting here that he recalls this as significant. He has a memory of sitting on his father's shoulders and of a *Dan Dare character* with a big head and a small body. *Homosexual . . .* he writes. *Violent sex. No Lore. Punishment.*

He recalls how his mother's face was distraught, while his father was determined to toughen up his child, fearful of his sensitivity. *I don't blame him,* he is quick to write. *He was not a bad man. But his son was sensitive and did not need to toughen up but to be cossetted by his anxious mother instead.* He draws himself as a character in this narrative that we as a family know all too well: *I look back to childhood, before alcohol made its excuses as yet another obsession – sex, fear, self-doubt, self-medication, the telephone – the alcoholic inherits his past and integrates it into his present and future, applying the same madness and insanity.*

Every time I return to his notebooks, I see the glint of some small shining diamond that, however hard I had looked before, somehow I had not been able to see. I wonder if this has been part of my need to protect myself. I am moved by the wisdom in my father's words, a tragic glimmer of the truth he worked so hard to obliterate. He recognises this time at boarding school as the point from which all else follows: *Here began the eventual alcoholism, here began the agonies of adulthood at the hands of the 'fucking' parents – God bless their tortured souls.* Or is this just an old trope – 'The sins of the father are to be laid upon the children' – more drama to obscure the more difficult truth? That there comes a time when we can no longer blame others for who we are and what we do.

Adultery

Soon after I was born my mum felt the solitariness of the new mother, longing for a chance to read the paper or go to the loo unencumbered by small tugging hands and constant chatter. She would watch the tick of the clock at the end of the day, impatient for my dad to burst through the door to take their toddler or baby from her, my elder brother and me. But there was a lingering unease, too. One night he was out late ostensibly rehearsing the publisher's pantomime and had not come home. She waited at their bedroom window with me in her arms. It was December and very cold. As the hours passed, she became fearful. Why was he so late? Where was he? It crossed her mind that her anxiety might pass to me, her precious two-month-old baby, held tightly in her arms. Heart to heart, my face searching for her breast.

Her instinct was right. Not long after, she found a long blonde hair on the passenger seat of his Citroen Maserati – his latest enthusiasm, a sporty two-door coupé with its iconic engine, stark white and space age, but prone to breaking down. Confronted, he denied everything. The first brazen lie of many. He told her she was mad. She was obviously paranoid.

Soon after, my dad returned from a business trip with a sack of potatoes. He lugged it into our small kitchen and told my mum he had bought the sack from a roadside seller. When questioned as to why, he said he thought it quite 'a cute gift'. She was perplexed. He had never shown any desire before to shop at roadside sellers and was not that keen on potatoes. It slowly dawned on my mum that this bearer of potatoes was not her husband. The idea was not his. Only a girlfriend, and an American at that, might think it thoughtful and 'cute' to stop at the roadside and buy a sack of potatoes for the little wife at home. This was my mother's first glimpse of my father's secret life.

Despite the suspected transgressions, my mum and dad were happy. Together they made a striking pair. They had met when my mum was eighteen and in her first year of university in London, living in the women's hall of residence off Bloomsbury's Gordon Square. Growing up, I loved to hear the story of how she thought it would be fun to take part in a new experiment to trial computer dating, with students at Oxford, Cambridge and London universities its guinea pigs, and how even though my dad was not a student at any of these institutions he still managed to wangle his form into the computer mix. Looking back with the wisdom of all we now know, it was significant he was not on her list of compatible mates, although he said she was on his.

When my dad walked through the door the first night they met, his eyes fixed on her, this young woman, exotic with her high cheekbones and long auburn hair, dressed in a red velvet cloak, home-made by her from an old curtain. She thought he looked so outlandish, tall, blonde and thin with chequered drainpipe trousers two inches too short, he must have fallen to earth from another planet. To me, growing up, the story of this quirky meeting was strangely thrilling.

But my mum was susceptible to romance. I remember as a stroppy teenager reassuring her, 'Don't worry about me. I am nothing like as romantic as you and won't make the mistakes you've made.' She had laughed at my youthful superiority and was quick to put me right, saying she thought she combined good sense and sensibility pretty well, thank you! I now know this is true, but as a girl she had a romance about life. She lived in an atmospheric manor house and read Jane Austen, and all the

Regency romances of Georgette Heyer she could get her hands on. 'Is it not unsupportable to be held down to a canter when you long to gallop for miles?' When she was fourteen, she started to write her own version, which began with her young hero, like Narcissus, gazing into a pond and admiring his reflection. It soon stuttered to a halt, but now I am struck by how premonitory it was. Pursuing her own romantic dream, how unprepared she was aged only eighteen for pinning her hopes on a dishonest, damaged and unreliable man. The eldest of a spirited family of eight children, she had grown up under her colonial parents' aegis of breezy fearlessness and lack of convention. The rambling house in which they lived was draughty and underheated, but full of dogs and children and laughter. She fell in love with my dad, certain that they were meant to be together. It all happened so quickly. Why not, if you really believed this was your destiny? And, anyway, this is how nineteenth-century heroines behaved.

The same year they met they were married. My mum still eighteen, my dad twenty-one. My mother wore a pin-tucked cotton lace dress, bought from Mexicana, a Sloane Street boutique that was all the rage. Her bouquet of flowers cut from the garden was tied together by her mother half an hour before they set off for the church. My father was striking in a lean frock-coated suit bought from the Way In boutique on the top floor of Harrods, newly opened and a mecca for the trendy young. The wedding reception was held in the garden of that old stone manor house where my mother had grown up, with its mulberry tree, shell house and a spreading Cedar of Lebanon. Instead of a cake, they had a Danish cornucopia.

It was so good in the early days. They were so young, they believed they could forge their own way through the world; that dreams really could become real. Their first home was a flat in a grand stucco building near Portobello Road, and a little marmalade kitten was delivered by a cat rescue woman who had cycled over with it in her basket. They took the kitten for walks in the communal gardens at the back of the house. My dad had finally turned his back on the career prescribed by his father: after failing to pass his law exams for the sixth time he decided to work in publishing during the day, and by night to reinvent himself as a writer. He was the governor of his fantasy then, conjuring his own world of escape and freedom, a make-believe, under his control. From the safety of the kitchen table, he entered outlandish fantasies of sex and violence and more sex on planets beyond the reach of man. He was beginning to live his life on his own terms. There was a small cultish following for his science fiction books, two 'space opera' sequences (the Steeleye series, and the Cabal series), and his young wife admired and adored him. He was also very good at his job as a salesman for two independent publishers. Was this not enough for him?

I look now at his early writing and wonder how much of it is an expression of himself. His character Steeleye is asleep, his wife beside him and two children in the next room, but there is also murder happening in the frame, 'blood gushing like a slow-motion film', a dream within a dream, a visitation, he writes, a stalking shadow, that should not have been there. The dark side was already seeping into his life. But through his writing, he had discovered the power of transformation.

My mother, cleverer and more beautiful, had her own sparkling prospects. She loved her work as an editorial assistant at *Vogue*. The late 1960s and early 1970s marked a time when British popular culture ruled the world. Photographers were like rock stars; David Bailey, Lord Snowdon, Norman Parkinson were princes swaggering through the Hanover Square offices of *Vogue*. One day my mother was whisked off from her desk to Battersea Park by Barry Lategan who, without the aid of a hairdresser or make-up artist, snapped her standing by a lilac tree in dappled spring sunshine. Amazingly, this informal photo became one of the coveted colour pages in the August edition. It was 1971. Serendipity like this seemed perfectly normal.

Everything for my parents felt possible. Opportunities abounded. My mother was at a dinner party when the then Managing Director of Weidenfeld & Nicolson said to her: 'Think of an idea for a book and I'll publish it.' She thought he was just showing off, but less than a week later she was on the phone to a canny friend who said, 'Take him seriously!' As Mum put the phone down the thought of Mary Shelley came into her head from nowhere. When her book *Moon in Eclipse* was published and Richard Holmes wrote such a generous review in *The Times*, my mother thought perhaps I really can do this. It seems fitting now that she should write a biography of a woman who brought to life a gothic science fiction monster, sensitive and longing for emotional connection, but cast out from family love and the human world. The monster's heartfelt cry, 'I was benevolent and good; misery made me a fiend. Make me happy and I shall again be virtuous,' echoes down the centuries. It also now casts light on my father's subsequent fall.

Then my brother arrived that same year. In the early 1970s childbirth was still heavily medicalised in most hospitals, and my dad was ushered from the room once the obstetrician arrived with the forceps. Loving a bit of drama, he reported that all he could see was the short white rubber boots worn by the students, some splattered with blood. In the real world my mother was distraught at having her baby removed to an incubator. All her instincts demanded she never let her newborn out of her sight.

With her new baby, Mum felt she had everything she desired. Her own family in her own house, purchased with the help of their parents, in the scrubby end of Islington, but full of light and space. A perfect scene, the golden threesome, their mini galaxy. She loved my father; he was the centre of her world, but she was not prepared for the overwhelming rush of love of early motherhood. She gazed at this big, healthy baby in her arms, amazed by what they had produced. 'Look at how beautiful he is!' she once said to my dad, expecting a similar rush of feeling.

But he replied flatly, 'You used to say that about me.' Perhaps it reminded him of old betrayals. Perhaps his search for other diversions, for more unwavering attention, drove him away. Family life was somehow effacing him.

On the wall in his hallway, my brother has a photograph of himself as a toddler in bed between my parents. While my mother smiles at my father, Dad more guardedly looks at his golden son, who dominates the photo with his plump arms outstretched above the Victorian patchwork quilt. In this image both my mum and dad are eclipsed by this gorgeous boy.

Only about a year later, my dad went to visit his sister in Syracuse, New York State. She was married to an artist who made his own oil paints and painted large canvases in their attic. It was snowing, winter, perhaps January – although it snowed for half the year, my aunt complained. Bright white light flooded through the bamboo blinds in their top-floor apartment. My aunt believed at the time that Dad had made the visit specifically to see her, although not long afterwards it became apparent he was in America for other reasons. The three of them settled on cushions on the hardwood floor and Dad played a cine film he had made the previous summer of my mother heavily pregnant with me, on a visit to his parents' house.

In the sepia slow shudder of the film, my mum dances in the garden with her mother-in-law. They hold hands and laugh. My granny is coy when she looks at the camera, waving it away, while my mother, confident in her beauty, throws her head back, revelling in the attention from the man filming. She glows in my father's gaze. Her face lights up in a flush of sunlight, and her eyes glint with diamonds. She is dressed in a cream smock, her hair loose and wild, her stomach bursting with the shift of new life. My curved body, seven months inside her, quickly growing. 'She's so beautiful,' my father said, partly to himself and partly to his sister. He then collapsed, his face clasped, sobbing into his hand, his body contracted into itself.

My aunt was shocked and confused at this sudden show of emotion. She guessed he must simply be missing us, his family back in London.

My mum was right. The girlfriend who made my father lug the potatoes home was American. My dad told Mum he was in love with her. By the time I had joined the happy family, it was already fractured. What had gone wrong? On the face of it, nothing at all. This beautiful young couple still loved each other, two writers now who found pleasure in their shared pursuits and who had made a loving home; two children, living, breathing, laughing, looking so much like their dad. But suddenly, it seemed, he was willing to throw it all away, as if we were a pair of shoes he had tried on for fit and decided, when faced with a new pair, that they were not so good anymore.

On the night my dad confessed, he dashed from our house to my mum's closest sister who lived only a street away, got her out of bed and demanded she come back to be with my mum. He then phoned my mother's father and, being the reliable, loving father he was, he prepared to drive three hours through the night if needed.

So much drama, pulling others into his pain, as if he could not bear to face it on his own. Was it easier for him if they all knew about it? Gathering his soldiers into a line of defence. Would it be more difficult, in this semi-public setting, to rewind and stay? But as the hours wore on, my brother and I still asleep in our beds, and our mother shocked by the madness, he dashed from girlfriend to home and back again. Then exhausted, he crumpled. He didn't mean it, he said, and begged for my mother's reassurance. My mum cried alongside him. It was the first blow to her heart.

And my father? He'd found something different, something new. A new kind of intimacy, one that felt more real perhaps than the steady comfort of his family. Did his unlived lives beckon? The doors of the anteroom he had yet to open. No one can have everything, but perhaps in this moment, here, in the early 1970s, a young man, discovering the delicious power to make women desire him, felt entitled to at least try.

Recently, I saw a photo of my mum and dad taken at this time. They are in my dad's parents' garden. My mum is seated on a chair and my dad is on the floor at her feet, with a dog in his arms, as if searching for distraction. She looks at the camera. She is dressed in a yellow T-shirt, and her hair falls around her face, as it always did, but her expression is guarded, and she is pale. Her hands rest on my dad's shoulder, her delicate fingers curled in on themselves, except for one, her index finger on her left hand, the hand that wears their wedding ring. This finger points downwards towards my dad's shoulder, towards the dog in his arms as a distraction, towards his genitalia. My mum shared this photo on our WhatsApp family group and my sister-in-law commented on how different she looks. Compared to the *Vogue* photo taken three years before. It is of a different woman, drained of her vitality. She is already weary with the weight of it all, and she never expected any of it.

Hers had been an uncomplicated childhood, so different from my dad's. Born on the other side of the world, in South Africa, my mum was of Norwegian descent on her father's side, from an enterprising family of shipbuilders, who in the middle of the nineteenth century emigrated from Stavanger and sailed in their own boat, intending to settle in New Zealand. However, they stopped off in Knysna in the Cape and decided to stay. When my mum was seven, and her mother was pregnant with her seventh child, the family returned to England, my grandmother's country of birth. They bought a run-down estate in Wiltshire to set up a poultry farm and my grandfather learned everything they needed to know from a book and advice from neighbours.

My grandparents dealt with any crisis with the calm competence of self-reliant pioneers, and their children grew up unafraid of spiders, mice or rats, bats or wasps, or any living thing. Now my mum is pained when a grandchild squeals at the sight of a daddy longlegs in the bath. This unconventional family was exhilarating to my father, who longed to escape the fearful, smaller scale of his own family life. They all welcomed him. One of mum's sisters describes him as golden that first time they met. She found him alluring and lovely. He stumbled into their rambling house, emerging through the tumble of dogs and children, unaware of his charm. My grandfather shook his head and laughed at my dad's ability to sell an old car for more than he had paid for it. 'We all fell for him,' my aunt has since said.

The house was full of activity and colour. Brisk with cold, the heat leaked from the old coke-fuelled Aga. They ate free-range chickens, eggs, unpasteurised milk and home-churned butter from their Guernsey cow, and vegetables from the walled garden. When the foxes got into the chicken houses in the field and killed enough chickens, they would invite the neighbours round for a big party, cut out the chewed bits, and serve chicken curry. The children roamed the garden and fields and were seen only at mealtimes, summoned by a bell tolled from the roof. Benign neglect left them free to follow their impulses and interests, building dens with hay bales, riding bikes down country lanes at night without lights and driving the family's converted army lorry through lumpy parkland, towing a sledge loaded with children and Rocky the corgi.

In the early days before they were married my dad took photographs of these unselfconscious children – rosy cheeks, freckled noses and smiles, unbrushed hair and sun-bleached clothes, growing into, or out of, hand-me-downs. He printed these portraits in his dark room, alongside headshots of my mother with 1960s kohl-rimmed eyes. At night, my dad crawled between the chilled cotton sheets with his fiancée, and they wrapped their bodies tight around each other to keep warm. 'I don't deserve it,' he would whisper. 'All of it. Your love; their admiration. How can I live up to it?' His eyes searching through the dark. My mother kissed him and held him close. What a silly question, she thought. She was destined for him, and he for her. Sent to each other from the stars. In her mind there was no question it would all work out right.

My mother's first years of childhood were in South Africa where she and her siblings ran free and barefoot. When her family first moved to Wiltshire, the children so valued the toughened soles of their feet as a sign of their individuality and resilience, they continued to run barefoot, but this time around the cinder paths of the walled garden. Thus adventurous, straightforward and brave, my mother's family met my father whose shame was always at his heels, who had never managed to transform hardship into strength.

After enduring another day of my dad's ricocheting from her to the American girlfriend, my mum finally acted. After the last guilty return, she picked up his favourite green velour fedora from the coat stand. He seldom wore his hat but, needing to make the gesture emphatic, she thrust it into his hands and said, 'Just go!' My father stared at my mother with tragic eyes, all the fight gone. Her decisiveness gave him clarity.

Of course he did not want to go! He didn't want to lose us. Not at this point anyway. So he begged her to let him stay. When she relented and opened her arms to him again, he put those worn old shoes back on, the ones that had taken the shape of his feet, reminded of how comfortable they were. He told my mother that the American had ugly hands. 'Your hands are so much more beautiful,' he said.

My mother made a lovely home on ingenuity and very little money. In summer, the front window box was legendary in the road for its radiance, shimmering with nemesia, pansies, petunias and brilliant trailing nasturtiums. Next door's old Albertine climbing rose joined in the symphony of scent and colour. We were on the sunny side of the street.

My parents picked up antiques from junk shops and auction houses. A Victorian scroll-ended chesterfield stood in the window, and in the dining room, through large double doors that were always open, was a wooden Victorian pub table with a brass-bound green and white tiled top. Against the wall stood a bench with a curved back. Mum had found a particular wall-paper, which she loved – huge watercolour roses in green-grey and soft pink, almost abstract in their size and like crepe to the touch. My brother and I ate breakfast here, me on a rickety high chair, porridge splattered on the bare pine floor beneath it. Later, we would playfight and flick food, bits of tomatoed spaghetti stuck to the wallpaper, just out of reach. American Soul spun from the turntable: Nina Simone, Brook Benton, Stevie Wonder.

My father's charismatic skills as a salesman had propelled him to success in publishing; he was quickly given his own list. But he soon grew restless and bailed out, to set up his own packaging company and to develop ideas for books to sell to publishers at home and abroad. He and my mum shared an office in the base-ment of our house. They would create luxuriously produced, uniquely illustrated science fiction books. Over supper one evening, my mother suggested a potential name for the com-pany. Her own mother had given her a French ceramic Pierrot, perfectly white with downcast face, a ruffled collar and elaborate pompom-buttoned shirt. Mum turned it round to face Dad and said, Pierrot. My dad tilted his head. The sad clown, the naive fool who lingers between innocence and death. The outsider, misunderstood and alienated. He nodded. Their company was registered in 1977 as Pierrot Publishing.

With my mother's advance for *Moon in Eclipse*, she paid for us all to have a holiday in an unfrequented corner of Corfu. We stayed in a two-bedroomed, whitewashed house on top of a dusty hill, cool in the shade, and with views of the sea below. Each morning on the wind we heard the bleat of goats led onto the beach, their tin bells tinkling, and every evening we dined at the local taverna. The owner Mathias gave me and my brother free ice cream. I was enamoured with Mathias. When we were in the restaurant, I would follow him; when he turned and looked down, I would be there. A chubby blonde three-year-old gazing up at him.

One evening Greek men danced to Zorba's song, their arms gripping, shoulder to shoulder. I watched astounded, transfixed by the music, laughter and setting sun, slow and rich on the sea. In the pink of twilight, my father reached out and touched the side of my mother's face, as she held his gaze and smiled back at him. The next day she painted him, as he relaxed on a deckchair in the bright yellow light, his golden chest exposed warm against a pea-green shirt. We no longer have the painting, but a photograph of him like this is in one of the family albums I carefully put together a few years later. He smiles at my mother with softness in his eyes. He was at the height of his attractiveness during this time, stopped by strangers on the street who mistook him for the young Donald Sutherland, who was also in his prime.

That afternoon, I went wandering off to see Mathias. I toddled off, when my parents weren't looking, down the lane, scorched in the heat of the sun. I found him setting the tables. Once my parents realised I had gone they came, panicked. My mother's face was stricken as she ran towards me, tripping on her flip-flops. I can still see her face now, devastated with the fear of sudden gunfire, her dream shot to pieces in a blink. I wrapped my arms around her. It had been so much fun. Mathias had given me an ice cream, and his wife had wrapped a green headscarf around my hair that tinkled with cowrie shells each time I shook my head.

The 1970s was an exciting and creative time for publishing, and Pierrot thrived: a high-concept publisher and packager, from first idea through to commission. My father was a quick mover, and charming with it, and he soon had a handful of talented writers and illustrators working on books for him. Brian Aldiss, Peter Dickinson and Harry Harrison drank coffee together in the chiaroscuro of our basement; Ian Pollock and Jim Burns joined them.

The strength of the company was in its forward thinking; my father always looked to the US for his publishing inspiration, where booksellers were more daring. Pierrot books were beautifully produced and originally illustrated, in oversized format, and were distributed not only to overstocked bookshops, but also department stores, record shops and gift stores – Dad's inspired idea to help the books stand out and get a more alternative readership.

Their first book was *Great Balls of Fire! A History of Sex in Science Fiction Illustration*, then came *Brothers of the Head*, an illustrated original novella by Brian Aldiss; *Mechanismo*; *The Flight of Dragons*; and Harry Harrison's *Planet Story*, all rich and visually accomplished adorning many 1970s coffee tables. My mother and her sister worked alongside my father, my aunt as Managing Editor and my mother as Assistant Editor.

Dad was particularly fond of Citroens during this time: when he traded in his Citroen Maserati, he bought more of a family car in the Citroen DS, otherwise known as 'the goddess' with its wide whale-like profile, sofa seats and low suspension. Then came the Citroen Safari, a five-door estate, and then a Familiale with its extra seat in the rear of the wagon, and deadly metal-bottomed folding chairs between these and the front, which clamped shut when we went over bumps or stopped suddenly. No seat belts in those days, I was once thrown into the back of the folding chairs when my dad entered a roundabout too fast. My nose bled profusely into my favourite pink woollen bolero.

But Dad still needed to have his private frivolity: his indulgence was a Jaguar XK150, an iconic car straight out of a 1950s movie, white with red leather interior, its swooping lines resembling a crouching Big Cat. Great for the open road, once it got started. Our neighbours watched, amused, at the daily ritual of him pushing it up our road to jump-start it, my mother at the wheel, in order to drive me and my brother to school. This car was stolen, according to Dad, from outside our house. He later came upon it in New York, he claimed, recognised from a cigarette burn on the dashboard, despite its American plates. But Mum never believed him. We lived on a quiet residential street, and their bedroom was at the front of the house – the engine was so loud we would have heard it. But anyway, it didn't start without a push. Even if the robbers had managed to get only a cough of ignition out of it, we would have heard. Then Dad suggested they must have lifted it by crane and silently slotted it into a container. He more likely sold it and then claimed it on insurance.

When I was about five years old, I moved into the small bedroom on the top floor next to the bathroom. It was high up in the sky and overlooked the gardens, and the backs of the terraces on the next street. As I grew, I liked to sit at the window and watch the little people opposite as they moved about like stick figures in the colourful light of a story board, cooking in the kitchen, singing round a grand piano, walking up and down the stairs. At night, I lay in bed and listened to my mum in the routine of her evening bath – the vigorous twenty splashes of cold water after she had washed her face with the iconic Erno Lazlo's black mud soap. We had a cat called Bertie, white and grey like pepper, and a hamster that we named Hamish Hamilton after the publisher. My brother remained in the room beneath me, also looking out onto the back gardens. He had a tank of stick insects and a wall covered in football heroes. On weekends we would sometimes drive to Cliveden and picnic in the long grass under the trees. On a sloping path in the woods, we learned to ride our bikes, any falls cushioned by a thick bed of leaves.

My brother and I grew up hanging about on our street. It always felt safe as we knew most of the neighbours, and in the spring and summer doors were left open so we could run in and out of each other's houses. We were friends with the kids from the family who owned the two Dobermans, which ran from window to window barking when we cycled past, and sometimes chased us on our bikes and thrashed at our heels. Another friend stashed porn mags under his bed and bored a hole in his bedroom wall to spy on his au pair in the next room. He and my brother stole his mum's car keys when she wasn't around and took her car for a drive round the block before attempting to parallel park. I liked to dance to the Jackson 5 with an Irish girl in her cold basement bedroom, and one time she lifted a floorboard in their living room to show me where her dad kept wads of cash. It was a quiet, friendly road where people settled. Our mum would call us in, and we would chase each other up to the bath. Long summer evenings flooded in through open windows, cats yowled in terraced gardens, there was urban music and laughter. We would hear our dad arrive home, and with his heavy monster hands on all fours climbing the stairs. We screamed from the bath when he appeared suddenly from around the door.

Dad brought us gifts from his trips abroad, clothes and sweets. Fluffy toys. Books and feathered pencils. A tube of white foam wedges that we pinged at each other. At Christmas, our stockings were full. We would wake to talcum powder Father Christmas footprints on the carpet leading from the loft door to our rooms. We were keen to believe the stories of far-flung snow-filled lands way beyond the rain that drizzled outside our window.

He brought gifts of love, or gifts of guilt. Not sure which.

Often when Dad was away, we three would escape London to spend the weekend with my mum's parents. Their house, tall and Georgian, overlooking the Clifton Suspension Bridge, had never-ending terraced gardens with cellars beneath, where they threw big family parties and receptions for their children's various weddings. We have a series of photographs of my grandparents dancing, holding close, in among the warm shelter of those stone subterranean caves. Quickly, after my brother and me, more cousins were born and, all together, it was as if there were a hundred toddlers tottering around the living room and up the stairs, in hand-me-downs and beautiful knitted cardigans over towelling nappies. While the sisters modelled my granny's latest hand-knitted creations, with twirling skirts,

Granddad, always outnumbered by women and children, lay outstretched on the floor, when around him the family swirled, his eyes closed and hands linked over his heart, taking his daily ten-minute nap.

At times, my brother and I would stay here on our own, practising our times-tables from a shared double bed, giggling deep into the night. In the morning, we would escape the chill on our bare feet by crawling into bed with our grandparents, still asleep, eager to feel their warmth beneath a heavy satin embroidered quilt. We would open the curtains to watch the morning light come alive from the three full-length windows.

I was warmed, whenever I caught a glimpse of our grandparents' affection, by their quiet, unshowy commitment. The two of them sitting together on the sofa, their shoulders touching. My gran would say something to make Granddad laugh. She would grab his hand firmly in her big hard fingers and drop him a sudden kiss, the two of them grinning at the surprise of it all.

My father stood tall, all six-foot-two of him. Big boned, he was an impressive man, effervescent and warm. When young, he was slim and elegant, easy with his body, before the allergies caused his stomach to bloat. His stomach was comforting in its size, firm not flabby, a pillow for my child face, and arms held tight around him. His hands were big, spongy to the touch, warm around mine. He was blue eyed. Soft eyed. Pleading eyes. Forgive-me eyes. Pathetic and needy, sometimes, too. And his laugh was contracted. A diminished sound that betrayed his sensitivity and told my brother and I when we had gone too far in our teasing, that he did not like to laugh at himself. It told us to love him, which we did.

As a child, I loved to cuddle him. My heart beat wildly for his. Little heart hands, lacing fingers. Little heart hands holding. Little heart hands bound together by arteries and veins and threads.

On nights when my parents had friends over, I would sit by the fire, placated by the smell of roast chicken and garlic, and keenly show off our family photo albums. I loved looking at them and liked to show them to others, despite their only polite interest. All the photographs were taken by my father and developed in our basement darkroom. In many, my mother looks happy. In one she is beautiful and tanned on our holiday in Greece, and I'm eating a melting choc ice in her lap. There's another of her broad smile filling the frame, with the end of a pencil pressed into her plump cheek, taken by my father when she was editing a book. Then there is one of my father and mother side by side, slightly out of focus, mute and hazy, my head floating in the fractured space between them. I stared at this one a little longer, wondering why it seemed so sad to me. Their friends often stayed into the early hours. I listened from the top of the stairs to joy and frivolity, though a part of me was armoured, reserved, my arms tight around my knees, the cocoon of me steady against the vertiginous spin of intoxicated laughter.

When I was five, we went back to Greece, to the Peloponnese, to visit another of my mum's sisters, who was living there caring for the horses at a new hotel. Her Greek boyfriend picked us up from the airport in his beaten-up Ford and the plastic seat cover was so hot it burned my thighs. Driving along the main thoroughfare, he swerved into ongoing traffic because he thought it was funny. I stared at my brother, eyes wide in fright, while clutching the back of the seat. It was the last holiday we were to have as a family.

I have a photo of my mother, serene beneath a wide-brimmed hat, worn constantly, even in the sea, to protect her skin. Her head floats over the water, shoulders submerged, eyes thoughtful, as she watches something in the distance. In another, we are on a speed boat, her mirrored sunglasses reflecting my father squinting into the glare. In a third, she stands naked in a mirror and pins back her hair: she is looking away from my father. Her shoulders are tanned, and her face is sad.

My parents were often behind closed doors during this holiday. Flies buzzed around what was left of lunch. My brother and I sat on a swing in the yellow heat, dust on our feet. We waited, listening to the lonely cicadas' song.

Left alone, we played for hours in the sun. Two Greek children with us on the beach, from the hard heat of the afternoon until the sand chilled. Looking up, I saw my mother's silhouette against sundown, and felt the sting of burnt skin. I lay awake through the night puking. A white curtain blowing in the hot breeze was no relief. Pain and nausea: fevered images of monsters throbbing through red, and beastly spiders.

In another photograph, my father lies back on a slab of rock on an overcast day: a yellow shirt, cotton trousers, sunglasses. I am beside him in my Osh Kosh dungarees; my hair twisted and clipped at each side, as my mum liked it, and my National Health glasses. My knees fall towards his, his away.

That day my father and I went for a walk along the beach, hand in hand. It is one of the few memories I have of being on my own with him. The simple bliss of looking out for jellyfish in the sand. But a woman called his name. I stopped and squinted up at her. She was tall, her body brown and oiled. She tipped her hips and her long hair swung when she smiled. My father dropped my hand.

'Who's that?' I asked trying to catch up with him.

'Just someone.'

That wrinkle of questioning. Things are not as they seem.

My father was unfaithful, a philanderer, a serial shagger; there are many words for people like him. Adultery is a shameful word, a transgression from the sanctity of marriage; like cheating, infidelity and unfaithfulness, it is not morally neutral. It derives from the Latin word *adulteritas*, meaning contamination. It is no surprise that my father lied about his liaisons in his twelve-year marriage to my mother, though he once boasted to his sister – probably falsely – that there had been 500 of them.

He took pride in being humorously subversive, doing nothing to hide his inappropriate comments to passing women when my brother and I, just children and alone with him, watched wide-eyed from the back seat of one of his fancy cars.

Some might argue he couldn't help it. It was not in him to be monogamous. He was permanently switched on, emanating receptivity, overwhelmed with all that attention. This was often his excuse. Like the baby boy in the pram, he had no control over the adulation of others. Except that my father's behaviour was more obsessive. He would have been forgiven for a simple flirtation or a one-off fumble, but he was like Pan, the horned god, led by his need for conquest, speaking in riddles so as not to be caught out. Or, I am wondering now, if my language, my mention of Gods, mythologising him, as if he were not like other men, is because I am still in the web of his own romance about himself, seeing him as he wished to be seen. For he *was* special, he believed, beyond the rule-bound life of ordinary men, and this world that we forced him to inhabit, with its expectations, its simple, respectful responsibilities for the sake of the family, was for mindless fools – not for him.

But he remained besotted with my mother, and never told her that he did not love her. They had a passionate relationship. How conflicted he must have been to cherish intimacy with her, only to adulterate it. Was it the split self he learned to cultivate for protection in childhood? His disconnection from his own deep feeling, which enabled him to hide, act, lie, pretend and love, simultaneously? As a child his voice was muffled by parents so driven to obscure their own uncomfortable feelings. The school with its unsympathetic masters and the anarchy of its parentless children, an animal farm, only acted to create an even bigger chasm between the man who stood before us and the hurt boy inside. But his fragile self had to be heard, to find some expression, so it became a provocateur, spoilt, demanding and concerned only with itself. It screamed out for attention. He was unable to resist the monster that was foraging, feeding and growing inside of him.

There is another, simpler way of looking at it. The way my brother does. Our dad shagged around. He was self-deluding, self-indulgent and led by his prick. He lied and cheated, broke my mother's heart. He was a bad husband. A shit of a dad. The sins of my father. There is nothing romantic about any of that.

Adultery. A Latin verb that means alter. To alter one's mind from the normal order of things. A house. A family. Love, intimacy, trust. My father would snatch clandestine time with another woman and then return to make love to my trusting mother. It altered his mind. It altered his heart. In the end his life was adulterated and so was ours.

My mother did not know about my father's worst deceit until years after he left. The 1970s was the age of Frédérick Leboyer, *Birth Without Violence*, and a refocusing on the child's experience at the centre of childbirth. One of the first obstetricians to practise what Bion and Freud had recognised previously, that babies feel pain, Leboyer wanted women and their carers to pay more attention to the transition between the womb and the world, and one way to do this was to create a softly lit and warm birthing environment. Suddenly, pregnant women and their husbands were signing up for antenatal classes, intimate sessions where parents met and discussed their anxieties over their pregnancies, with an emphasis on the father being part of it too. My mother was one of them, determined to manage the birth of her second child differently.

She and my father found an antenatal teacher who lived locally and led classes from her living room. These classes became the focus of my mother's week; my father came too when he was around. Expectant mothers formed a circle, supported by their partners, in a space that was calm and safe. At the centre sat the antenatal teacher, dressed in a pair of black tights and a T-shirt, and in this new spirit of frankness and demonstrable knowledge, she gave birth to a plastic baby.

This woman became more than just a teacher, she also became a friend. Someone who helped rebuild my mother's confidence in her body and its ability to give birth again after the shock of her first. My mother and her new friend spent time together, talking and sharing their anxieties of early motherhood; they would drop in on each other for a cup of tea.

My brother turned two at the end of 1973, and, heavily pregnant with me, my mother stayed up the night before to make him a birthday cake of a train with liquorice wheels. Loving liquorice, she ate the excess wheels and claims it was this that started labour and propelled me into the world on my brother's birthday. My mother's sister swept in to look after my brother, so my mum could go to hospital, his party hastily cancelled.

The night of my birth, she was alone in the birthing ward. Entering second stage, she sang a song, urgent and under her breath: '*Oh what a beautiful morning, Oh what a beautiful day. I've got a beautiful feeling. Everything's going my way.*' It had been suggested that this would help with breathing as you crest the waves of contractions. But her mind was also on my father, apparently away up north on business, and whether he would get there in time.

As a child, I thrilled to hear the story he told of his heroic attempt to reach us. How he had leapt into the car and drove as fast as he could down the motorway, blind to the fact he was running out of petrol. On the outskirts of London, the fuel gauge hit zero. He glided to a lay-by, got out of the car and ran. He ran all the way, he told me, to get to us in time. I imagined his long legs in narrow trousers, hair flapping crazily in the wind.

'*All the cattle are standin' like statues,*' my mother continued to sing. '*All the cattle are standin' like statues. They don't turn their heads as they see me ride by. But a little brown mav'rick is winkin' her eye.*'

Yet in my mind's eye, when my dad finally arrived at the hospital, I see how he avoids us. How the age-old picture of a mother cradling a newborn child throws his shame into relief. He is there, but also not. How could he be fully present? She was the mother of his child, and yet, as we were to find out later, my father's mind was elsewhere, with the antenatal teacher and friend. This level of deceit draws a new path, another landscape, with guilt close behind. All of us feel bad about ourselves when we lie. We withdraw, avoid the lover's eye, and see fault in others in order to justify our behaviour – *Look at what you've driven me to.*

I have come to understand that intimacy between two people is fragile. It relies on trust. Standing shoulder to shoulder, faults exposed – will you love me despite everything? – two people prepared to be vulnerable. Trust breeds openness, complete communication in everything, that light and easy syncopation, spinning off in all directions and always being caught. The peace of low voices in the dark. A warm hand finding you in sleep. It is the opposite of detachment, self-protection, keeping secrets. It is the opposite of closing down.

I know what it feels like when intimacy breaks. When you conspire with someone else, and the lies follow. True intimacy is precious, it is hard won, and yet how easily it is lost. Is it the guilt of deception that ruins the flow of trust you have grown to take for granted? All that instinctive openness suddenly gone? You can no longer stroke your lover's hand without first thinking about it, you can no longer look honestly into their eyes. Or is it more nuanced than that? A crime that goes beneath the flesh, beneath consciousness even, to that numinous space that none of us really knows. To adulterate, to corrupt, to spoil by adding something impure into the mix. Intimacy is undone when a third party enters the frame.

Later, in the dark corridors of my own struggling marriage, I found myself having an intensely visceral response to Steve McQueen's exploration of sex addiction in *Shame*. I was in the cinema and could barely breathe for crying. I cried at the aggressive sex scenes, Michael Fassbender's character snorting coke before he screwed a woman against a penthouse window – a woman who, if he had been less broken, less damaged, might have meant something to him. I cried at his emotional entrapment, and at the implied sexual abuse of him when he was a child. And when I returned home I sat in my peachy bedroom with my Art Deco wardrobes and the softening light – my cats curled in my lap, my children asleep in the next room, and my husband, their father, routinely turning off the lights for bed – aware of my privilege, of the life that should have felt nourishing and rich. I felt deep sadness for this man, so disconnected from feeling that he had to fuck for release, who fucked into a void. I cried because he was doing this to himself.

But my mother suggests that my dad's serial unfaithfulness was more to do with his need to feel special than any kind of addiction, a kind of adolescent excitement at his power to be desired. 'He liked to think of himself as a sex God,' she says, able to laugh about it now. 'If he had mirrors in his bedroom, he'd be gazing at himself – far more interested in his own performance than the woman he was with.' All these women were wounded, anyway, and it was up to my father to heal them with his sexual prowess. But I can't ignore the fact he later became an addict, and that his pursuit of other women was excessive.

In the years after he died I read loads of books on addictive behaviour in my attempt to understand. Dr Gabor Maté particularly spoke to me: his description of his patients in downtown Vancouver drifting through the streets like hungry ghosts, anaesthetised, mostly, he believes, from childhood trauma. It is the trauma that has closed their feelings down and, he argues, the illegal drugs are taken not to suppress the pain but instead in an attempt to reawaken the capacity to simply feel, to be human again. 'The addict's reliance on the drug to reawaken her dulled feelings is no adolescent caprice,' Maté writes. 'The dullness itself a consequence of an emotional malfunction not of her making: the internal shutdown of vulnerability.' The word vulnerability comes to us from the Latin *vulnerare*, 'to wound'. Maté suggests that in order to cope, the brain shuts down 'when pain becomes so vast or unbearable that it threatens to overwhelm our capacity to function'. It is not just drugs or alcohol that offer a synthetic remedy for this wound, it is also the all-consuming lustre of infatuation, the thrill of new sex, it is the ignition of arousal, the insistent throb of anticipation. Dopamine floods the system. Whether or not my dad was addicted to sex, he learned early to turn to pleasure, to assuage discomfort or pain.

Only with drugs and alcohol, the brain becomes accustomed to the synthetic high and thinks it has enough, so it gets lazy about making its own, and this is when the physiological addiction cycle begins. I am reminded of Patrick Melrose, Edward St Aubyn's compelling personification of self-destruction, returning to New York to see his father's dead body, but instead running headfirst into a multi-day bender. How he plunges his arm into scalding water just to feel, while blowing all his money on a luxurious hotel suite, his own private hell.

The story of my father's dalliance with my mother's antenatal teacher and friend came from my mum, but I don't remember where we were or what we were doing when she told it to me. I have a vague recollection it was a lesson in friendship – 'Beware of your women friends,' had been told to her by a wise old psychoanalyst. 'It is from there that the betrayal most likely comes.' My mother had a great love for her sisters and turned her female friends into even more sisters, and she remembered her outrage on their behalf at this slur. Friends don't betray us. Women do not betray each other! But how naive was she?

My dad did not tell my mother about this betrayal until a phone call about six years after he had left. When he had dropped his bombshell, I hope his conscience felt lighter. But my mother's trust had shown her as a fool. 'You must really have wanted to hurt me,' she said quietly before putting down the phone.

But it was never about her. He had not even given her a thought.

Recently, my mother and I talked about this again. So many years had passed. Was it really in the house? Was it really when you were in hospital giving birth to me? Possibly. Could have been. *Yes. It must have been.* Our house was always light filled and fragrant with flowers. The windows open, the door on the latch so the world could come right in. 'She cleaned our house. She wanted to do me a favour.' A gift from her for my mother's return with a new baby. Trusting and open-hearted, my mum had considered this the most thoughtful thing a friend could do. Her gratitude was perhaps amplified because she was not the most fastidious of cleaners – she had once set the cooker alight grilling bacon in a deeply greasy pan. The hearty helpful Islington firemen stomped into the house, followed by all the excited neighbourhood children, our friends.

My father had many affairs, some that mattered more than others, and this one, I am sure, meant nothing much at all. Just an opportunity presented and taken, thrilling in its transgression. But it mattered a lot to my mother. Perhaps it meant more to her friend, too.

She had always admired my mum – '*your skin is so much more beautiful than mine,*' she had said, envying too what seemed her golden life. In the years after this betrayal, she even bought a house a couple of streets away. So odd, considering the friendship had already cooled by then. My mum had never understood why it had become awkward until that phone call from my dad. She was shocked, of course, but kept it close and the friendship quickly withered to nothing. She never confronted this woman at the time. It was easier, I imagine, to forgive my father than to forgive her, a woman, as close as a sister, someone who had been invited into the intimate spaces of our life.

But perhaps the deceit was visited upon me too. This was how I came into the world, born into betrayal and lies, my father not really present for me from the very beginning, so blinded had he become by his compulsions, the endless cotillion of distraction, action, shame. I never had the whole of him and spent the formative years of my life distracted by longing for someone to offer me all his heart. But I had no idea of what to do when it finally came. Preoccupied, always, with that inflexible state that Roland Barthes so lucidly explores in *A Lover's Discourse*, that 'I am loved less than I love.'

As my father danced from woman to woman, forgetting names, forgetting the impulses that had driven him, the fleeting moments of pleasure and oblivion, did he wonder if it was worth it for this? For what? Was he even aware of how this would affect us? He was the eternal child, gripped by the endorphin flush, the libidinal instinct, the need to have every passing whim fulfilled: I want; I shall have. This is my due.

'I love you,' he said to these women, just to have them look at him in that way again. They might have believed it. They might have left marriages and families, made catastrophic changes in their lives just to have this sparkling man utter those sweet words again. I love you. They were all women with lives, with pasts and futures. Their bodies were full of heat and hope, of laughter and tears.

He hooked up. He fucked them. He came home to my mother. Until the whole macabre dance came to a sudden reverse and a spectacular end.

My father wrote to my mother. The year after I was born. From Helsinki. He had woken with a start from a terrible dream. *Such dreadful dreams I have been having about you.* A dread, which, he admitted, must have existed in his mind – that his wife fancied a poetic young man, *Twenty-one years old and full of teenage romantic foolishness*, he wrote. He feared, in this dream, that he had to compete with this ideal, and my mother retorted with *that painful air which I have seen – 'you don't understand – I need this romanticism'*. From inside the dream, all he could do was panic, shout and scream with such a dreadful pain, *that I want to kill the stupid fellow. What makes it worse*, he added, *is that the children are neglected by you and I feel fear and sadness for them.*

I am so stupid, he added. *I never see that such dreams only come with insecurity.* But this understanding did not extend into a deeper realisation that this was merely a projection of his own actions, of his own guilt, pursuing the unattainable ideal and neglecting everyone who really mattered in the process. Even at the worst moments, our mother put us first. She had laughed when asked by a friend: if she was on a sinking raft with her husband and her children, who would she sacrifice? 'Why, him of course. I'd throw him off without a second thought!' She would do whatever it took to protect her children and we wrapped ourselves in this truth.

Adultery. An altered state. A fantasy, seductive in its fragility and elusiveness. In that moment, he could obscure all reason. He will not have known the trouble he was storing up, that if he kept on searching for this momentary high, he might reach a state of tolerance where the high was not high enough anymore. But he continued to exist in the moment, speeding and out of control. When, years later, he ended up in intensive care for the third time in a number of months and was told he would die within the year if he didn't stop drinking, I begged him, and he could only laugh, 'But it's so much fun.'

'How can it be bad when it feels so good?' he was prone to saying. If he said it enough times, he would believe it. He twisted and changed. He altered his shape. He grew another head.

We did not know at the time – but, then again, perhaps we did. We are all instinctive beings. When my mother was pregnant with me, my dad was already cheating on her. Like a child born of an addict, did the agitation course through my veins? My origin myth. Subservience to a tantalising absence. My father's first touch of my cheek. I was marked then, by the fallout of all of this.

Runaway

My parents had a sublime bed. Super king-sized, six-foot wide, seven-foot long, with a mattress from Heals and an Art Deco cherrywood and peach silk headboard, shaped like a wave. It was so beautiful my mother even wrote about it for *Brides* magazine. All four of us could fit into it at the same time: Mum, Dad, my brother and me, even the cat, curled up unperturbed by the bump and shift of knees and feet. We had Christmas morning in this bed, opening our stockings, and Mum would sometimes play a game where she'd pretend-wrap me and my brother up in brown paper to make a parcel ready to post us through the letter box. I have a vague memory of early morning warmth, tucked between my parents, Dad still here. There were not enough of these mornings. I imagined this enormous bed was the soul of our house. Mum's smelly creams and beauty regime and her dream diary tucked away in the bedside cabinet. Dad getting dressed in the morning in an elegant suit, clipping the leg of his trousers for the mammoth cycle ride from Islington to Kensington High Street, flying with the tails of his raincoat flapping in the wind behind him.

But one day, when I was six, he woke up and decided to leave. This time for good. He just disappeared out of our lives, with no mention of when he would return. He bought a single ticket to India with a Dutch woman he had met at a peep club in Soho. She wanted to introduce him to her guru, Bhagwan Shree Rajneesh.

My brother and I crawled into bed with our mum in the morning but the space beside her was empty. There was more room for us, and yet our world had shrunk. My brother was eight when my dad made his real escape. Perhaps Dad needed this operatic rupture of flight to a new identity in India to finally drag himself away. I wonder if he had become particularly restless when my brother turned seven, the age he was when he was abandoned for the first time on the boarding-school step? Or if he saw himself in his son, the son who would one day vanquish and replace him. But perhaps it was more mundane. His business was in financial trouble, his frantic juggling was beginning to fail, he was alarmed by his sexual incontinence, and felt shackled by family and responsibility. Of course he would run away to an ashram in India where all your past could be erased, and your future is created from your imagination. We were now reduced to three, just as his family had been all those years before – an awkward asymmetry.

In Pune, the Indian sun was warm and rich with light. Sannyasins, Bhagwan's disciples, lived in wooden huts and abandoned Raj apartments dotted around the enchanted Koregaon Park, sleeping beneath high ceilings and clattering fans. They wore lunghis, home-dyed in colours of the first rays of the rising sun, maroon, orange and pink; traditional Hindu holy dress but without asceticism, Bhagwan's followers slung their malas around their necks or under an arm while they danced or made love. They worked as a community, cooking, cleaning, making crafts, running therapy groups, while their red-ragged children played in the dust and dirt, but mostly they meditated. They faced their fears together beneath sweeping canvas canopies, their shoulders rocking, and arms stretched up to heaven, to the rhythm of live drums and a backdrop of palms, heat-haze and bougainvillea. They breathed, they danced, they hollered, they then collapsed on the ground, still with silence, forming pink stars with their spent bodies.

Bhagwan was seductive with his long soft beard and flowing robes. He was beautiful, too, with a smooth conker head and mesmeric welling eyes. He was provocative and irreverent. In those early days he dressed humbly in white. 'The mystic is a drop-out,' he pronounced in one of his discourses. 'The real revolutionary is not fighting anybody. He simply sees the absurdity of things and drops out.' Like the first hippies of Haight Ashbury in San Francisco in the 1960s, Bhagwan believed change was only possible from inaction. A soulful step away from the system.

This was as seductive as nectar to the swarms of Westerners looking for relief from the mundanity of their lives, the dullness of the cities where they lived, in jobs they found tedious, the ties of bills and mortgages, the captivity of parenthood. Bhagwan's central philosophy, that you can only be responsible for yourself, was my father's sweet honey. In the late 70s, there were thousands like him wanting to be a part of this new religion. In the early days Bhagwan had mostly an Indian following, but it soon grew to include crowds of Europeans and Americans, mostly middle-class, educated and wealthy, emerging from the sexual revolution and LSD with its experiment in transcendence. But most of all they were turning their backs on their parents' generation, characterised as the oppressors. Many felt that the hippies' attempts at liberation had failed, and it was time to look within. After so many years of repression, conditioning went so deep that the individual could barely recognise it in themselves. It was in their bone marrow and their blood, in every breath and blink – the enemy, according to many, now lay within. This was the era of mysticism and psychotherapy, and Bhagwan packaged up both and offered it as a gift in his elegant long-fingered hands.

In 1978, 1979 and 1980, thousands of people came to the ashram, like my father who 'took sannyas' in 1979. A redeeming feature of Bhagwan's movement was that it promoted diversity, all creeds, all nationalities, all colours. He wanted to create the 'New Man', a uniting of West and East, an experiment that his disciples were thrilled to be a part of. They were the chosen ones and in the wonderful mood of 1970s naivety they really believed that they had the power to change the consciousness of the planet.

Bhagwan held the conventional trappings of family life in disdain and gave his disciples permission to free themselves from their yokes. He encouraged his disciples to say: 'I am not going to be a part of it. This way or that, neither for nor against. It is *so* stupid that I cannot even be against it.' What a relief that they could finally laugh at everything that had previously seemed so loaded with duty; what joy they felt!

Bhagwan Shree Rajneesh was first known to his disciples simply as Rajneesh, fantastically translated by his followers as the 'Blessed One Who Has Recognised Himself as God' or, more accurately, from the Sanskrit as 'The Blessed Lord of Darkness', then just Bhagwan. Later, after his first run-in with the US government, he changed his name to Osho. He was also notorious as the 'Sex God', a branding first given by the Bombay Press in the *Poona Herald* following a series of lectures he had given on sexuality, *From Sex to Superconsciousness* in the summer of 1968, which conflates the egoless state one reaches during intercourse with religious experience. It was these lectures that led him to become notorious in India, a reputation that never left him. In his 'spiritual gangsta' days on the ranch in Oregon, when his robes turned glitzy and gold and he did a daily drive-by in one of his ninety-six Rolls Royces, as if he was royalty, or, worse, on the set of *Dynasty*, he became known, in various non-sannyasin circles, as Bhagwan Shree Rolls Royce.

But Bhagwan did have charisma. My father spoke of his energy field, how when he was close to him it felt like he was tripping. At Bhagwan's *darshan*, his intimate evening gatherings in those early days, some of his disciples would start to involuntarily shake. He simply had the power to make people fall in love with him.

The movement took its influence from several philosophies and religions, a kind of potato smash of Eastern Hinduism, Zen and Western psychotherapy. At the heart of traditional Hindu philosophy, as quoted by the Indian scholar Sri Shantananda Saraswati, is the belief that 'to begin to be what you are, you must first come out of what you are not'. This was its premise: shed the ego, and with it your neuroses, the artificial constructs inherited from the constraints of society and generations of family, and the everyday demands of living in the civilised world. You will then discover your essence – the true you. Bhagwan believed in an ideal state, primitive and innocent, and he wanted his disciples to aspire to this freedom, too, through love, surrender and sex.

Bhagwan's devotees should live in harmony with everyone and with nature. His people would be 'creative' – able to transform their repressed energy into something productive such as music or poetry. They will live in love. To be a sannyasin was to be open – absorbent as a sea sponge and light as a feather on the wind. His followers appeared to drift in a perpetual state of 'bliss', trance-like, dreamy and disengaged. Bhagwan discouraged 'listening'; instead people should meditate, let his words swim on a wave, be receptive to the energy around them, creating their very own buddhafield. A few years earlier the Beatles had brought guru devotion and transcendental meditation into the mainstream with their own chosen one, Maharishi Mahesh Yogi tapping into Western culture's hunger for personal fulfilment and looking for an escape from the mundanity of societal roles. Bhagwan grabbed hold of the same noose and loosened it with his fingers.

During his 90-minute morning lecture, when he paraphrased religious scriptures combined with Western philosophy, jokes and anecdotes, Bhagwan sat before his coral-clad followers and imparted his wisdom with a mocking knowingness and hands pressed together in namaste. His unbreachable sense of his own superiority was assumed also by his disciples. It was not in humility but with pride and disdain that they surveyed their 'unenlightened' families and friends who had been left to clean up the wreckage of their abandoned lives.

★

In my late twenties, researching my first novel, I wrote to my father, who had recently moved to California, and asked him to explain a little of what was the appeal. Why this? We, as his family, had been one of the many left behind, standing on the other side, puzzled and bemused. In defence of our hurt we had turned to ridicule what we considered a cult, to laugh at the wackiness of the long beards, the beatific smiles and hum hugs.

Just a few years ago, I found the letter he sent in reply, telling me of his early jobs climbing the publishing ladder, from sales to running his own business; his restlessness in his marriage with my mother (he spoke of his infidelities as a kind of compulsion); why he became a sannyasin. Of his time in Pune, he wrote about a moment before dawn, joining a line of men and women gliding through the dark, dressed in warm coats over red robes, hoods, socks and comfy shoes. It was the daily procession to the morning's 'dynamic meditation', of chaotic breathing, shaking and hoo-ing, as a prequel to stillness. *Everything was silent*, my dad wrote, *except the gravel beneath our sandals. Occasionally we'd also hear the Indian chai-wallahs beside the road with their carts. It was the most magical moment. It will stay with me forever.*

Watching the Netflix documentary by filmmaker brothers Chapman and Maclain Way, *Wild Wild Country*, my heart surges when one of Bhagwan's closest allies, a Californian lawyer, speaks of what it felt to walk through those gates in Pune for the first time, stepping out of the heat and chaos of the Indian streets and into this lush and green oasis, where groups of red-robed people were talking and hugging. 'A sea of people moving in waves,' he describes it. 'I wanted to be there,' he says, his eyes filling with tears. 'I had arrived. After a life of feeling I don't belong here, even with my wife and children, I felt like I had come home.'

I realise now that this shaking up of his life and his sense of himself was the beginning of my father's odyssey, in search of a hoped-for discovery of a more private self, in the process attempting to shed his past like old skin. It was a reprogramming, perhaps, of that early suffocating influence between home and school, and the frantic distractions that followed. Many British disciples were escaping their public-school educations, the prescriptions of Western religion, too. I have since been told of a dean from one of the leading independent schools who turned up to teach in his red robes and mala of beads and recruited his students to join him in his spiritual mission.

It was clear that my father was searching for an ideal home. In that same letter, he admitted he had been a mess when he first joined the movement, having gone through various therapies to try to address his restlessness. He wanted to be stripped back, given a chance to start again.

In Pune, my father felt free to be himself. He could wear a skirt, a faded pink bandana around his head; he could eat watermelon all day or fast himself to a standstill. Nothing would curb his excesses. Having been encouraged, as all the newly arrived men were, to have a vasectomy, he could follow his impulses. Have sex with whomever and whenever he pleased. There was no need to hide anymore. It was the new norm. With repression and guilt removed, there was no longer any need to rebel. He could look at these impulses and examine their usefulness. 'I like sex,' he could say, staring at his naked reflection in the mirror. 'What's wrong with that?'

Did he feel he might redeem himself? Finally rediscover the golden dawn, the light of his original wholeness? Maybe he was trying at this point to reunite with that innocent child who searched out only pleasure when he still felt it was possible. But it was anarchic here, as it had been at boarding school, a grown-up animal farm. *Bhagwan created a kind of structured carelessness*, as my father describes it. *If another person was suffering from some emotional problem – jealousy, anger, fear, doubt – it was their problem.* I see this echoed in the way Ma Anand Sheela, Bhagwan's notorious secretary and the driving force behind much that turned sour about the movement, reveals in the documentary how her skills at deflecting responsibility were slicker than any politician's.

It is very hard to describe it all, my father wrote. *Not because I don't want to, but because the reality was only in the feeling and the being, and not in the mind and therefore couldn't really be memorised at all.* I have since recognised that this is the language of the heart – the soft oblique realm of the unconscious. I do believe he felt he had found a neutral place, finally, in which to face himself, to exorcise any regret or guilt. It does not have to be this way, Bhagwan had told them: he who clapped at his devotees to finally 'Wake up!' It must have been so seductive.

And us? My father phoned only once during the six months he was gone. Apparently, there were no phones at the ashram, and of course mobile phones were still an entrepreneur's dream. Mum laughs when she recalls that one time when an Indian receptionist asked her to accept reverse charges. I imagine his voice in among many others, the shrill of parakeets, tears of laughter and joy circling him like a heartbeat. 'You have children here,' my mother said with deliberate calm. 'Please think of them.'

We, his family, were forgotten amid the neutral grey of north London, an afterthought; left behind with only the slow rhythmic drip of waiting. Had we become merely an anecdote of that time when Dad failed to know himself? His maroon-clad friends would have nodded and smiled in recognition. They were all moving on.

My mother says that this is when I changed. Aged six. From bold, bright and confident, to mute and pale. I folded into a shell, forgot my smile. I have memories of school, sitting on the scratchy library carpet behind my friends, and of losing my voice, a perpetual lump in my throat. We did not know where he was – India was an alternative universe, not somewhere we could imagine. It might as well have been the moon. A day to a child can feel like a week, a week like a month, a month like a year.

'Why did he leave me?' I was to ask my mum again and again, rejection like a barbed arrow in my heart, her reassurance making no difference. 'What did I do to make him go?'

I had no concept of the greater world, or the complexity of desire, or the myriad reasons why he bolted. My parents had loved each other; we had been a family. Rejecting that felt like a personal betrayal. At bath-time, as the day unravelled and I felt the comfort of night draw in, I cried, and my mother despaired at how sad I was. 'You were heartbroken,' she has since said, and my grief was like that of an abandoned lover when he had simply tired of me.

In the absence of anything else, my brother and I told ourselves that he was dead.

My mother, on some level, told herself this too. She wrote a novel in the early 1980s, the years that followed Dad's disappearance, a kind of thriller suspense, never submitted it for publication. She was not aware of it at the time, but it expressed strong feelings she was not able to process. Her heroine is haunted by her lost love, full of sadness and erotic longing. Despite his apparent death in a car crash, he still, through the power of memory, appears to control her life and heart.

When Dad finally returned six months later my brother and I met him on Hampstead High Street. I had stuffed my hands into my duffel coat to try to stop the shaking, my toggles done up, navy tights, Start-rite shoes. My hair was cut into a bob and heavily brushed, shocked with static. My brother wore a blazer, and a long Doctor Who scarf. It was a grey October day; that perpetual flat-toned ochre of autumn. Our father stepped from his car and stood facing us from the edge of the pavement, teetering between two worlds. He glanced back at his new girlfriend in the car.

He looked so different. He appeared smaller than his six-foot-two, tanned and thin from dysentery, his shoulders a hanger to oversized clothes. But it was his smile that spooked me. It was all dreamy, and his eyes were glazed, focused on some other horizon. His girlfriend peered at us from the car, dark fuzzed-up hair, clothes of orange to faded red; she was a stranger to us then. He was dressed in a purple Ellesse vinyl-mix tracksuit with plastic elbow patches and gaiters, and a long-beaded necklace. For a father who liked cruising the men's department at Harrods, it was clear to us that this outfit had been chosen by her. Sweat gleamed on his forehead, despite the London chill, as if he had brought the heat with him. His beard was wild and flecked with gold.

'I've been reborn!' he told my brother and me that day in Hampstead, his eyes shining. 'The man you knew before is no longer.' I dug my hands deeper into my duffel coat and stared up at him. 'I have a new name,' he said with affected elation. 'From now on, I will be known as Purvodaya.'

Pooh-va-what? My brother and I frowned, caught suddenly by an abrupt blast of fleeting sunshine. But if you're no longer the man you were, does that mean you are no longer our dad?

There was an element of ridiculousness, even to us at such a young age – our father a caricature, standing on the stage of someone else's play. My brother nudged me, and we met each other's eyes.

A few days later, my dad arrived at our home with his girlfriend. She sheepishly settled at one side of the kitchen table and my mother at the other, and Dad looked indulgently from one to the other and proposed that he wanted to come back, and wouldn't it be a good idea if his girlfriend could move into the family home, too? He would move back into the marital bed, and she would sleep in the basement. It was a charming thought – he pirouetting between each of his women like a polyamorous happy prince.

My mother made them tea. She felt sorry for this silly sweet girl – she was still inclined to think of women as sisters – and her anger was only for my father. To him, she said emphatically, 'No. You are completely bonkers.'

With his new guru's words fresh in his mind, he probably dismissed my mother for her conventional mind. Why couldn't he still be with her, the woman he loved, and love another woman at the same time? She would have known this also as Shelley's philosophy, expressed to his wife Mary when adding another romantic liaison to his life, 'True love in this differs from gold and clay, that to divide is not to take away.' But my mother did not join these men in their contempt for the bourgeoise trappings of monogamous marriage.

My mum tells me now that Dad was also partly spurred to return because she had caught the attention of our handsome neighbour. With his black hair and saturnine looks, he could not have been more different from our dad. Trustworthy and reliable, if a bit austere, he was clever – a double first in Physics from Oxford – and a doctor at a renowned London teaching hospital. But most painful for my dad was his car, a red Alfa Romeo Spyder, the iconic Italian sporting coupé, which was parked outside our house.

In our north London 1970s existence, most fathers were absent. On our street, in the corridors of our liberal multicultural state school, where were the dads? There was the Puerto Rican cab driver who escaped his family to tour with a jazz band; the producer who searched greater fame in Hollywood; the neighbour who ran off with the Bulgarian au pair; the solitary Yugoslavian poet who eventually threw himself under a train. My father was part of a wandering tribe, off on their travels to search for – who knows what? – the promise of a more fluid and self-centred existence than family life could ever offer. The majority of those who wandered were men, mostly fathers. My mother sat at a kitchen table with her friends, cup of tea in hand, and they all acknowledged it. This epidemic. A middle-class phenomenon of an excess of choice and too little grit.

But our house was our castle, our street our moat. We formed our own community. My mum and her neighbours relied on each other for childcare, and we a gang of kids who played football on the road, ran in and out of each other's houses, stripped off naked to play doctors and nurses, and danced wildly in bedrooms, before settling at someone else's kitchen table to eat boiled eggs and soldiers or cheesy toast fingers. My mum threw brilliant birthday parties – all our friends from school in a colourful jumble on the living room floor, musical chairs, and statues, dancing to Stevie Wonder – *Happy Birthday*. Her favourite trick was to leave us supine as sleeping policemen (the first to twitch was out), while she finished decorating the cake, shushing us each time we wriggled a foot or raised a head. A new neighbour moved to a flat next door, a performance artist whose best friend was Matthew Kelly. In the summer they would beckon us in from the open window, off the dirty streets, feed us biscuits and squash. For my eighth birthday, a sweet young Matt Lucas ate fire in our garden, his bald head shining bright in the neighbouring lights.

My brother and his friends scaled scaffolding to enter derelict buildings. They hung about in disused gardens, and befriended a homeless man, smuggling him bread, milk and bananas. They stole the stars off Mercedes hoods and lobbed eggs from the top windows at passers-by. Sometimes my brother took pot shots at tin cans on our wall, far too close to the neighbours, with his air pistol, secretly given to him by our dad. On hot days I would spend hours on my own, chalking hopscotch onto the pavement, or squatting to inspect the ant trails, dreaming up imaginary worlds. Real fires flickered through the darker months, and Christmas trees twinkled. Apple-bobbing parties. Marshmallow clouds. In the summer we were out all day. In gangs with buckets and sponges, we knocked on neighbours' doors to ask if we could wash their cars for extra pocket money; when they went on holiday we fed their cats. Each night, we closed the door, and it was our mother who kissed us to sleep.

Our father's adventures were only made possible by our stillness. A reliable central point, static and unmoving, the eye of the storm. Regardless of this, we followed him, somehow. Or he was with us still in the tasks of our every day. I would imagine him watching me from a magical globe and spoke to him often in those long hours of knocking about at home, as if he might be interested in the quiet ordinariness of my day. *Now I'm making toast. Would you like some?* A sigh, smoothing my hair. I would mutter to myself, half my mind on my performance to my dad who will think I am quirky, so sweet, such a silly little thing.

He was also somewhere in the depths of my mother's longing, in the heat and quiet sadness we all felt.

I see us three at that time, strong and solid like a pyramid, our foundations firm in the ground. But we are static, resolved. I am struck by Barthes' exploration that absence is only possible as a consequence of the other. 'It is the other who leaves. It is I who remain . . . like a package in some forgotten corner of a railway station.' Somewhere in the depths, I was suspended, while my father searched out truth from obscure corners of the world. My dad was a runaway who had found happiness in freedom, while I was left in his thrall, almost like Echo who cannot speak unless another has spoken, mute, diminished, waiting for his return.

Dad didn't only abandon us. Pierrot Publishing was left to disintegrate ignominiously in the shadows of our basement. My mum and her sister were left to face the creditors and take the small, once brave, company into bankruptcy. There were shameful sums of money owed to authors and printers. Plans made, forward projects booked, authors and designers let down, lives affected, hopes crushed. It was tragic and terrible. And yet the architect of these woes was in the land of lotus eaters, twirling in the dust.

Pierrot's strength was that it was run like a family. Everyone was shocked at my dad's sudden abandonment, disappointed and grieving, but also full of empathy for my mum who was left with the ruins. Even *Private Eye* covered its demise sympathetically.

But it also left us vulnerable. My mother was asked to reveal our assets. Told to turn over the keys to our car. What of the house? Our home had been set as guarantee against an unpaid bank loan, and my father had fled, leaving his debts with no regard of how it would be paid, and no real concern where we would end up. Our beautiful home. Our beds. The wardrobes. The tiled table. All at risk, because of his recklessness. My mother's father stepped in and borrowed money against his own house to pay off the bank. Without him we would have lost our home.

I recently found a postcard in a box of old photos and letters. A satirical illustration, twenty caricatures of the Queen with one of her corgis, like a black and white contact sheet. It is by and from Ralph Steadman and addressed to my father who used him as an illustrator for one of his books. He refers to some changes Dad has for a new book, a version which had been seen by Ted Hughes. I am struck suddenly by how rich my dad's life had been and how, if he had wanted it – if he had believed in it, or himself enough – he would have continued to be an innovative publisher. This was his doing. He had created this world and was its charismatic leader, whose entrepreneurial endeavours others wanted to follow. And yet he gave it all up for the promises of a self-proclaimed guru in India, whom he would never truly know. My dad had regressed to a child again, looking up to a father for guidance on how to live, only this was a father he would never grow to supersede. The guru/disciple relationship is designed that way. What if this new path infantilised him, made him dependent, and denied his agency?

There was no kindness in the abruptness of my dad's flight. Freud might have seen it as self-preservation. His protection of himself from the pain of us, of love lost and the accompanying guilt. But what of that pain? What does it look like? Maybe he acted it out in those meditation rooms. He kicked and screamed and swore. He probably fucked it out with all those strangers, as if he could purge himself of us through depleting his life force. And what of his children's suffering? When my mother asked him this on a crackling line to India, he said, with his new-found confidence, 'Their pain is their responsibility. They can choose to suffer. Or they can choose not to. It is nothing to do with me.' Since my father had become 'enlightened', any criticism or outrage expressed by my mum at his behaviour was patronisingly dismissed as merely more evidence of how unevolved she was. Luckily, the brittle line broke up after her spirited response, and she didn't have to hear his smug condescension.

A year after Dad left us for his guru, Pune was thrown into disarray when it was announced that the ashram would be relocated near Antelope, Wasco County, Oregon, in the United States. The movement had outgrown itself and needed bigger premises. Bhagwan liked the idea of moving to America, the country of promise, and with growing publicity, good and bad, and books published in his name, he was becoming something of a celebrity. This was 1980 and many of his disciples, like my father, who had left their families, uprooted their lives, or taken their children with them to India, now had to consider 63,000 acres of rugged farmland, known as the Big Muddy Ranch, as their new home. What followed was an enormous project to build a self-governing city, Rajneeshpuram. At its height its population grew to 2,000. With architects and city planners among them, the sannyasins built the infrastructure; electricity, plumbing, an airport, pizza parlours, an enormous meditation centre and settlements of A-frame houses. The moment the disciples arrived at the ranch they were put to work. It took years and a huge communal effort to reclaim the land and turn the desert green. Bhagwan arrived once it was all ready for him, flown in on a private airplane, in August 1981. But, soon after, he declared he was going into silence, taking a backseat for almost the entire time he was there.

Dad went to Oregon but did not stay long. It was chaotic in the months of its evolution and you needed to pay substantial sums of money to be there. Disciples were driven to drug smuggling and prostitution, or to re-mortgaging their homes, if they were lucky enough to still have one. My father, with nothing to his name, decided to visit his sister, so he flew into Syracuse airport, New York, with his girlfriend, homeless without money. He was so thin that my aunt barely recognised him, his hair and beard overgrown. She drove them to her home in Fairhaven – a wood-structured house full of bright white and shadows, which looked out on a frozen bay, skimming distance from Lake Ontario, with five acres of forest out back. She lived there with her second husband, with whom she was on the verge of separation, two young children between them. The winters here are harsh – six months of heavy deep snow. It was quiet in the enveloping white. The mood was melancholy.

I see them drifting, my father and his girlfriend, arrived from the more civilised climate of Oregon, now with blurry morose faces peering out from hoods, in a sea of white. They are not smiling. They are adrift and lost. On the periphery. The bitter cold of outside.

They stayed for six weeks. They both tried to make money reading Tarot at the local 'physic fair' but otherwise Dad hung about the house, distant, purposeless and moody. My aunt has since said he made no sense during this time, 'spoke such mumbo jumbo, pure gibberish, all that hippy shit'. Despite this, he projected the authority of someone who had found the way, a leading light, he himself a swami. He parodied his guru. His sense of superiority, of being in command of a higher truth, was already established. His sister found it irritating. To make things worse, when they eventually left, her hard-working husband was furious at Dad for leaving a phone bill of $600 and no money to contribute.

A similar mood of entitlement was sweeping over the surrounding culture of the ranch. The sannyasins harassed the local residents of Antelope when challenged about their lifestyle and misuse of the land. They had bought it under false pretences, claiming they would only develop it as an agricultural farm, as its conditions allowed, knowing full well that this was not the truth. The Rajneesh people lied from the very beginning. The residents made it clear they did not want them there, these strange hippy folk taking over their town in their faded red puffa jackets and sweatpants. 'They all had "that look" as if they were hypno-tised,' one local recalls. 'When they came around the town, we'd cross our arms.' While the sannyasins were driven by the belief that they had been chosen to transform the consciousness of the world, the local Antelope residents, mostly conservative Chris-tians, believed all that free love and open sexual cavorting would bring down civilisation. Jonestown was still fresh in the Ameri-can consciousness, and with it the fear of cults and brainwashing and the inexplicable deeds that could come about with power concentrated in one person, and surrender of the rest. When a group named 1,000 Friends of Oregon, whose members included Bill Bowerman, founder of the waffle sole that eventually grew into Nike, threatened to have the buildings of Rajneeshpuram removed, as they had all been illegally built, Bhagwan's deputy Sheela got angry. 'I will paint the bulldozers with my blood!' she exclaimed in her defence of the city they had built with their bare hands. In retaliation she started to buy up the town of Antelope, in order to create a stronghold: 'Sheela with her gold pens and diamond rings,' a resident described her. She flashed big money at those who could not resist and before long the sannyasins had taken over the sleepy town. They changed the name of the café, the hub of the Antelope community, to Zorba the Buddha, and at night they would shine their car headlights into the remaining residents' houses in an attempt to intimidate them into leaving.

Sheela admitted that they sought 'loopholes in the law'. They even formed a police force (which they called the Peace Force) justifying their right to arm themselves. I am struck by their attitude towards the locals, people who justifiably considered the area belonged to them, their home for generations. The sannyasins waded in with an aggressive and colonial superiority, dismissing them as yokels, uneducated, 'stupid and ignorant', as if their opinion counted for nothing. 'It was just a ghost town,' Sheela is recorded as saying, but Antelope was where many settled down to retire, a place where people belonged. In an interview, one of Antelope's residents who managed to find incriminating evidence against the sannyasins by raiding their bins (which eventually contributed to the picture of immigration fraud that the FBI built up around them), was quoted as saying, 'they were educated beyond their intelligence'.

I think again of my dad and his boarding-school peers, of the British elite, most of the men who rule this country, and their unassailable sense of entitlement, perhaps also 'educated beyond their intelligence'. What my father won't have realised at the time of his escape was that in searching out this community, which on the surface felt like the antithesis of all that he had experienced as a boy, he was in fact exchanging one institution for another, each with its own hierarchy and reward systems, its own set of rules and power games; but this time he was one of the chosen few, surrounded by people who were less powerful and therefore could not hurt him. He was beholden to no one. Back in the safety of the 'special' crowd, he had exchanged his black school uniform for loose cotton and lunghis, dyed purple, orange and red.

Living a communal life was all that my father knew after all. It was a shield in his armour; here, he could be both absorbed and diluted.

But reality soon caught up with him, and he returned to London to get a job as an insurance salesman to earn enough money to return to Oregon or set up his own community. He and his girlfriend looked for an apartment to rent in Hampstead or its surrounds. However short of money my dad was, he never spared himself a smart address.

They lived in a top-floor flat in a white Victorian mansion house on Grosvenor Avenue, overlooking Primrose Hill. It had one bedroom, but a grand high-ceilinged living room, with shutter dividers so my brother and I could sleep in relative peace, while my dad and his girlfriend watched videos. We watched *American Werewolf in London* in this apartment. That night I was too scared to close my eyes in case a werewolf came bursting through the curtains.

Sannyasin friends came to visit, like globes of sunshine in their yellows, oranges and reds: an American gay man, dark and moustached like Rock Hudson, his open-necked shirt exposing curly chest hair. Together we counted Dad's money. Ten-pence pieces, a few fifties, and lots of coppers. I piled them up in towers and Dad tossed a coin to see whether we should spend his last pennies on milk and bread or tickets to the cinema. I was thrilled that the cinema won.

They moved to a ground-floor flat in Lyndhurst Gardens, which was dark and brown, and had a sitting room that appeared to stretch round corners, to a kitchen and out again. My brother and I slept on a bunk bed in a tiny back room, close enough to hear the horror movies. We once walked in on the *Exorcist* scene where she levitates from the bed, all white eyed and bloated. This flat was close to both of our schools and we would visit in the week and do our homework together at the big central table. In the curve of the living room was an L-shaped sofa of brown velvet, on which we jumped from seat to seat, while 'She's a Maniac' from *Flashdance* blasted through the stereo.

They moved again, this time to a basement apartment in a house on East Heath Road, on the bend as it passed through Hampstead Heath. A wooded area on one side and a line of houses on the other. The road was busy, and my brother and I would bomb across it the moment it was clear. It was dark and cold with corridors and narrow rooms where you could always hear the traffic. Here I found three photographs in Dad's desk drawer: one of him naked and lying on the bed, his engorged penis slug-like on his stomach. The other two close-ups of his girlfriend's dark bush.

We watched the science fiction cult movie *Flash Gordon* with our dad. We watched *Flesh Gordon*, too – its erotic spoof. We watched *Confessions of a Window Cleaner*, following a window cleaner on his bed-hopping adventures with housewives. We watched the first ever animated feature film to receive an X rating in the US, *Fritz the Cat*, a satire on the free love movement and ideals of hedonism. We watched *Emmanuelle*. I was aged nine; my brother eleven. Our mum had no idea.

The move to Oregon had put Bhagwan's religion on the international map, and communes were popping up all over the world. In 1982 Dad and his girlfriend left London to go and live at Medina, a sannyasin community in a stately home in Suffolk with acres of woodland. Up to 200 people lived and worked here between 1981 and 1985.

On sporadic Fridays, our dad would collect me and my brother from school and drive us there for the weekend. We would emerge from the car in our school uniform, dazed from the journey, and dazzled by the sudden blast of colour and light. The commune kids would crowd around us, scruffy and skinny, in ill-fitting clothes. I stumbled back when they fired questions, about my school, my age, whether or not I had hit puberty. The hint of sexual knowingness that crossed their faces both thrilled and frightened me. At my insistence, Dad bought me a maroon bomber jacket and purple cords from the commune shop. On our next visit, I struggled to get into them on the backseat of his car.

People liked to dance at Medina. It was another form of meditation, of surrender. When sannyasins danced, they closed their eyes, swayed their arms above their heads and swung their hair. My brother and I hung about on the margins, too embarrassed to join in. While the adults formed a sweaty throng, the community's children sought out their own entertainment: they skidded along the slippery floors, chased each other up and down the stairs, climbed trees and ran barefoot across the lawn. In his memoir *My Life in Orange*, the late Tim Guest captures life at Medina vividly: 'As the children of the commune, our role was to run free, to be uninhibited, to say yes, to look beautiful, innocent, uncorrupted.' And many of them appeared to be just that. Their confidence was radiant. I stood back and glanced shyly from behind my NHS glasses.

My memories of Medina are of open spaces, communal meals, washing up, panpipes, wafts of incense, people drifting about in loose clothing and calling one another 'beloved'. In my only photo from this time, I am dressed from head to toe in red: red sweatshirt, red cords, red Nike sneakers. I am in a field of children, all in pairs with their arms around each other. There is one pair of girls at the photograph's centre, their ankles tied together, laughing, playing a two-legged race, oblivious to me walking towards them from the left of the frame. I am alone, clinging hold of my fingers, looking for a friend. This captures how I felt most of the time, off-centre, wanting to belong.

My brother remembers feeling very homesick here. The acute absence of our father, at a time when my brother still felt he needed him and might get a little back. He remembers many long hours hanging about; lonely in one of the bedrooms Dad camped in, listening to 'Telegraph Road' on repeat. Our father shoving a pound note into his hand before disappearing again.

Along with the men who were encouraged to have a vasectomy on joining the movement, many women were sterilised, some when they were young. Children were considered an obstruction to their parents' personal development. But what of the children who were born outside the commune and had followed their parents to live here? Those families were encouraged to give their children up to the greater good of the multiparent family, to become children of the commune. The kids at Medina slept in a mixed dorm, forbidden from the age of five to sleep with their parents. Some children were sent here from abroad and had to live away from their families. Tim Guest's mother spoke of how she had believed that the community would be a better parent than she could be. But according to Tim, he felt he spent his 'whole life on tiptoes, looking for my mother in a darkening crowd'.

The school here was chaotic and colourful, and while English and Maths were compulsory, everything else was optional. 'It is up to the children, they will lead us,' was the general approach to teaching. But not many lessons went on; most of the time the children were expected to work for the community, to cook, do the laundry and clean. Above all, the most important lesson was in life: children should learn from each other and the adults around them. Only the adults now appeared to be in regression. At times they dressed in pyjamas and walked through the grounds fondling teddy bears and speaking baby talk.

The one and only time our mum visited Medina she was shocked and hated the fakery of it all. Instinctively, she felt that it was not a safe place for us. My brother was protective of us both and felt the impact of our mother's recoil when we were there. But we continued to visit at odd weekends, as she felt she could not keep us from our dad as long as we needed him. She was afraid that if she did, he would become a messianic mystery and all the more seductive. This was a recurring question that hounded her throughout our childhood: should she cut ties with him in order to protect us, or let us negotiate this rocky path in the hope that we would learn from experience to reject it ourselves?

And we did need him. Like clockwork toys we slowed down in the weeks between – later, once he had moved out of the country it was months – and our weekends or holidays with him were like a key winding us up again. I, particularly, was anxious leading up to seeing him. But – though our mum never would have said it at the time – it was always us who did the running. Our father couldn't care less if he saw us again. Our mother let us go, but always stood at the ready, holding her sword tightly in its sheath, her hand gripping it firmly.

During those weekends at Medina, both my brother and I became aware of sex. There was no particular moment or revelation, it was just around us every day in displays of open affection and in conversation among the kids and the adults – inappropriate things being said, late-night noises. We learned that sex could be indiscriminate, that love did not necessarily mean monogamy and that kids did it, too, with each other and with adults.

Dad and his Dutch girlfriend were still a couple here. But during the many empty hours that my brother and I spent waiting outside the meditation room, playing Donkey Kong on our consoles, we would catch a glimpse of Dad in a crowd of similarly sunset-clad, bearded men, with a new pair of female hands clasped around his back. He told us they were in a consensual open relationship, but then I would walk in on his girlfriend naked and furious, about to hurl his marble Buddha out the window.

Every time we visited they had moved bedrooms. We slept in the Active Meditation Centre, kept up most of the night by hysterical laughter and sobbing, or in the communal attic, where futons were divided only by clouds of sheer purple organza, and where couples copulated openly. I once crept up the stairs for a forgotten something, only to find a man fucking a woman, while she lay back in a cloud of cosmic boredom, entertaining herself by reading a book. Bhagwan preached that sexual perversion lay behind all mental sicknesses, that civilisation repressed an essential 'life energy' by calling sex a sin. In the days before the harsh reality of AIDS gave sannyasins pause for thought, long-term relationships were not the norm: *Everyone was screwing everybody else all the time*, my dad later wrote to me. We never told our mum what went on there, as we didn't quite know how to formulate it ourselves, and didn't want to risk not being able to see him.

Bhagwan cherry-picked from Eastern philosophy and twisted the vine to fit his promotional tool of free love. In one of his discourses, he made his position clear: 'Once your own understanding of love blossoms there is no question of attachment at all.' He referred to traditional Indian Aboriginal tribes whose teenagers – aged thirteen to fourteen, on the cusp of sexual maturity – had sex with every one of their peers before settling down to marriage. 'With one condition – and this is a beautiful condition – that no boy should sleep with [the same] girl for more than three days . . . So, there is no question of any jealousy, there is no competitive spirit.'

In this context Bhagwan saw attachment as something to be overcome. To protect yourself from jealousy you should free yourself from feeling. In other words, teenagers should experiment. But he added a gloss to this sentiment by conflating sexual freedom with love. Vedanta, the teaching of nonduality at the heart of Hindu philosophy and Buddhism, understands non-attachment to be central to freedom, yes, but freedom from the mind. Love is in the body and is something else entirely. A famous statement in the Bhagavad Gita – one of the great philosophical treatises, tells us: 'When a man dwells on the objects of sense, he creates an attraction for them; attraction develops into desire, and desire breeds anger. Anger induces delusion; delusion loss of memory; through loss of memory reason is shattered; and loss of reason leads to destruction. But the self-controlled soul, who moves amongst sense-objects, free from either attachment or repulsion, he wins eternal peace.' To desire is to covet. The principle of non-attachment in Eastern philosophy is let things be. It has nothing to do with sex.

It is hard to trace whether Bhagwan spoke about sexual initiation in his discourse, but there was a definite culture of older men being with younger women within the communes, and of men pursuing minors, virgins. There were mutterings of older men 'deflowering' these girls, and it was certainly common enough that my father considered it a good thing, that the inexperienced girl (as it was almost always girls) would benefit from the man's maturity. Perhaps this initiation was seen as a safety net for these girls to have a wiser, more experienced teacher, but in reality it is peverse and sinister, and a total abuse of power. There were men who watched me while I played at Medina, making no attempt to hide their inappropriate admiration. 'She's cute. She's going to be a beauty,' they'd say to my father.

'He likes you,' he would tell me, as if it were normal for a man to look lecherously at a nine-year-old.

But my brother also had experiences like this. One of Dad's lovers, small and blonde, hung about longer than the others and was particularly keen on him. Once she and Dad had decided not to have sex with each other anymore, she landed on my brother's lap outside the meditation room and stroked his face, questioning what he might look like as a man, 'Handsome, like Purvo,' she purred. He felt deeply uncomfortable. During movie nights, when the kids all cuddled up on cushions in the dark, my brother was accosted by some of the more forthright girls. He was just eleven years old. Much as we loved to be with Dad we must have been relieved to return to the safety and predictability of our real life at home.

In a Dutch documentary, *Child of the Commune*, directed by Maroesja Perizonius, which touches on her time boarding at the Medina school when she was aged thirteen, she and her mother dig out a form from the school that requested consent for a girl of Maroesja's age to be given 'appropriate contraceptive devices', either 'chemical or mechanical', 'should she request or should it be considered medically appropriate or otherwise desirable'. Maroesja had very similar experiences to me – unwanted attention from men who were far too old, when she was far too young to know how to handle it – but she was on her own in this place. It was her only home, and she had no parental figure to turn to.

In *My Life in Orange*, Tim Guest describes the year Medina closed down, when a lot of the children who had lived there ended up in Oregon, at Rajneeshpuram. The children landed, probably stunned and dizzy from its size and extreme climate. The ranch was also on the verge of collapse – the FBI already planning to raid the place, digging up all sorts of frightening evidence of murder and madness; the atmosphere would have been paranoid and aggressive. The place was bristling with guns.

'That year . . . at the Ranch, many of the Medina kids lost their virginity,' Guest wrote, 'boys and girls, ten years old, eight years old, in sweaty tents and A-frames, late at night and mid-afternoon, with adults and other children. I remember some of the kids – eight, nine, ten years old – arguing about who had fucked whom, who would or wouldn't fuck them.'

My mother was right to be worried, but she won't have known any of this.

'Burn your bridges – go forward,' was one of Sheela's lines. It was a movement that thrived on provocation, and the sannyasins made enemies wherever they settled. Their conflict with the ruling Janata Party in Pune culminated in a knife attack; later, after driving out the residents of Antelope through bullying and intimidation, the sannyasins' offensive behaviour went further afield, spreading like a disease through Wasco County in their attempts to win seats in the local elections, and to eventually 'paint the State red' – and they did not mean turn it Republican. In an attempt to manipulate the votes in a local election, Sheela masterminded a plot to poison residents in the county seat with salmonella, cultured in the sophisticated Rajneeshpuram labs. Some 750 people were taken ill, forty-five of them needing hospitalisation. It was the first bioterror attack on US soil. During Rajneeshpuram's last months, the autumn of 1985, there were so many guns on the ranch, not only hand rifles, but Uzis and assault rifles, that the National Guard was on standby. It was like some kind of crazed sci-fi political thriller – my dad could not have come up with this plot. After fleeing to Germany with her female entourage, Sheela was arrested and imprisoned.

The movement was like a pressure cooker, building up and up until it imploded. Rajneeshpuram collapsed just five years after its inception, and Bhagwan was arrested before being deported back to India with a $500,000 fine, narrowly avoiding prison for circumventing immigration law to arrange fake marriages. The US government stayed on his tail, preventing him from renewing his visa in India and then any other country where he tried to settle. Finally he was permitted to return to his home country where he lived his last years in poor health, dying of a heart attack in January 1990.

Recently I read a book about Bhagwan written by an anonymous sannyasin who chose to call himself Sam – mostly, I imagine, because he admits to being a drug smuggler in order to finance his stints at the ashram. But it is an intimate account of that time. He writes of his guru's contradiction, that he was complex and mischievous, 'that's what makes describing him so tricky, for whatever you say about him you have to add that the opposite could also be true. Regal, he was, but in a flash he was Dennis the Menace.' Despite his vow of silence for much of his time in Oregon, Bhagwan's movement, cult, whatever you want to call it, became a mirror of him.

There is such divided opinion, even now: some of his disciples are still devoted, despite everything, some have denounced him as a fraud, a charlatan. Scandal was inevitable. How could it not be given their beliefs, the outlandish and dangerous behaviour, the philosophy of provocation, and contempt for the laws of the land. The Way brothers in their documentary show early footage of the therapies, which were extreme – groups of naked sweaty people locked together in a room become more like feral animals, shouting and hitting, knocking each other to the floor. There are stories of sexual and physical abuse, of corrupt hierarchies, based on social and financial standing. There are accusations of hypnotism and undue coercion: that the therapies were designed not for their disciples to push themselves to the limit in order to know themselves better, but instead to lose their minds and judgement and become compliant. There are even reports that in those last days at Rajneeshpuram, everyone was drugged into complacency, that the kitchen staff were adding heavy tranquillisers, like Haldol, to orange juice and to the food, fed to children as well.

Disciples were certainly distracted and exhausted by the daily grind of work. There was no time for socialising, nor meditation; everyone was too busy to stop and notice what was going on.

When the murderous extremes of behaviour of Sheela and her female lieutenants were exposed, the majority of the thousands of disciples had no idea that the whole place had been wired, that every phone conversation they had ever had from the ranch had been potentially listened to and recorded; or that there was a medical lab on site where various poisons were made to be used on anyone who stood in the way of their push for power. One member of the community who followed her mother to Rajneeshpuram when she was seventeen years old recalls, 'There was a culture of control and fear. You knew that you couldn't complain. If you said you were exhausted or if you were negative, they'd tell you to leave.' And by then so many had burned their bridges and had nowhere to return to. A couple of years into her time working there, they were ordered to wear a uniform, a purple shirt and slacks, anonymised, stripped of their individuality. It is an irony that so many people chose this self-proclaimed progressive movement because they believed it would save them from the repression of their past, only to find themselves in an even more oppressive environment.

In the end, the scandal overshadowed any of Bhagwan's teachings. Sheela had truly driven the movement into cult status with her dogma and threats of reprisals; she even renamed it Rajneeshism, the philosophy of the Lord of Darkness. By choosing to be silent in those last years, Bhagwan retained his aura, while Sheela stepped forward to replace his status as guru, but of a different kind. She was the classic narcissist, the trickster, taking on a persona which was impenetrable, with a constant strained and fake smile on her lips. But it is also worth noting that Bhagwan had accepted the name Rajneesh with its dark connotations for himself. Even in his most outlandish days of collecting Rolls Royces and *Dynasty* robes, he could always claim it was to illuminate the ridiculousness of it all, that no one must be attached to him, his disciples only had themselves. His most loyal defenders would believe that in choosing to be silent in those last years and letting Sheela rule, he was allowing her to be her most authentic self – a megalomaniac. But I believe the harshness of the land at the ranch and its development into a self-governing city was just too big for him, too extreme and hard-edged compared to the gentleness of the original ashram with its emphasis on meditation; his silence was a type of opting out, he himself became the 'drop out' that he had encouraged his disciples to be.

When AIDS became a worldwide threat, it was announced that the New Man of Rajneeshism would be saved from death, as together they would form a protected island, while the entire rest of the world would perish. This only strengthened the fear and control of community members, further separating them from the outside world. It was not helped by misinformation that AIDS could spread through saliva (everyone was advised to wear rubber gloves when having sex and to avoid kissing). Maroesja remembers mass AIDS testing at Medina, of even the toddlers and children, as a new rule came into effect that you had to have a negative AIDS test to be admitted to any of the communes. I was with Dad one summer at the height of hysteria when this new edict came through and, even though he thought it was ridiculous, he did buy in a bumper pack of yellow Marigolds.

The American psychotherapist Daniel Shaw, who himself spent years in a cult and writes about it in *Traumatic Narcissism: Relational Systems of Subjugation*, has identified a 'cult phenom-ena', based around the relational dynamic between leader and follower, and the guru's narcissistic need to attack his follow-ers' subjectivity in order to stay in power and for his ego to remain intact. 'They control and exploit followers by seductively dangling carrots ... such as success, fulfilment, wealth or en-lightenment. Along with the carrots comes the relentless use of sticks, such as humiliating character assassination and threats of expulsion, meant to persuade the followers that their own sub-jectivity is inadequate and corrupt compared to the leader's, and therefore in need of extensive correction that only the group and its leader can provide.'

But I am also aware that it isn't easy to reject such a profound and intensely felt experience as this, particularly when so much has been given up and left behind. Among those who do leave cults, a common feeling is shame, at their own blindness, their hunger to believe, and grief at getting it wrong. Grief, too, at leaving the community where they had belonged, and at the destruction of a dream. My father did renounce it in the end, in anger and regret – *what a bunch of stupid assholes* – but not for some years to come.

My brother and I were lucky that we were not raised in the commune. We were lucky to have our mother, the safety of our four walls and the ordinariness of that. But I was enamoured with my father – so absent, so unavailable; and therefore, so longed for – which made me vulnerable. My father had chosen a corrupted spiritualism that enabled him to behave with malignant self-centredness and consider himself unaccountable. We all choose the philosophy that suits us best. He adopted his guru's ways, parodying the mystic, the master, with his quixotic and superior musings on the 'enlightened way'. His frequent batting away of our feelings – *you are responsible for how you feel. You and only you. You can choose to feel happy or sad. It has nothing to do with me* – pushed us back in on ourselves. It became his mantra, making us question our feelings of love, need or fear, all so natural for a child finding her way in the world. The cult did not accept negativity of any kind, and our dad was not prepared to question himself. How convenient it now all seems. My father had safeguarded himself from the gritty truth of his failings, cloaked his damaged ego in grandiose proclamations. He walked around with stars in his eyes. I, like so many of the other children with parents who gave themselves up to Rajneeshism, became the victim of his fragmented overweening self. The pendulum of his self-regard swung back again and knocked me off my feet.

Betrayal

Following the implosion of Rajneeshpuram, and the closing of Medina, in late 1984, Dad and his new young wife left England to live in Italy. They moved into a beautiful Tuscan villa, with thick walls and green shutters, marble floors and heavy mahogany doors, and set up a sannyasin community of their own. The house was classic Italian and impressive, with its two staircases and bright, light-filled rooms. My dad's plan was to run a book-packaging company from here, and his friends would all live and work in joy and harmony. He and his wife were celebrated as fulfilling the sannyasin entrepreneurial spirit. My father was good at this kind of thing and it brought him influence and recognition within the community. It was a happy time for him.

The winter he moved there the phones were down. He wrote to tell me there was no heat and electricity and they were working by candlelight and cutting down olive trees to burn on the fire, such a sweet fragrance. I had just started secondary school, but was missing him terribly. In January, my second term, I went on a school ski trip and wrote to tell him.

We'll both be in Italy! he wrote back. I was desperate to see the house, and be part of this new adventure alongside him, and he promised to come and find me, only – and I didn't know it at the time – we were on opposite sides of the country. *Just phone when you arrive*, he wrote, and so every day I dialled the number he'd given me. I tried it with the code. I tried it without the code. I swapped round the numbers in case I had written it down wrong. 'Pronto. Pronto. Pronto?' I stood by the phone and re-dialled, locked in that debilitating but familiar longing. Maybe the phone was finally connected; their business up and running. Maybe he had been out somewhere and had just got home. Maybe he just needed to buy a phone and stick the plug into the wall socket. I must phone him before he goes out again. The maybes were endless and paralysing. I didn't want to do anything or go anywhere because I might miss his call. I sat in the snow at the top of the nursery slope shivering with the cold, watching my new friends fly down with freedom and confidence. I wanted to follow them, but I was so frightened of losing control.

Finally, my brother and I visited Dad and his wife the following summer. I was eleven years old. I had cut my hair short for my first day at secondary school, and now it was an outgrown and curly bob. I have a photograph of myself grinning from a mattress on the floor in the room I shared with my brother. I am wearing Levi 501s and DM boots, despite the heat. Hugging my knees, I smile with a sparkle that makes me think he has just done something silly like fart into a tennis ball cannister. My cheeks are pink from the sun, and my mother-of-pearl glasses reflect the light.

My favourite part of the house was its belvedere, a viewing platform where you could dance and twirl between party tables, or sit brooding on the wall, feeling the feathered breeze as it came in over the trees. It had terraces of vegetable gardens and cypress trees that swished in the wind, and beneath was a road that wound in bumps and curves towards Florence. My brother and I were to come every summer for the next seven years. It was among the happiest and most confusing periods of my life.

For the first time, here, I experienced how intensely beautiful a place could be. I threw back my head and closed my eyes to the hot sun and inhaled deeply the smell of baked soil and dust after a passing storm. I walked everywhere barefoot, from the cold marble stone floor to the gravel on the drive. I heard the swifts and house martins each morning, as if they were singing just for me. I discovered herbal tea, and coffee brewed Italian style, strong and milky with a dollop of honey. I smoked my first beedi and drank my first cup of wine. One of Dad's friends, a tiny Italian woman who wore cotton slip dresses and had a daughter who taught us Italian swear words, took on the role as cook. She made omelette, and quiche and potatoes, and salads with radicchio, and laid it all on the communal table beneath the umbrella pine. There were enough places for eight, or nine, ten, eleven, twelve, those who lived here and daily visitors from Miasto, a larger commune near Siena just over an hour away. We ate under the stars, me beside my brother, our father and his wife, and their friends, full of bright talk and mellifluous laughter. The cicadas sang our chorus.

I discovered the scent of the night, rich with tarragon, and the creeping darkness. Glimpses of fresh Indian silk; a glitter of gold; bells ringing from anklets and bracelets. We listened to Huey Lewis and the News, to Sade, to Peter Gabriel, to Steve Winwood – *Higher Love*. Spinning around the kitchen table, we wound round and round, hands clasped, and laughed until our heads spun and our cheeks hurt. I discovered the feeling of rapture, warm blood and eyes open to the light – all that they let in. This was happiness, but it was an ecstatic happiness that exploded in your heart, intense in its fragility. My father had landed again, using his instinctive leadership skills and charm to steer this particular ship. Here, finally, he had reclaimed his position at the helm.

There were no boundaries here, no rules or walls to knock against. Dad and his wife would have a row, and everyone would know. They would make up and everyone would be talking about it. Live it, feel it, be brave. If you love me, tell me. If you're angry, shout. You wanna fuck me? Act on it. Bhagwan had told them: 'Just be natural. Never feel guilty about anything.' They took it literally. A visitor would leave her shoes at the door and make love in the afternoon. The window open.

My dad was immersed in this new life, but distracted and absent to his children. Two years older than me, my brother had learned to enjoy this freedom. He has no real memories of being with Dad during this time, but no longer felt it was a loss. He ridiculed the hippy sannyasin goings-on and kept his own distance, taking advantage of the absence of parental supervision.

Dad hired us 50cc Piaggio Ciaos, part bike, part scooter, which needed peddling to get started and lost power going up hills. My brother loved to ride down to the outskirts of Florence, to a supermarket where he would stock up on his favourite foods: Babybel, Yop and cheap stuffed green olives in brine. He knew just enough Italian. I joined him on my own 50cc Piaggio. When my brother got a bit older, Dad hired him a Vespa.

Occasionally, my brother and I had friends from home stay for the first week, and we'd spend long hours scripting and directing films made with Dad's video camera. We set up a pretend doctor's surgery with chairs in a circle in the sun-dappled courtyard. My brother, the doctor, tended to his friend, whose leg was wrapped in a bandage made from a T-shirt, always unravelling. We scripted a film about Madonna, on the insistence of my friend who knew all the words to all her songs. Somehow Madonna morphed into Marilyn Monroe committing suicide by jumping out of a top-floor window. 'Cut!' I shouted with my shaky camera work of the back of my friend's head as she pretend-lurched towards the view. The next shot had her lying splayed out on the pebble drive below, her colourful dress askew, covered in dust. Play-acting kept us occupied for hours.

But this didn't stop me from going in search of Dad, and I was more susceptible to his friends and their attention than my brother ever was. When I finally caught hold of him, a fleeting moment when we could be alone, he would put his bear arms around me, and the longing would disappear. My brother was aware always, even on his adolescent adventures, of where exactly I was and who I was with. He thought it odd that I was drawn more to the adults. He tended to take the micky out of them, as his way of deflecting, warmly, always, so they laughed at themselves, rather than taking offence. 'Oh, Purvo,' they would say to our dad. 'He's so like you.'

After supper in the garden, I would stay to listen to their grown-up chat, and as it got dark my brother often disappeared. He would be off somewhere playing with the cats or would take his Vespa out, helmetless, and in the dark he would drive to the top of the hill, any opportunity to be off and someplace else. He would return with mosquitos trapped and whining from his hair. One night, a flame suddenly burst down the side of the house, a streak of gold through the black night. We all looked round from the table, the last of pudding, vats of wine and candlelight, and spotted my brother and a friend pouring lighter fuel from one of the top bedroom windows. It left an impressive black burn mark on the beautiful terracotta wall, until it eventually washed off in the storms.

But my brother also recognised, and admired, my persistence with our dad, my determination to keep on trying, nagging like an echo, 'who always answers back'. I did ask for his attention when I needed it. I did not always get it, but I tried.

Solitary and imaginative, I was swept away by the mood and beauty of the place, and enjoyed dreaming time alone, lying on my mattress within the cool white walls. I had discovered writing some years previously when my dad had given me my first diary and encouraged me to write down all my confusing thoughts, and here the words flooded out of me. I would sit in my room or beneath a tree and furiously scrawl across the page, exploring the characters I had created, and their worlds, drawing from the exoticism of all that was around me for my inspiration. From the belvedere, I leaned into the wind that whipped over the hills. I watched the swarms of local young men, helmetless and zippy on their mopeds on the road beneath us and fantasised about what it would be like to kiss them. I let the wind embrace me, believed it might hold me.

My dad and his wife had the best room with French doors and a balcony, overlooking the pebble drive. An en-suite bathroom of marble and stone. My stepmother would invite me in to talk to her while she did the ironing. She would wash my hair in the marble bathroom, where I would sit with my back to the open window and its view through the wrought-iron gates and up the drive between the olive trees either side. She would thread lightener into my hair, which smelt like pure camomile and turned my hair blonde in the sun.

She had been a student when she and my dad met, also a sannyasin. Between Medina and Italy, Dad and his Dutch girlfriend had moved back to London near Hampstead Heath, and this young woman had come to stay as a lodger, taking the small room that overlooked the garden. She was multi-lingual, dark and exotic with cropped short hair and a delicate face, dark wide-set eyes; she wore multiple earrings up her ears in silver and turquoise and bangles that sang when she moved. Small boned, she was a neat hourglass, and wore pink suede trousers and cashmere jerseys, owned Agnes B cardigans in all colours, and ironed her knickers, putting them away in neat piles. She was just eighteen when she met my dad; he was thirty-seven. I was ten. She felt like a sister.

Very quickly the two women had swapped rooms. This new beautiful eighteen-year-old moved into the big room at the front of the house and into my dad's bed, and his now ex-girlfriend, who didn't seem to mind that she had been replaced by a teenager, moved into the small room that overlooked the garden. They called themselves the white witches and lay around on Dad's bed cackling. I was enthralled by Dad's new girlfriend. When I lay about on their bed, she spoke openly to me of how pleased she was to be with an older man. 'Don't choose a boy your own age,' she would say. 'Boys take a lot longer to mature than girls. Best to double your age.' I nodded and listened and drank her words thirstily. I totted up the years in my head and worked out that my first boyfriend should be twenty. I wonder now if she was trying to justify her choice, this sudden shift in her destiny. She had dropped a dark and sparkling-eyed young man her age, for my dad on his insistence. I remember how awkward it was for her the night she dumped him at the sannyasin disco in Gospel Oak. She loved him, she had quietly told me.

I was a sponge, saturated with her and her elegance, and the bridge she balanced between teenage and adult. She showed me how to wash and blow dry my hair. How to use deodorant. How to feel pride in looking and feeling fresh and clean. Before they'd moved to Italy, in a moment of shared conspiracy, she took me to have my ears pierced – a salon in Selfridges where they used a needle rather than a gun, despite my mother having forbidden it until I was fifteen. She gave me her clothes, and I learned how to dress beautifully when with her, in fine fabrics, the finest colours, from the smartest shops. But I also started to cry during these weekends. I was not sure why. I would sit in the corner, hugging my knees, breathless against the tears, which were urgent and unbidden.

My dad always gazed at her with love eyes, and I would ask why he didn't look at me in that way. 'Do you love me more or less than you love her?' I would ask, repeatedly. 'Do you love her more than you love me? How much do you love me? Why don't you love me as much as you love her? When you say you love me differently, what do you mean? How is it different?'

My father was possessive of her; he was nervy and eager to please. Perhaps he was overwhelmed by her youth, her intelligence, the precariousness of that. He had fallen in love with a child. He encouraged her to leave university – midway through – to abandon her studies, and instead to go into business with him. He knew how much she admired him, her genius daddy, and he convinced her of his greatness. She lit his cigarettes, taking just one puff before passing it back. She giggled, a breathless feminine song bright with her confidence of being the one he desired, loved, cherished. A blushing knowledge of her power when his eyes were on her.

Perhaps the world shifted all the more because there had been so much at stake. She gave meaning to the sacrifices made – the people hurt; the lives he had upturned – to make himself available for this: a delicate beauty, a butterfly, alive but potentially fleeting. She must be with him always, in every waking hour. He was not in command of his feelings when he was with her.

Within a year of meeting they were married. My father's impulsiveness playing out again just as it had all those years before when he married my mother the same year he met her when she, too, was eighteen. The chance to hit the reset button – decades later, another eighteen-year-old, a new life. My brother had said he didn't want to attend the wedding, but I was determined to.

The video from their wedding sat on the TV stand beside the Betamax player. I did not want anyone to replay it, dreaded being reminded of how I had ruined their day. The video had been recorded by one of their sannyasin friends and it opened with a purple rose at the centre of a heart, softly focused, a backdrop of Indo-European music, synth and pan pipes. The purple matched the bride's dress, which had puffed sleeves; her hair was soft and feathered around her face. She and my dad's arms were entwined. The man who took the film tried to crop me out of the frame, but couldn't, because every shot he had of them was also of me. I clung on throughout the ceremony, even when they took their vows there was a small bespectacled me, my hair plaited by my mother, just as I wanted it with ribbons, crying and clinging onto my dad's arm, grabbing at him when he surreptitiously tried to elbow me away.

Soon, I couldn't breathe I was crying so much. I was gasping for air, snot and tears all over my face. I loved her, but I was heartbroken. My beloved father was in love with someone else. Someone beautiful. Only eight years older than me. A more intelligent, more beautiful daughter.

When I was in my twenties, I read Kathryn Harrison's *The Kiss*. A memoir about her estranged father laying claim over her sexually. The first time they meet after ten years apart he kisses her goodbye and 'pushes his tongue deep into my mouth: wet, insistent, exploring . . .' I was struck by this book, not because my father ever showed any sexual interest in me, but more that he too had somehow trapped me in a state of longing for him and he did nothing to help release me, and nothing to protect me from the confusing landscape of his voracious sexual appetite.

Sitting on my father's lap when I was just ten years old and so pained by my jealousy of this young woman who had all his attention, I have a memory of facing him, not away, a porn movie playing on the TV behind me, an orgy, three women in a line, naked, their backs and bottoms bobbing on strips of grey legs, all hazy motion, moan and groan. My dad says flippantly that perhaps we should turn it off. My brother turns to me and says, 'This isn't really what sex is like.' I'm undoing the buttons on my father's shirt, or am I doing them up? I don't know which. I say simple words to him – or do I? I say, 'Some children have sex with their dads.' He doesn't respond, nonplussed. I climb off. The film is turned off. The lights go down. Did I really say it?

If he had stepped back and seen me then, aged ten, trying to work out the landscape of love, might he have understood what confusing messages I took from observing him and his open sexuality? That by unbuttoning his shirt I might have been flirting with a latent desire to possess his attention in the way his lovers did? To have all of him. Why didn't he want to protect me from this? Pathological narcissism is not love, writes Daniel Shaw. It is the opposite of love. It is not acknowledgement and acceptance. It is not empathy and understanding. It is not mutual recognition. It is, according to Shaw, 'a failure to see a child as being subject in his or her own right'.

Harrison writes: 'In years to come I'll think of that kiss as a kind of transforming sting, like that of a scorpion: a narcotic that spreads from my mouth to my brain. The kiss is the point at which I begin, slowly, inexorably, to fall asleep, to surrender volition, to become paralysed. It's the drug my father administers in order that he might consume me. That I might desire to be consumed.' He is the narcissist. His daughter is subjugated, and infected by his poison, paralysed by his need to maintain his unreflective position as the focus of her gaze. He traps her, so he can continue in his power, superior, untouchable.

My father did not want or need this kind of enslavement, but he needed my puppy-like devotion so he could continue to behave as he wanted, the indulged man accountable to no one. But I was also a nuisance to him, hanging on his sleeve, so often unable to contain my noisy grief, and it reminded him of what he had done.

My mother turned to a psychoanalyst friend at this time to ask for advice about me. Her friend reached for Freud and Jung, suggested I had been suspended in the Phallic stage of my sexual development: I was 'father fixated', she said. The Electra Complex, according to Carl Jung, is about the daughter's sense of competition with her mother for her father's affection. My father had left abruptly, and perhaps I had not yet mastered my understanding of his role in this world as father to me. Any progression I might have made was continually undercut and muddied with his more urgent compulsion to be a sexually active man, desired by women and adored. He was unknowable. He was puffed up, he swaggered, embodying virile conquest. A fantasist and in some ways a ludicrously fantastical figure, no wonder we laughed at his preening self-regard. Women on the Underground were always pressing themselves against him, every face that turned his way was full of admiration and desire.

There was no recognition of his sacred role in showing me that the love a daughter and father shared was not the same as the sexual love between adults but was just as powerful. Without this clarity, I had little chance of falling out of love with him, to learn to simply love him as my dad, and reject him like a daughter should finally do. He kept me at a safe distance while he played the romantic fugitive, a charmer, elusive, hard to know and even harder to pin down. I *was* fixated. I could not see beyond his facade, to know who he really was, a fool of a man, sentimental and making mistakes, blundering through life, but on an epic tragi-comic scale. There was no real fatherly love, prepared to make compromises and rein in his own needs. There was no discipline to rail against. He was the adult.

In Italy, Dad and his sannyasin housemates worked from the attic room, white desks pushed together, computers and fans. Their books were hardback and square with glossy photographs, New Age, and alternative, quasi spiritualism. My dad's ex-girlfriend came to live with them and wrote a book on magic that included far-fetched cures for 'lack of sexual activity' and 'relationship depression'. Among the other books they produced as a household were *Living in Balance*, which promoted a mix-ture of yogic and Bothmer technique to aspire to a more holistic life, and *Wonderchild* – which my father wrote on enlightened parenting, a subject he believed himself more than qualified. Coffee-table format hardbacks, they were nicely presented and designed with high-quality stock photos, along with photogra-phy that was taken and developed from inside the house by my father and a photographer friend, all the images nicely cheesy in their 1980s soft focus.

The house had a buzzy, creative atmosphere: people up early to meditate in the rising sun before work started. When my dad and his fellow sannyasins were in the open-plan office, I liked to sit alongside him with a typewriter on the table in front of me, the fan whipping my hair, typing up pages and pages of written scrawl from my notepads. I started many stories here, and two novels.

In the afternoon, my brother and I drove our bikes down to the taverna to buy panino prosciutto in fresh salted focaccia. Over dinner and wine, lit by candles, we were told about the Florence Monster who had been killing courting couples annu-ally for years, and hacking off their genitals. Young people in love who snuck away to the hills to make love in privacy. Just like it had been at Medina, sex was once again everywhere. Only now it was not only in conversation over dinner and late-night noises, but in the gorgeous countryside beyond, a fallout from Catholic repression, as my father and his friends dismissively claimed.

Italy. Tuscany. This beautiful house. A dusty path leading through olive groves, wild cats skulking beneath bushes, and an orchard of almond trees. We had so much freedom. Driving mopeds at speed around blind corners. Being thrown off. Getting lost. The heart and its acrobatics. Fresh mornings in early shade. The dead heat of the day. Warm winds. A greying, yellowing of the sky before sudden flash floods. It was a place of extremes. It was where I learned how deeply one can feel.

Like tender new shoots unfurling into the light, the air, so fine, on our new skin. We tremble in the soft breeze, and as the sun shines, we open up some more.

There were wild cats living here. There was a tabby we named Calvin Klein and a black and white kitten we called Obsession. Calvin Klein had kittens. There were five of them, tiny fluffy things that ran about on the drive outside the house or scattered chaotically, unsteady on soft legs, in a trail behind their mum. One night, late, one of Dad's friends arrived in his thick-tyred Mercedes and he drove over one of the kittens on the pebble drive. I was standing at the window of the living room when he reversed his car right over him. I saw tiny legs stick out from beneath the wheel, heard the horrible squeal of a kitten being crushed.

I imagine now that the lights dimmed, the mood changed, although I know everything continued as normal, everyone oblivious. My father and his friends held hands. They stood still, caught in a hug mid-movement. They closed their eyes, standing in the kitchen. Beside them a kettle boiled, a big pan of brown rice bubbled away on the stove, rosehip teabags sat stewing. They stopped what they were doing. They closed their eyes and hummed.

Another friend brought capsules of ecstasy from India. Bags full of them. One summer they were all high. The truth drug, they called it, and dropped it in the evening, glazed eyes and enhanced midnight noises. Dad and his wife went out for dinner and, wide eyed, he talked gibberish to the waiter. They all laughed. Dad offered me a capsule. I turned it over in my hand and shook my head. I had not taken drugs, other than once spluttering and vomiting after cider and a puff or two on hashish. 'No, thanks Dad,' I said. I was twelve.

One day I fell off my 50cc scooter, alone on a dusty path out of walking reach of the house. An old farmer found me, led me to his front porch and squirted antiseptic on my cuts. I knew nothing, such minimal Italian, but had hurt myself too much to walk. I had no idea how I would get back to the house, which was a few kilometres away, my bike an injured lump on the ground.

Then he came, my brother, appearing out of the heat haze like a lone hero. He had been worried about me when I had not returned and had feared the worst. But then he told me of his premonition: he knew what had happened and where I was, although I was far beyond our usual biking route. I have no idea how this happened, but somehow he found me.

I hobbled to him and climbed onto his bike and he drove me back to the house. He laid me on the sofa in the dark wood of the living room, the shutters cooling from the heat of the day. He put a sheet over me, gave me water and made me food. He had a strong instinct to tell our dad who was having his siesta. My leg and arm were badly cut, and he was worried that it would get infected if it was not looked at. He woke my dad and was shocked when he didn't get up to come and check on me. He did eventually, but not quickly enough. 'It took him too long,' my brother has since said.

That night, in a lot of pain, I went in search of Dad, limping down the dark corridor. A light flooded from beneath his door and I stood with my ear to the sounds of whispering. I found them both cross-legged in among huge cushions in the softening light, with wide, dilated eyes and beatific smiles. 'Your dad took that silly drug,' my stepmother said, and he whacked her playfully, looking sheepish, seemingly happy but also oddly sad.

'*You* understand me, my daughter,' he said with softness in his eyes. He turned to his wife. 'She knows me,' he said. 'The only person who really knows me.' This is when he said those fatal words to me – the truth drug, was it? – as I held my throbbing leg.

These words attached themselves to that barbed arrow in my heart: *Lily understands me. She knows me. The only one.* Did that make me better than her? More special? Had I somehow transcended his instinct to push away those who came too close? Had I managed to catch him, finally? I wanted to believe him then, and for years to come, throughout the rest of his life. I still ask this question now.

But – 'it took him too long,' my brother had said. 'I will not read your book,' he told me. 'I will not indulge him anymore. It's bad what he did.' Always pulling me back – reminding me to stand firmly on my feet, to stop looking up, seeing only the glitter in those stars and ignoring the blackness of the night. These are the words that he has said. The evidence is there, he will say. It is all here. Our dad – drugged, drunk, out of his mind. Letting us down again.

I sustained real wounds from that scooter accident, and I still have the scars. I was not taken to the hospital, no doctor was called. Instead, someone in the house gave me antiseptic powder that I puffed onto my arm and leg, and which formed a kind of caked pus-white plaster. When it was time to go home to England, I was pushed onto the plane in a wheelchair, and then again at the other side wheeled off to my shocked mum. I see myself tanned, in my stepmother's beautiful clothes, my hair in a fuzz from the crimper I loved to use. But I am motionless, passive, puzzled. For months afterwards my jaw seized up, so tight I could barely open it to eat an apple. I have often wondered about this time, my inability to open my mouth wide, to scream and shout. It was treated as possible tetanus, but I saw it as a physical expression of my silencing, unable to vocalise to my father my need to be considered, my need to be heard.

I would return home after each summer, bronzed, blonde, beautiful and stunned. It took a moment to re-orientate, the sun at a different angle, a lens refocused. Back home and at school, growing through my teens, I found myself drawn to the troubled kids. Those who bunked off school and hung about the off-licence, handing coins to passers-by to get cider and cigarettes. There were sannyasin kids at our local schools too, with names such as Rajan and Rupa, who turned up at parties, with their long thin limbs and otherworldly confidence. I hung about them despite – or perhaps because of – their lack of interest in me, just to feel the sick sensation of adrenalin, that subtle rearrangement of air. They spilled stories of an unnatural freedom of drugs and no curfews.

My friends and I sat in bedrooms. We smoked fags and drank cider. We went to house parties, and sometimes further afield to warehouses, which were dark and crowded and loud, walls shaking. The sweet smell of hashish and the shock of a fight, a crowd dispersing. When I returned home late and smelling of cigarettes, my mother grounded me. When my school informed her of my truanting, she chased me up the stairs with a rolled-up newspaper, and I could not go out for a month.

I missed my dad.

At the end of a holiday with him, I would sit at the top of the stairs and cry. 'I don't want to go,' I would say. 'Why can't I stay?' He stood in a bright square at the base of the stairs and looked up, his body the core of a warm glow, shimmering within the white sunshine that flooded in through the doorway. He lifted his hands and dropped them again. 'Why not?' he would say, smiling. 'You can stay if you want. You can do whatever you please.'

I was twelve, thirteen, fourteen. Did I want him to rub a salve on my wounds, soothe me with his words, tell me what he thought I wanted to hear? Or did I simply want him to acknowledge my feelings, the difficulty of switching from him to home, and the difference of these two opposite worlds that didn't cross over, were like oil and water. The confusion I felt at loving this place so wholeheartedly and it simultaneously causing me so much pain. I wanted him to acknowledge me. To recognise me as the child I was, understand my needs. I wanted him to help me pack my bags, a tender moment shared, and drive me to the airport with his eyes on me, and his heart touching mine, those little heart hands. I wanted to cry and be understood. I wanted a father not a friend. I wanted him to miss me so much that he might ask me to stay. Instead my brother and I chucked our clothes into our bags, accepted his cursory goodbye and were driven to the airport by one of the hangers-on.

From home, I wrote to him. I used my best handwriting to copy the lyrics of my favourite song: *I'll keep holding on. I'll keep holding on. I'll keep holding on. I'll keep holding on. So tight.* I cried when I wrote down the last words: *That's all I have today. It's all I have to say.* I was not sure if I should send it because I was worried it sounded like a love letter. It was a love letter.

I waited for his reply.

However sophisticated I thought myself, on sunny summer evenings and weekends at home I still liked to hang out with my friends on the street. Sitting on the walls outside our Victorian terraced houses, chatting and watching the world go by. Any excitement would bring the children running. A transparent wisp of an old lady who occasionally escaped from the old peoples' home opposite and came to our door worried about quislings; a police car slowing to speak to a group of footballing boys who had just put a ball through a basement window. When my brother did this once, he and his friends pooled their pocket money to pay for the repair. One evening, Barry Humphries took my mother to the West End to see a play and all us children congregated outside our house in the hopes of seeing Dame

Edna. Recently, I asked Mum, how did it happen? 'I really don't know,' she said. 'I'd only met him a couple of times previously and really liked him, and he told me he was passing through having been in LA writing a script for Les Paterson.' As simple as that. He took her to see a Peter Nichols play about middle-aged adultery, and they both thought it terrible and spent the evening pulling it apart over a curry at Shazan. 'I thought he was one of the most elegant people I had ever met. Sweet and funny and thrillingly clever,' she told me.

Aged thirteen and back in Italy one summer, I discovered that I was attractive to a particular kind of man. One who was enchanted by the innocence of early adolescence, made more vulnerable by paternal neglect and need; one who was able to objectify others and manipulate them for his own means. I was open and unprotected, thrilled by the creative energy of the house and the beauty of the landscape, in need of a father's love, and yet spellbound by all that was new.

One hot summer's morning, a man arrived at my father's house. My father's friend. His eyes lingered on me from across the table. I noticed him too, so dapper in his white suit. He looked old for his age – he later told me he was thirty-eight – as his brown skin was leathery. He was elegant and tall, and held himself well. He smoked cigarette after cigarette. Had a stammer, too, found it difficult to talk, his face growing pained with each unexpressed word pressing on his throat.

That first day he invited me into his campervan, and we lay together on the bed. I stared up at the ceiling as he read me his poetry. He told me that I inspired him. I was aware that the door was open, as I could feel the air on my feet; I could hear my brother kicking a ball against the house, the dull thud thud thud. I did not feel comfortable, and yet that need, that longing, overpowered everything. I was uneasy, and yet there was a part of me that wanted his attention.

It was only days later that he kissed me, late at night when everyone was asleep. We stood in the kitchen, the cold tiled floor under my feet, and the strip light overhead exposing the looseness of his weathered skin. I held myself stiffly as he pressed his chest against the new breasts under my T-shirt. He was dressed in a vest, his skin in folds. The wheeze in his chest and croak of his voice. 'I want to have sex with you,' he whispered. I was a virgin. His kisses were hard and brittle. I found him physically revolting. He told me he was not well. He said he had a urine infection. I looked down at my feet and watched a scorpion, its tail extended, scamper millimetres from me.

Despite this, I felt an awful longing to be with him that week. We went on walks. We sat beneath the stars. He spoke of his love life and its troubles. I had no answers for him but was oddly soothed by his company. He said I was special. His speech got better. Like a river, he said, flowing with ease, flooded with new life. He said it was because of me. I was beautiful in my sadness. Something in my eyes. 'Sad, but special,' he said.

My heart beat fiercely when I was with him, and I felt sick. But he told me his heart beat too. He pressed my hand against his chest and said: 'Do you feel it?' He told me it was because I was in love with him. I had no idea what love felt like. No idea what this was. But I was sad when he was not there. I stared out of the window and waited.

One afternoon, confused and desperate, I confided in my father and his wife. We three sat together on their bed, the place where I had searched out refuge from the heat, from my solitude, so often. Where I would lounge and stretch out while my stepmother tidied or rearranged the clothes in her drawers, or where Dad would read my Tarot. I had wanted that same comfort that afternoon, but I got something else instead: 'You could learn something,' my father said. 'He's a good man. He'll be gentle.' He stood up as if he was getting ready to leave. I looked up at him, perplexed. But I did not want to have sex with this man. I was thirteen. I didn't want to have sex with anyone, but particularly not someone my dad's age, with a wheeze and a stammer, and leathery folded skin. I wanted his attention; I wanted a father maybe, but – I was discovering – a certain kind of man wanted something in return. This was not a safe place for a child. I needed my father's protection.

I turned to his wife, thinking she would defend me, but instead she said: 'Sometimes it's good to be with an older, wiser man.' I was shocked that they both seemed to know of this man's intention, and yet did nothing to stand in his way. *I give you her hand*, I wrote into my first novel where I explored the betrayal of a father literally giving his daughter away.

'But, Dad –' I said. 'He told me he's got a urine infection,' as if that were enough of a reason not to.

Dad paused. 'Ah,' he said. 'I saw his pills on the kitchen table.' He laughed. 'It's not a urine infection, sweetie. It's gonorrhoea. Yeah, I guess –' he said, almost as a throwaway comment while walking from the room, 'it's probably not wise to have sex with him.'

My cheeks caught fire. I was speechless. My heart ached, and then it shrank. I did not tell anyone about this.

But I think back now and wonder, actually, if I didn't really want anyone to stand in the way. I remember thinking I was mature enough to handle it on my own. This must have been the reason I didn't tell my brother because I knew he would think it mad. He was the moral force, despite being only fifteen, he was the echo of our mother, the marker of our London life where these things simply did not happen. This madness belonged here only in this make-believe world. But I did tell my dad. Was I testing him? Did I want him to show me at last that I mattered more to him than anything? And yet I must have known deep down he would do nothing.

I did not have sex with this grotesque man. I knew myself well enough to know I didn't crave that. But I felt compelled by something bigger than me, and it was to feel that a man wanted to be around me, it could have been any man. I simply wanted to feel noticed. I wanted to feel liked. So, I resigned myself to my only defence: I learned, over the course of the next week, to disappear. When he overstepped the line, a tentative kiss or his fingers tracing the fine skin on my arm or knee, I retreated into my shell, deliberating over the discordance between what I needed and what I had to endure. The need was for significance, like a craving, only not for this and not from him.

But suddenly, I was overwhelmed with feeling. The birds outside sounded harsh to me on the edge of that knife. The light sliced my eyes. I squinted when he touched me. I held my chest and tried to crush my beating heart. I did not like the sound of it on my breath, how it might show itself up in my words, so I said nothing.

'You are shaking because you love me,' he whispered.

He took me away on a day trip to the lake, lay me down on a pebbled shore and kissed me, and I was aware only of the birds spiralling up above in the vastness of the sky. There had been others there when we had arrived, silhouetted stick figures on the opposite edge of the lake, and I don't know if they had stayed. What would they have seen? A pretty setting of tranquil water lapping the shore, the hard afternoon sun startling in its shape and colour, the subtle gradations of shade. A middle-aged man with thin hips and black trunks, leaning over a child and putting his hand on her flesh, his tongue in her mouth.

Another day and he drove me to a beach, women waving to him as we rolled the campervan slowly along the dusty path, their silk trousers so light they ballooned on the breeze, orange socks beneath open-toed sandals. They called him Beloved. *Beloved Beloved* on the wind. There were other young girls here, with pretty Indian names and unidentifiable accents. One was chocolate-tanned with jade eyes, and another had hair as fine as a bunny's coat, her skin, hair and eyes appeared to be all shades of white. They were bold enough to run into the sea in just their knickers, their pubescent breasts as brown as their feet. They stood before us, their wet bodies glistening in the sun. 'Are you in love?' a girl asked standing over us dripping with water as we lay in the sand. Another said: 'Do you love her?' He shrugged his shoulders, as if it was not so unusual.

These girls were familiar around him, and he with them, as if they had known each other a long time. It made me uneasy, the way this man, more than twice their age, felt like a family member, only he was not, and their bodies in their newness were sexualised in the tilt of a hip or a knowing look in their eyes. In the depths of my consciousness I knew that these girls had also been preyed on like this, and they had grown so accustomed to it that it had become nothing more than just the way it is.

They threw on their T-shirts and wrap dresses, pushed brown feet into flip flops, and piled into the back of the van, to join us at the house. He had not bothered to tell me they were coming. They sang loudly from the back, Joan Armatrading. 'Love and Affection'. But I was the one in the passenger seat. Then the music slowed – *You've got somebody who loves you*, and I turned to look at him just at the moment he looked round towards me.

Back at the house, my father photographed the girls for his book *Wonderchild*, sitting together in the garden, cross-legged among the urns, a blur of wild flowers and bees, their eyes closed, index fingers touching thumbs in a staged meditation. Dad had promised that I would feature in his book about parenting. I was his daughter. It would not have felt right without a picture of me. While these girls in their brightly coloured T-shirts tied into a knot beneath their young breasts, their tummies as brown as chocolate, made it into my father's book, there was no photograph of me. Was I invisible to him, just like I felt myself to be? Did my need repel him?

That night, feeling desperately anxious, I returned to my dad to ask for help a second time. He was asleep, a big lump in the bed. I stood at the door and spoke clearly into the darkness. 'Dad,' I said, so he could hear. 'I want him to leave. Will you please ask him to leave? It's upsetting me. I don't want the attention he keeps giving me. I can't handle it,' I said. My voice was shaking, betraying my truth. Dad lifted his head and groaned. 'Dad?' I tried again. He shifted over. 'Dad?'

'I'm asleep,' he said.

I backed out of the room.

I remember that the corridor felt cold and long, the darkness of the wood-panelled living room with its heavy mahogany furniture and dusty fireplace, the sofas and the TV, but recently something else came into my mind that I had forgotten. There was someone else there with me when I went back downstairs. A boy, my brother's age, who was a friend of ours since the Medina days, and had come for an extended visit. I turned to him, and told him what had happened, and that I needed this man to leave – he *had* to leave – but I was nervous, my heart a flutter in my chest, because I didn't know how to say it, and I did not want the man to know how scared I was. The boy sat with me. He took my hands and told me not to anticipate anything. 'It's pointless,' he said, 'as you will never say the words you plan to, anyway. Just trust yourself to say the right thing,' he told me. 'It will happen.' So I took a deep breath and stepped out into the darkness, tiptoeing across the gravel drive, to knock on the campervan door.

The man croaked to call me in. I was shaking when I glimpsed him bleary eyed, sleep creased into his face, up on his elbow in the sharp light of his bedside lamp. But the boy's words were still in me – his support and trust in me and my instinct steadying my hand.

'I want you to leave,' I said. It just popped out, five perfect words. 'In the morning, when I wake up, I don't want you to be here.'

He patted the bed for me to come in.

'When I wake up in the morning, I want you to have left,' I said again, my voice in shreds. 'Will you promise me?'

He looked at me, and smiled, entertained by my emotion, the shake in my voice which he probably thought was a sign that he meant something to me. *You repulse me!* I wanted to shout. *You fucking creep.* He shrugged. 'Okay,' he said.

When I awoke the next morning, I had a sick sensation in my stomach at the thought that he would go. I wanted him to go; I wanted him to stay. I was thirteen. I had no idea of what I wanted. I stepped into the shade of the corridor and glanced out of the window. His van was still there, and he stood beneath the umbrella pine, dressed for the day in a white vest over white trousers. I had asked him to leave before I woke up. I had been brave enough to do it alone. And he had promised me. My father was there, too, with his arm around him. They were speaking in hushed tones. Was my father comforting him? 'You don't need to go,' he might have said. 'She's a worrier. She's melodramatic. The problem is in her, not you.' *It is her, not you. Not me. The problem is not mine. It is hers. Her needs. Her feelings mean nothing.*

In that moment it was sparklingly clear that my father's friendship with this man was more important than his relationship with me. All my words. My bravery so hard won. All undone. He would sacrifice his daughter to keep this friend at his side – who was not really even a real friend.

By the time the creep left, I had already apologised. I had said sorry and begged him to stay. I had held out my hands, with all my power there in my palms, like a million tiny grains of sand, so much of it, and I had offered it to him. *Take it*, I said. *All of it.* So easily, tipping the sand into his hands. It had been mine, that power, for a short time – I had felt it – but then I gave it away, as if it were worth nothing.

Occasionally, I trawl a website set up for those who lived at Medina. It is not up to date. My father's entry fails to say that he died thirteen years ago of alcoholism. But there are blurred photos of the kids who lived there, and many of them I remember. I study these pictures and the rushed, misspelt notes beside their faces. On the first page, I am shocked to read: *She died in*

1997, after a long battle with drugs. I scroll down: *He died of AIDS in London in 1994.* I scroll down: *Unknown. Unknown. Unknown.*

There was a Facebook page dedicated to a woman who died from a tubal pregnancy. She had been sterilised in Pune as a young woman and years later fell in love with a man and decided to risk a reversal so they could have children. She became pregnant, but then died of internal bleeding. When I saw the post, I was pregnant with my second baby. It is a much more complicated procedure to reverse a sterilisation than a vasectomy, and there is significant risk of tubal pregnancy.

I have since had conversations with some of those who were raised at Medina, and there is a quiet mention of abuse that took place at the commune school, by one of the teachers; but there is also suspicion at my questions, a shake of the head at further enquiries, and a reminder of my position on the periphery. This particular story is not mine to tell. But I know that many of these children were not all right, and I also know there is a lot of secrecy still in the communities, loyalty, protection of each other, fear of being misunderstood or ostracised.

But what I can conclude from the evidence that I have in front of me is that in his attempt to exorcise the sin of conventional sexual expectations and taboos, Bhagwan enabled instead what became a perversion of love. He and his disciples chose to ignore the corruption and abuse of the children who embodied the innocence they were meant to revere. By not acting they became complicit.

The Wonderchild of my father's book was the 'New Child' – the child of Bhagwan's New Man – 'more silent and meditative than our generation was ever allowed to be', my father wrote in the introduction to his book. His text parrots many of Bhagwan's ideas on how to rediscover the magic of innocence by re-engaging with ourselves, our children and the environment around us. My father sets out his premise: 'To give us adults the chance to play with children so that we no longer need to think of them as our children that need our protection, for children need no protection, they have it bound up inside them from the moment of their birth and before, and it is the adults who take that natural protection away from them by making them adults who have forgotten how to be children.'

I can barely tolerate this incoherent rubbish, the fuzz and evasiveness. Such careless words. He writes about children as playthings: adults should play with children for their own use? They must not protect those children because children have an innate sense of how to protect themselves? In fact, by protecting them we risk taking away their innocence – warning them of the risks of the world will only contaminate them. This book has nothing to do with children, and everything to do with adults justifying their neglect of those children. It is the provocative twaddle that Bhagwan had become notorious for, but my father was no guru.

Tim Guest wrote in his memoir that the role of the child of the commune was to be free and uninhibited. I would add to this that they also had to become precocious and outspoken, grown up before their time, in order to create a protective cloak for their own shoulders. They had no choice. On the surface, a child was considered divine, a gift from the gods, one that should be held with care. A child was autonomous, it did not belong to its parents. But mothers, according to Bhagwan, should not get pregnant until they were stable in themselves. 'First you do the work on yourself.' Otherwise they risked dumping the bag of crap they had been carrying around all their lives into the child's lap for them to carry. But what of all those damaged people who had already become parents who flooded through the gates of the ashram for his guidance, their red-ragged children following behind? Bhagwan believed children were a distraction to their parents' spiritual development, so many were simply pushed aside. During Sheela's time, it was announced that the children of the movement were better off without their parents, and so were packed off onto shuttle buses that ran between the European communes to schools often in other countries. Some were very young. Many were left to navigate the rocky terrain of this experiment alone, or with only older, equally abandoned, children to guide them. They were entirely outside the care system, often with no one responsible to turn to.

Their parents had been told that the commune was better for their children than they themselves could ever be, but a commune full of these same damaged people believing the mantra that you are responsible for no one but yourself was hardly going to take care of a random group of children, some already desperate and lost. Sannyasins may not have been alert to it at the time – so consumed were they by their devotion and pursuit of self-knowledge, but they created the perfect environment for grooming and sexual abuse of the weak by the powerful.

Back at home in London after that summer, I phoned that friend of my father's, who I knew had returned from Italy, and asked if we could meet. He was in me still, disturbing, repulsive, but insistent. I wore a black miniskirt to school, conscious of it crawling up my thighs as I walked, snagging on my tights. He met me in my lunch break and took me to his house that he shared with his girlfriend, which was only a walk away. He held me, and I shook. I told him I wanted to run away. I didn't want to be back home. I hated school. I hated living with my mum. I hated everything. He held me, my small body between his legs. I was so nervous that I wanted to go to the loo, where I did a poo, and tried to flush it down, but it bobbed to the surface. I flushed again. It was persistent, my poo. It would not leave. When I went back downstairs, I stared at the wood floor, worried that he would discover it. I didn't want him to see it, my secret, so I started to cry.

He stood up. 'Come with me,' he said, and he went to his wallet. 'We can run away. Get a flight to Italy. Live in my campervan.' He passed me a wad of cash. I stared up at him, holding it in my hands. 'I will meet you at Pisa in a few days.' I thought of the heat and the cypress trees, listening to Joan

Armatrading in the passenger seat, staring over at him as he drove down dusty twisted lanes. Mosquitos flying blindly into headlamps. He held me. He kissed my forehead. 'You want to come?' he asked. I nodded.

I returned home and before I had a chance to think about it, to see the sweetness of my room, inhale the scent of my comforting nurturing home, I packed my bag. Not allowing myself to feel anything, I told my mum I was leaving to go and live with Dad. She sat with me, stunned, in the walls of my green-painted room, with its border of small yellow flowers and tear-outs from my mum's fashion magazines of Christy Turlington, Iman and Cindy Crawford. She cried and begged me to stay. 'No,' I said over and over. 'I'm going. I'm old enough to decide.'

'But how?' she asked.

I felt a sharp bubble constrict my throat but thrust the cash at her. 'I have the money,' I said, and told her that a man – Dad's friend – had given it to me. *I'm leaving.*

She pleaded, 'What about your brother and me? We've always been a family, us against the world.' Somehow she was on her knees. Her child. The third peg of this stool that she had so carefully built, that she crafted and shaped, held so resolutely in her hands; it would topple and be useless. All that she had cared for; all that hard work. *Please.* She cried, calling on my love for my brother. 'You can't leave your brother. You can't leave me. You can't go.'

I shook my head. I turned away, clenched my fists, vigorous fists. *I'm going.* Made all the more certain by her anguished words.

'What about school? Your future? Your friends, your life here?'

I could not look at her.

Then she stopped.

Her head dropped to her hand.

If you love someone, her mother had once said. *You have to let them go.* My mother had been here before. My father, fleeing. The same. He wanted to escape her, to live with someone else. He wanted to go – then he didn't. He loved her – then he didn't.

My beautiful mother, so loyal and true, that central point that stayed so firm, our star.

She was suddenly calm. 'Okay,' she said. 'If you want to go, then you must go.'

I looked up. Was she testing me?

'But know that we are always here for you. We will always love you, and you can come back any time.'

I stood before her, my bag between us, my mother pale and waiting. All I was putting her through. I felt heavy with the weight of it. It suddenly hit me between the shoulder blades, and I sank into a chair. All the fight had gone. I collapsed like a deflated balloon. 'Of course I don't want to go.' It was my home. I was loved. It was not that I didn't want to be here. It was the pull of Italy and my dad, driving freely along the sun-baked roads, the bliss of summer still in me.

But what about my mum? Someone she loved more than her life was threatening to leave, again. She was paying the price for being the one who stays. Only this time I was her child, and I was threatening to go to a place that she did not know to a man she could not trust. She was my sole parent. All her energies spent on protecting me and my brother. She was what I needed; I only really knew it at that moment.

'You never thought I would do it, did you?' I asked her recently.

'I hoped not,' she said. 'But you are so obstinate and head-strong. When you set your mind on something, it's hard to stop you.' She paused. 'But I wouldn't have let you out of that door.' We both laughed.

'You would have pulled out your sword by then,' I said, imagining both Mum and my brother, backs flat against the front door.

That night in my room, she asked me about the money. 'Who gave it to you?' I told her a friend of my dad's. A man, I said. Someone I met in Italy. I added nothing more. She would not know for years what that man had really been.

I asked, quietly, 'Can we keep it?'

She was emphatic. 'Of course not, darling.'

I so wanted to keep the creep's money and burn it all on Oxford Street.

The next morning, on the way to school she drove me to his house and we posted the money back through the door, with a polite note saying: 'Thank you for your generous offer.' My mother had helped me write it. 'But I don't need your money.'

Many years later, one cold and bright autumn, this man contacted me via Facebook when I was walking along the cliff tops in a treasured place of mine at the western point of Cornwall. I was an adult, married with two children, and on a rare holiday with my mum. A message came up on my phone as I stood at the tip of a promontory; it read: 'I heard you wrote me into your novel. I'm intrigued!' As if he was flattered. 'I've just ordered it from Amazon. Would you like to meet?' He had perused my Facebook page and worked out where I lived. He suggested we meet at a local café.

I stood at the tip of the world, the wind whipping my hair into a frenzy, and I couldn't stop shaking. All those feelings flooded back, the repulsion, the fear, the weakness of being so needy and small. I passed the phone to my mother and said, 'What do I do?'

'You write to him,' she said plainly, 'and you tell him what he did. You tell him never to contact you again.'

That night by the fire, I did just that. I told him that he had groomed me, that it was sexual and emotional abuse of a minor, that it was wrong. I said if he contacted me again, I would go to the police. When I pressed send, I felt a small celebration at asserting myself, at wrapping a blanket, so heavy and warm, around that small girl who had felt so alone.

The liberation at the heart of #MeToo was that the toxic silence was broken. The shame of being victims of abuse was slowly being released into the antiseptic healing light. It was passed from the abused to the abuser, 'You have it,' we could finally say. 'Because it's yours. You must carry it, so I don't have to.'

I can barely forgive myself for awarding Dad's friend so much space here on the page, for being a part of my story. Why should I care about such an inadequate man, so pathetic that he needed to prey on girls of thirteen?

But he does have significance, because he revealed my real traitor.

It was my father who did the real damage by refusing to shoulder his parental responsibility, revealing his obliviousness to the anguished voice of his daughter. As the psychoanalyst Sándor Ferenczi maintains, trauma happens when the child finds no response from those who are there to care for her, or worse still when those same people deny there is anything wrong. There was no empathetic witness. But shockingly, my father made me question my own perceptions and interpretation of reality, just as his had been undermined all those years before by his parents, at his school. In failing to protect me, he was not able to adhere to the emotional contract between a parent and a child.

I would not be silenced by this experience and over so many years I tried to get answers from my father, just a simple acceptance that he had played a part in this crime. But it was useless. 'You can choose how you feel,' he said, again and again. 'It has nothing to do with me.' Not dwelling on the past was an integral precept in the Eastern tradition from which Bhagwan spoke, but it was not intended as a dodge. When in The Tempest, Prospero says: 'Let us not burden our remembrances with a heaviness that's gone', he was releasing those who had atoned, not those who denied or refused to see. Bhagwan gave his followers permission to do anything they wanted and to dust the wreckage from their heels. My father never once acknowledged this dereliction and certainly never apologised.

★

In my study at home, I have a photograph of the front door of my father's villa in Italy. It is a heavy wooden door, both functional and ornate. Behind the door was the flag-stoned floor, so cold beneath my bare feet. The stairs rise in their elegant curve, traced by the wrought-iron handrail that ends in an ornate curlicue. I remember sitting on the loo beneath the stairs, out of breath from dancing around the kitchen, flapping my T-shirt to dry the sweat. Finally giving in to a long held-in pee, desperate to go back to the party. It was so much fun, I could not pee fast enough. Here, from my study, I can still imagine the distant beat of Roxy Music, *There's a Band Playing on the Radio, With a Rhythm of Rhyming Guitar,* and the sound of crying laughter, and I can feel the thrill I felt in that moment, of being young, of being in such a creative place, at the crest of my life. In that small echoey, stone-floored toilet I clasped hold of my body and hugged myself. It was a thrill I was to chase through my teenage years, which filled me with longing, to be alive, to feel whole.

The Long Wait

Recently, I dug out one of my old diaries. A fat black A4 book filled with scrawled writing, letters and photographs that cover the years I was fifteen to seventeen. *Had a lovely afternoon sitting in Polly's kitchen and we ate so much toast and drank so much tea, and we talked and talked and talked* – I read remembering her kitchen, always warm and welcoming, the original Art Nouveau tiles on the walls that her mum collected; the many hours I spent in their house – how Polly and I never ran out of things to say. *Her mum then forced us to go out for a walk and we went to use the phone box outside the shops and phoned Delilah, and we looked round and there was a man sitting in his car with his willy out. We looked at each other and burst out laughing, trapped in that tiny phone box, and I don't know if it was the British Telecom sign – the big T that did it, but once we started we couldn't stop, pointing and everything, and the man looked really embarrassed and drove away. We then bombed it out of the box and ran up her street screaming. I love Polly. She's my bestest friend in the whole world and I know she will always be there for me.* There's a lot of this – of friendships made, passionate expressions of commitment, but there are also many pages of conflicted feeling and longings for boys, with my first attempts at working out love. Only what I read has nothing to do with love as I understand it now, just a hardwired circular anxiety, spinning around in the attic of my mind, the dos and don'ts, the wonderings, the fear, the questions, does he, doesn't he? *I don't think I like him.* I read about some boy who I barely remember now. *But I want him to like me. I asked him: Do you like me? He laughed and nodded and then mumbled something. Sometimes he looks at me like I'm a little bit nutty.*

I discovered clubbing around this time with another friend, Bee, whose dad was a doctor who lived on Harley Street. The Saturday nights when I stayed, we would sneak out after the lights went off, whispering and smothering our laughter as we slipped through her basement bedroom window. We linked arms and skipped through the streets as they came alive, high on the neon thrill of Soho. One night I met a man on the dance floor of the Wag. It was 1988. I was fifteen.

Bee and I tripped down the mirrored stairs towards the music, a flash of red lipstick, our young cheeks afire, let loose in a blast of warm wind. Seventies funk powered up and pulled us under. All those beautiful people at the bar, fashionistas and wannabe models glittering in their jumpsuits. We stood ablaze, giggling and trembling. We so wanted to be like them. We were underage, and everyone could see it, in our Ms Selfridge stretchy dresses and concealer-blocked spots. But we were pretty, and we had flirted with the bouncer, who had winked as he nodded us in.

The man wore a floral nylon shirt with big lapels, tight jodhpurs over shiny black boots, head wriggling with dreddy worms. He twisted his feet to Kool & the Gang, and laughed to himself, all shimmy and shine. *Yeehaa*, he shouted and narrowed his eyes, pouting to an invisible camera. He smelt of cocoa butter. In a haze of Blue Curacao and Bailey's Irish Crème, he told me he was a Vidal Sassoon hairdresser.

He liked my hair, a lion's mane, long, blonde and unbrushed. He asked if I would be his hair model. He told me he was thirty-two; I lied and told him I was sixteen.

He also told me he was a Muslim and had been celibate for three years. In my diary, I recall: *In a way (if this is true) it makes me like him more because I feel safe. Everyone who knows him in the club thinks differently though. They think he is lying about his celibacy and has many girlfriends.*

★

I waited for this man at his hairdressing salon. I waited on the padded, leatherette bench seats by the door and watched the women having their hair cut. Sometimes I flicked through a magazine; sometimes I went to fill up my polystyrene cup from the water cooler; sometimes I picked at a small hole in the seat cover, slowly making it bigger. I waited in the basement. I stood at the bathroom mirror and tried on different coloured lipsticks. I sprayed hairspray and walked into its sticky mist. I hung about, always alert and ready. I waited among other young women waiting to do hair modelling. Sometimes we spoke, but often we didn't. One evening I waited all night long, sleeping on the sofa while he fussed over models for a photo shoot.

I lost my virginity uncomfortably, in a white room, on a white bed, with a white lace bedspread. He told me it was his friend's flat. His friend's bed. That he slept in an upstairs room. 'She lets me sleep in her room when she's visiting her mum,' he said. He continued telling me this each time I visited, and slept in her bed, used her towels, took milk from her fridge. He never showed me his room upstairs, and I never asked to see it, because I wanted to believe him.

His lies hooked me into a circular dance of questioning, because however much I tried to convince myself I could trust him I had a horrible feeling, deep down, that I couldn't. The discord between what was said and what I felt knotted my mind in obsessive thoughts, as I blindly tried to grasp the validity of my feeling. But my feelings had let me down before, so I didn't trust them.

I lied about him to my mum for months, and hated sneaking off in order to spend the night with him when she believed I was at Bee's. When I finally confessed – I don't think I was entirely honest about how old he was – she listened and held my gaze. She was not happy about it, but she said she wanted to meet him. He was small and cheeky and wore funky clothes. He didn't look his age. But still, Mum says now, she was horrified.

I might have kidded myself he was youthful and that there was not that much between us. I was so mature after all. Look at what I had been through! So much exposure through my dad – all that stuff with that creep in Italy. Witness to my stepmother marrying my dad at just eighteen and he more than twice her age. All that frivolous, thoughtless encouragement that I should be with someone equally older than me. It had distorted my reality and I really believed in my teenage superiority that I was more sophisticated than my friends, striding towards a higher destiny. But the hairdresser was an adult, and I was a schoolgirl; all this confusion was happening during my GCSEs.

When my mum learned of his true age, she didn't know what to do. She never turned to my dad for conventional support. He didn't care about her distress or have any interest in what I was up to. So she turned to a friend of mine. This friend was clever and wise and often at our house in those days, returning home with me after school and playing long convoluted games of Canasta in my bedroom as it got dark outside. She sometimes stayed on downstairs after supper to help tidy up and chat to my mum while I skulked away. Seeing my mother's upset over the hairdresser, my friend told her that I was the most sensible girl in our class, that I knew what I was doing. She pointed out that locking me up would never work and might even push me into running away.

I had already given my mum a fright by not coming home one day from school. Frantic, she rang each of my friends. When there was no sign of me, she and my brother walked the streets into the early hours, waving torches along the canal in case I had fallen in. She rang the police to report me missing, and they asked for a photo, and my brother chose a horrible one of me looking cross and spotty, so I would be furious should they ever find me. That night my mum and brother barely slept. In the morning, they rang around my friends again and a parent answered. 'Oh, yes, she's eating breakfast!' They had no clue I had spent the night, smuggled into her bedroom. When my mum told the police I had been found and she was about to drive over to pick me up, they told her they would go. It would be better if they had a word with me. They gave me a telling off as I sat sulkily in the back, but I found it kind of cool rocking up at our house in a police car, and craned my neck to search the street for any neighbours who might be watching.

Now, observing my teenage daughter with her friends, I am struck by the confidence that emanates from them when they are together, a chorus of knowingness and eagerness to step into the unknown. But they still put stickers on their phones, hearts and flowers and bubble writing that says World Peace. The forward thrust of their enthusiasm cloaks their innocence and inexperience.

I have asked my mum since about why she didn't put a stop to the relationship, and she has admitted that she was afraid of pushing me to wilder extremes. I was feisty and unhappy, and I was truanting. She did what she could, demanding curfews and grounding me if I missed them or another letter arrived from school, but if she had been any more draconian I would have threatened to leave. She was still wary and wounded. Our bonds of love and the stability of us three, so hard won, had threatened to unravel, and she was frightened that if I was to flounce out of the house for good, it would be the final unloosening. She was also protective of my brother, and he of her, and she didn't want him to feel any more responsibility than he did. She tells me now above all else, she felt compelled to keep me close.

While my brother shut himself away in his bedroom to write football scores on index cards, I thrashed about. I was angry and I blamed her. I wouldn't accept the new man in her life. The man she would eventually marry. He was a linguist, a scholar; he stood for everything I, in my rebellion, was attempting to trash. He also didn't have much experience or patience with the gyrations of a melodramatic teenage heart. I was not impressed when he moved into our house and was jealous when his younger children came to stay. He shouted at me that I was making everyone's life a misery when I failed to tell my mum where I was one day, and she was sure I had run off again. I was outraged when he answered the phone to my boyfriend and told him to go sniff around someone his own age. The cheek of it!

I see a vision of my mother and me in our Islington kitchen, flooded with daylight. Sometimes I would return to her side and we would quietly bake cakes together. My favourite was farmhouse fruit cake, which was moist and crumbly. I would leave it in a large tin for sustenance over the coming week. In this image, my mother stands back from me as I crack eggs into a bowl. She puts her hands in her apron pocket and watches. What did she want for my life? What did she bring to mine from hers?

She was the daughter of a woman who had experienced an un-trammelled childhood in Isipingo on the coast, south of Durban in South Africa – the sand dunes and their insect life a constant source of fascination – and later the Kloof Gorge area of open wilderness, rich with wildlife. My grandmother and her brother could spend most of the day in the wildest country, building dams and fires, finding tadpoles and trapdoor spiders, tracking animals and climbing trees; one fire they made got out of hand and they had to use all their childish courage and ingenuity to put it out. When my grandmother's brother broke his leg on one of these adventures, she carried him on her back over a mile to get home. She was eleven and he a sturdy nine-year-old.

We loved our grandmother's brave and exuberant character. She didn't believe in ageing, only in forever altering her aspect to the sun. She was up for any adventure, and her artistic and creative self, and love of colour, was expressed in her houses and clothes and the expert jerseys she knitted for us, each a work of art. She was a brilliant gardener and maker of all things, her big strong hands barnacled with rings which she would let me try on and sometimes keep. This outdoor life nurtured her extreme competence and resilience and love of the natural world, and this she passed down to all her eight children, born within nine and a half years, with my mum as the eldest. When she was well into her eighties, and I was in my early twenties, my grandmother expressed an interest in joining me and my boyfriend at Glastonbury and sleeping in his van; in her nineties she was determined to remind herself of how to drive so she could go off on day-long adventures on her own.

Above all else, my mother's upbringing gifted her joy, security and endurance. She had always found it difficult to give up on anyone or anything. When she and my father finally parted, she was relieved to be free of his neuroses and her debilitating suspicion and fear, but a part of her loved him for the best he had been when they first met; while another part loathed him for the self-centred and destructive monster he had become.

Perhaps my mother believed that if she was my anchor, calmly loving me despite my anger, that I would finally follow her lead. I would slip into the cast that she had so carefully made for herself. I would study and go to university and live a creative life. I would meet a good man and settle down and be married. Which is what I eventually did.

But what she failed to see was that my heart had already been broken. I did not have the privilege of an uncomplicated loving father, with trust as a foundation. I could not safely abandon myself to love.

At times my mother had no idea of what to do with me. A few years later, we sat together on the sofa and she was so perplexed at the tears that flooded out of me, frightened by my weakness to their force, how I could not stop them.

I was with the hairdresser for over a year. While I clung hold of him, the rest of my life steadily fell apart. I screwed up my GCSEs – like my dad had, I walked away with just four. My truanting had got so bad that I would turn up at school only to leave again and sit alone in the skate park. I might go to my English or art class, those subjects I found easy and which gave me nourishment, but I would miss those in which I had fallen so far behind. I had lost the thread of what was being taught and the classroom filled me with panic. Soon I couldn't get through a whole day without missing some of it, an entire week without the gap of a day or, more likely, two. I signed sick notes in my mother's hand; I intercepted the post. There were certain subjects that I missed entirely. When it came to my Maths GCSE, I covered my exam sheet with drawings of punks. I spent many hours alone in the cold and concrete, staring at the sky, which in my memory is perpetually grey, with low cloud, dribbles of rain. It was not fun sitting in the park all alone, huddled in my bomber jacket, tearing at the loose threads on the slashed knees of my jeans. I fell behind at school, scared I would never catch up. I knew it wasn't cool.

When I walked out on the hairdresser, I was nearly seventeen. He had moved into his own flat by then, a basement of a large house in Holland Park which he shared with another hairdresser and his make-up artist girlfriend. Often when I stayed the night, I would go to bed before them and listen to the sound of the telly in the next room. One night the phone rang, and when it was not answered it rang again. I heard the answerphone click in. An American voice came through the speaker. A steady: 'Pick up the phone,' building in urgency. 'I know you're there. Pick up the Goddam phone.' She was crying. 'You can't keep ignoring me. How can you walk away? How can you ignore my calls? I'm pregnant!' she shouted. He stood in the doorway of his bedroom, his silhouetted head shaded in lies. So, I got out of his bed, got dressed and went out onto the street. I walked to Holland Park Avenue, dazzled by the lights, and hailed a cab to take me home. That night, I had a bath while my mum did her teeth and, between tears, I begged her to stop me from going back. Her patience snapped, 'Oh for heaven's sake, just get rid of him. End this bloody business.'

It worked. I cut off all contact. I knew I didn't want this relationship, but still I could not quite harness the power to turn my back and do it alone, caught between the legacy of my father's neglect and my mother's endurance, which paired with weakness becomes passivity.

In my diary I read about how I wanted to be with boys my age, but I was not sure if I could. Their immaturity irritated me – *they are all quite idiotic and childish*, my stepmother's voice echoing in my mind. Would they be put off by my honesty? My straight talking. I'm so different! I went to Pizza Express with a boy from a local school and when I ordered extra anchovies on my pizza and ate them with my fingers, just because I wanted to, he blushed and shuffled in his chair as if he was ready to leave. I didn't want to be like every other girl he had taken out, because I didn't feel the same as them. But what if my superiority was an armour that I had constructed in order to protect myself? Falling for a boy my age meant ease and laughter, being stupid together, exposing your true feelings in all their mess and complexity. Learning together, making mistakes, loving, being loved, everything at the same pace. I had been pushed too young and too soon into adult complexity and cultivated an air of nonchalance to cover up a vertiginous sense of being out of my depth. Within the sannyasin community, I had got used to damaged people causing more damage by screwing around, making their partners jealous and then sitting around talking about it. This was not normal, and it was not what kids my age were interested in doing.

I want to feel special, I wrote in my diary. *But I am creating tension by thinking about this so much. I can't be myself because I'm afraid of how it will make others feel. I'm scared. He told me I was special. I want to feel special. He said I was beautiful. I don't want him as a boyfriend, but I want him to be attracted to me. It makes me so angry with myself. It's so stupid. I am so stupid. I've worked myself up into a frenzy. It's totally unnecessary. I can't work. I can't think about anything else. Why can't I stop?*

★

Meanwhile we had more drama on our street. My brother was driving down the motorway back to university when he heard on the BBC news that our mum's ex-fiancé, someone she'd had a relationship with when I was aged around fourteen and who had been in the public eye, had been found dead. His death was initially thought suspicious. My brother knew this meant trouble and immediately turned around at the next services and drove home. The press and photographers had already descended, like a wolf on the fold, and would camp outside our house for the next week. Mum shuttered the windows and pulled the blinds and forbade us to talk to them. She did not want any fabricated stories emerging about a heartbroken ex-fiancé. But then our cat needed to go to the vet, and my brother and I had to leave the house with it in the basket. Reporters called out cheerily, 'Are you smuggling your mum in that?' We were cloistered. My friends started to pile round, seeing this as an opportunity to have their photo in a newspaper. In their coolest jackets, with immaculate make-up and blow-dried hair, they would pause decoratively on the doorstep as the flash bulbs fired. But then a better story came along and the paps disappeared like magic.

My next boyfriend was six-foot-seven, and a skinhead. He wore skinny Levis over size-12 steel-capped boots. When we first met, he lived in a squat; a tall, thin Georgian house at the back of Camden Road with floor-to-ceiling windows and wrought iron railings. His living room was dark, I seem to remember, as if every surface was covered in brown corduroy, heavy curtains closed to the traffic outside. On that first day, a group of us lost ourselves to mellow skunk and dub with its reverb and echo. Minutes turned into hours, no one really speaking. When we got up to leave, he told us a bunch of kids had broken into the house the night before and had left a huge scythe in the loo. He stopped at the bottom of the stairs to let me pass, and I felt dizzy when I looked up at him.

A week later he came to meet me at the café where I worked. When I saw him standing outside, I wiped the sugar from my hands and took off my pinny. In his van he asked if he could kiss me.

He got a studio flat in Pimlico. From the kitchen window, beyond the red-brick flats opposite, you could see the corner of the Thames. The first time I visited, he made me supper and we lay together on the sofa listening to his records. When I said I had to go, he told me to wait until the song was over, but he had turned the speed right down on the turntable, so it seemed to go on forever.

He said he would collect me in his yellow transit van. We would go to the pub or for a kebab. I stood ready and waiting. I had dressed up especially, maybe a figure-hugging T-shirt or a new pair of jeans, but I would try to look casual on the doorstep or sit back on the wall and pretend to read a book. Eventually I would end up standing in the middle of the road craning my neck for the sight of anything yellow.

He worked in the music industry and went on tour. Sometimes I followed him. I followed him to music festivals and sat on the scaffolding as he did the light shows. I took drugs that he gave me and danced beside him as he worked. Sometimes the drugs took me places, other times I waited for them to come up and the more I waited the more I got stuck with myself. *Like a kettle that never boils; like a phone that never rings.* I followed him to gigs in Amsterdam and Cologne. I sat in hotel rooms and watched the colour leech from his skin when he took another line of coke. I waited until the sun came up, and when I finally went to bed, I waited to fall asleep. '. . . *be still and wait without hope/For hope would be hope for the wrong thing . . . But the faith and the love and the hope are all in the waiting . . .*'

He was seven years older than me. I was doing well! He was big-boned and dog-like, with a Great Dane's heart, but also full of bark and growl, in constant argument with a world that he experienced as unjust and out to get him. He was uncompromising and would shout me down when I challenged him. I was not confident enough to stand my ground, and so turned mute when I was with him. But he was my protector: I loved that he had big hands. That his knee joints were flat like tables. That he loomed taller than any other man I knew. I would call on him when I felt threatened by a boy trying it on at a party, or a male friend testing his limits, and he would appear as a warning, looming over them, his forearm against the wall. He was my wild man, my Big Foot, and he reduced those around him to shreds. I was guilty too of making more of these stories to test his feelings for me. I would cry and tell him my fears of being left so suddenly out of the blue, of being abandoned, and he would shout and swear and say it was all because of my dad – that my dad was a bastard. 'If I ever meet him I'll thump him, knock his block off.' I didn't much like it when he said that, but I did quite enjoy getting a reaction, that my feelings mattered, that I could upset someone. That *I* mattered. We were together for only a few months this first time, but he would be back in my life for many years to come.

He and his work partner moved into a new office in Islington. There was a ledge up high and he lifted me onto it. My feet dangled, some seven feet above ground. They laughed and pretended to leave the room. They went through the door and closed it behind them. 'Bye,' they said and waved. 'See you later.'

When I allowed myself to be single, I could see clearly again. After a bad start in sixth form, I clawed my way back. In a rebellious moment, a group of us girls had flounced from Camden School for Girls, flicking our hair as we went, and turned up to do our A Levels at a co-ed school, Le Swap, a sixth form with three schools in one. It was vast and echoey compared to the compact familiarity of our old school, and we knew no one. On the first day we sat in the classroom that overlooked the edge of Hampstead Heath and the green beckoned. We walked straight out of school after register and formed a huddle on the Heath.

When the teachers didn't report our absence, we spent every day in that first week drinking wine and listening to Otis Redding on a grassy hill that overlooked London, and before the end of the first term we had all dropped out. Luckily, my English teacher from Camden got in touch and the school offered me a place if I studied my A Levels in one year. My other friends were not so lucky, and some of them had to go to cram schools to get their exams, some never did.

Back on track and quietly relieved, me and a friend sat in her bedroom eating boiled rice and prawns, poring over books, *The Story of Art* by Gombrich, and *Ways of Seeing* by Berger, and by teaching ourselves Art History that year, I discovered, for the first time, a love of critical thinking and of knowledge.

I had been sitting for an artist, a Royal Academician called John Ward who was Mum's friend. She had won her own portrait painted by him in a raffle held to help restore Vanessa Bell and Duncan Grant's farmhouse in Sussex. These were the quiet months, when I retreated into myself and found some peace. I loved going to the Wards' house in Kent, every other weekend, for a few months, where his wife was always in the kitchen, cooking pies and making salads. There was a big wedge of Stilton under a cheese cloth, which I chipped away at each time I passed. Artists would visit, and sometimes interesting local friends, sitting relaxedly at lunch, their cheeks slowly reddening over red wine and bloody grouse. I was John's life model, dressed in Victorian blouses and fine silks. He loved painting women, fabrics and flowers, and would cut daisies from the garden for me to hold. His studio was thrilling. It was a Medieval Hall house, double height and mysterious with winding corridors that led to the rest of the house. Filled with half-finished paintings on easels, mannequins, abandoned still-life displays of shrivelling fruit and dried flowers, shiny gold trumpets and trombones, any shapes that interested him and might find themselves into one of his paintings. It was all lit by the most shimmering light from its massive north window.

I have since found a letter I wrote to a friend from here, which I never sent. *I am sitting in my own room at John's house enjoying a strong milky coffee (I just sneaked a fag out of the window). I think this time I am spending here is doing me a huge amount of good.* My days consisted of sitting for John in the morning *He wakes me at 7.30am!* and an hour's walk, in all weathers, in the afternoon with John and his dog, Jiff, followed by an afternoon sitting in the garden or sleeping. I spent hours lying on my bed listening to the Grateful Dead on my Walkman. *I sleep about 11 hours each night – it is all part of the cleansing process.*

He painted and drew many portraits of me over the years, all of which were sold at the Royal Academy Summer Exhibition or through independent galleries in Mayfair, specifically the Maas Gallery. Once at the Summer Exhibition, my friend dared me to stand by my portrait to see if anyone recognised me. They did, and I stood there blushing and sheepishly waving.

All I have to do is lie back in a rocking chair, reading, which is very convenient! I wrote to my friend that weekend at John's. He was working on a pastel which was to be called 'Lily reading *The Maker of Heavenly Trousers*', which I still have in the form of a postcard. Sometimes I stood in for other models. *I have to hang around until 11am because John is painting the Mayor of Canterbury's gold gown. Yesterday he made me pose, pretending to be the mayor, with his hat in one hand and his gloves in the other.* When my mum sat for him he was in the middle of painting an official portrait of Prince Charles and needed to put some finishing touches to his ceremonial jacket, so he asked my mum to pose in it. She was amazed at how slight Prince Charles must be.

I did a lot of painting here, too. John let me use his oil paints. I painted portraits of myself staring intensely from the canvas, a knowing look in my eyes. I have a portrait on my study wall that I painted during this time, and the girl who looks down on me has a directness that surprises me, as if she knows where she is going. Her eyes tell me I am so much more than the mess I have created – and who cares anyway, because the mess is part of me. I think again of Jung's 'complex of inexorable opposites – day and night, birth and death, happiness and misery, good and evil . . .' There is power in acceptance of all and everything we might possibly be.

In John's studio, I was moved by choral music he liked to play, and I started reading again. My mind settled. In place of that chatter of self-doubt, it took to sweeter wanderings. *Here I am surrounded by trees, grass and flowers, with only two people in sight. I got such a strange feeling when I last returned to London seeing the thousands of people all looking so stressed and I thought of what a crazy routine they all have. Not like the simple routine I have here: breakfast, work, coffee, model, lunch, model, walk, work, tea, TV, supper, bed.* When I posed for John, I saw visions of bluebell woods that soothed me, happy images of the vast sea and sky, drifting through me with the music, my imagination bubbling up from the depths. I didn't feel so frightened.

My diary entries became calmer too. The energy had shifted. It was no longer high up there in the eaves, full of indecision and compulsion. Instead, it settled somewhere closer to my heart, a feeling of contentment that what was happening did not need to be worked out, it just was, and what it was, was alright. I went with my body's rhythm, I trusted. In photographs, I grin to the camera with the delight of a child, an innocence reclaimed. I am youthful and shining.

I got good grades for my A Levels, enough to study the subject I really wanted: Art History at Manchester University. I was really proud of myself.

My dad and his wife were back. They had recently returned to London from Italy and gravitated to West End Lane. Their dream of wealth was beginning to materialise from the success of their book-packaging business, and they rented a modernised flat on the top floor of a mansion block, with white carpets throughout, and halogen spotlights that made the kitchen and bathroom sparkle. They bought tea sets and porcelain, lovely matching napkins and tablecloths, as if they were settling. I remember the apartment clearly. I stayed there a few times when they were away, tiptoeing around in fear that I might break something. A friend came to call, and we drank cans of beer and watched telly. But I don't remember ever being there with them. Eventually, burglars rampaged through the place, and in their muddy boots they ruined the white carpet. They pulled down the double-lined linen curtains and bundled up the stereo and TV, and my stepmother's jewellery, and left with their swag.

During the long university holidays, I worked for Dad, in an office in Kentish Town. I carried out secondary research on his books, and sometimes answered the phone. I sensed a change in his wife, a loneliness and longing. She would question me about my social life. My friends. My eating habits. She told me I was looking pretty. Slim. She liked my trousers. My boots. My blouse. We spoke of our similarities. Like sisters, we said.

I leaned against the radiator in her office, the clatter of the metal blinds behind me, while her eyes shone bright in the cold city light and she told me of her unhappiness.

'Your father doesn't let me do anything.'

'I go out to meet friends, and he follows me.'

'He thinks I'm having an affair.'

She was in her late twenties, and I wonder if in me she now saw the freedom she had given up by marrying a much older man. He had taken her youth. That idea she had, all those years back when I was ten, that girls should choose men who were so much older, was no longer convincing. Did I represent for her the unlived life, the young woman in control of her destiny? Having spent so many years admiring her and envying her my father's attention, it was unsettling to have our roles reversed. How interesting that we project onto others those things we long for. Here was my beautiful stepmother, with so much youthful potential, trapped by my father, whose possessiveness was driven by his own unacknowledged guilt. She wanted a family, and my father did not. He had had a vasectomy after all. She was eighteen when she met him. She had given up her studies. Now, he expected her to give up on her desire for children, as well.

Soon after the burglary she and my dad moved to another mansion flat, bigger this time, and on the other side of Finchley Road, nearer the shops, cafés and restaurants of West Hampstead village. I could take the train to Finchley Road and Frognal. I would walk to their house and ring the bell, and be let in. They would sit side by side in their study, my dad's desk on one side and his wife's on the other, working on a book together, music on the stereo. Vangelis, the futuristic calm of the synthesiser spreading like water. There were speakers in the study, in the living room, in the kitchen, the sound surrounded you like a dream. I liked to open my dad's fridge and pour myself a glass of milk, take a biscuit from the tin as if this was my own home.

My first experience of love had been a fractured thing, with men who were not my equal. I had learned early that my feelings were dangerous and so I should not trust them. Years later, when married, with two young children, I still walked this path despite it making me ill with anxiety and sadness. I still found myself searching for this familiar feeling of unrequited love. For years there was a writer who looked like my father, who made promises he couldn't keep, who was elusive, just out of reach, with whom I was infatuated and clung to a secretive email dance. I found him one day at work and sat opposite him at his desk and my nerves fought a war inside me. I was a woman – a wife who had every intention of being loyal, a devoted mother, responsible for two young children; I was an adult – and yet I shook so violently in that office chair that I could not meet his eyes; and my mouth was stripped of all moisture, making it impossible to speak. My head was bowed with the weight of old pain and humiliation, that same wound forever open. 'You can go now,' he said eventually, thinking he was helping me because I was unable to help myself, but his words cut right through me. I did not want to be that woman, so damaged and weak, who could not make this decision herself, who had to be told to leave because she didn't have the strength to do it on her own. I stood up and walked as steadily as I could towards the lifts. All I remember is that I was wearing my favourite trousers, an expensive pair of designer jeans my father had bought me on one of his visits, and I was so conscious that he might think them too big on me, that I was unable to fill them.

It is shocking how readily we repeat these patterns, how we are drawn on a visceral level to the people who remind us of those who have been so central in our lives. But it is those to whom pain and suffering adhere that have the greatest pull, perhaps because we long to try again to make things whole. Their familiarity is seductive: I have met you before; you are part of my history. We move towards the fire despite knowing it will burn. 'It will be different this time,' we tell ourselves in our delusion. I can make it all work. If he changes for me I will straighten this kink in my personal history. I will be The One.

But it was not all that I was. In our Islington home I occupied the big bedroom on the top floor, which had once been my parents'. I slept on their super king-sized mattress, pushed against the wall. In the evenings, I set up a canvas in front of a mirror and painted myself, my eyes staring intently back at me, and I painted those eyes as carefully as I could with intent brushstrokes. They were strong thoughtful eyes that challenged the viewer and reminded me that I am many things. I am not only what I allowed my father to make of me.

When I was not painting, I sat at my desk and wrote stories with urgency. They always spun around complex family dramas, lots of kids living freely, their father absent, flying about in his shiny red car with a woman as young as a daughter by his side. The mother was a constant. This rambling family lived in a large terraced house in North London, modelled on my grandparents' home in Bristol where they had raised the youngest of their eight children.

One particular story that refused to end and grew as long as a novel was about an incestuous love affair between my main protagonist and her brother. The boy was my imaginary hero. He was the only one who understood his sister, and his love for her was complete. I was close to my brother. Perhaps this was my way of exploring that trusted love between a young woman and a young man, an unthreatening place to me, but something painful and unresolved, I know, for my aunt and her brother.

While I sat at my desk, my body relaxed with my notebook in my lap, and my feet tucked up on my chair, my mother sat at her own desk at her word processor on the next floor down, writing another biography, this time of the relationship between the sisters Vanessa Bell and Virginia Woolf. I wrote, she typed. The house fattened with our words, its walls a container for the worlds we recreated. My mother was surrounded by notes and transcriptions of letters from the Tate archives and the New York Public Library. This sisterly relationship was most brilliantly documented by Virginia Woolf herself, and my mother spent years delicately unravelling it and stitching it together. Having read her book, Vanessa's son wrote to my mum – 'it is almost too true and too moving to be read by a close relation'. She occasionally read out bits of Virginia, perhaps hoping to encourage me. 'Life is not a series of gig lights symmetrically arranged. Life is a luminous halo, a semi-transparent envelope, surrounding us from the beginning of consciousness to the end.' But I was not ready quite yet to treat my own life with care.

The Abyss

I am twenty. The year after I finished university. Picture a downstairs bedroom, lamp lit with curtains drawn. Bubbles. A posh pair of tall glasses, drunk and then refilled, the hit at the back of the throat, the withdrawal of breath as it pops up the nose. Music on, a pirate radio station. Two girls on their feet and at the mirror, 'Do I look alright? Should I wear this? That? You look better than me. So pretty. So slim. You do. You are!'

Others arrived: two boys hiding their height with slouched backs and their faces half-obscured with hoods. Eyes down on the Rizlas in their palms, massaging weed, barely looking up. One was her boyfriend, taking her out tonight. New Year's Eve. I was heading off to World Dance, a rave at the London Arena with my Great Dane. We had found each other again. I knew he would step into that sad echoey void that I carried around inside me, the one that bruised and ached, that my dad had dug out all those years ago with no regard, so I'd reached out. When he took me back, I buried my head in his dogged loyalty. It was wildly exciting too, as he was king of the light show. For your regular punter, it was the night of their lives – thirty quid a ticket, but free for me. I liked the thrill of being part of the VIP tribe.

Out came the scratched CD case, the gym membership card and the rolled-up note. The rush up the nose and bitterness as it dribbled down the throat. My friend pulled a face, and we both laughed, the sudden numbness of tongue and teeth. The music was louder now – with us up and about, a shimmer of lipstick, dancing, laughing, a bump and a grind and a hair flick. If only you could feel this buzz forever.

Then I was on my own. He said he would meet me, and there he was at the door. I loved his height and authority. He had a backstage pass, all the privileges. I scooted to the front of the queue, past the kids with coloured hair and tracksuits, smoking and hugging their coats – so used to it now – and he nodded to the bouncer and took my hand, leading me up and above and through the crowds. I was walking on air. It was dark and blue inside, the air conditioning on. Those faces all around, oversized T-shirts, whistles round their neck, flushed already with adrenalin and that distant sweaty look. It was hard-core, drum 'n' bass, and the sound was everywhere in this vast space, made for bands and basketball. Quick beats pummelled my head and thundered my heart, but I was above it all. I clung to the skimp of my clothes as I followed through the smoke. I wanted to be out of it, up there in heaven.

He went up the scaffolding tower first, his long legs on the steel bar. I followed, lodging my heel onto the clamp. I would not look up, as I knew I would not see the top of it, up there in the arena's clouds. I put a hand after each foot and, all glitter and shine, shimmied to the top.

A strobe blasted from the platform in a tube of green light, flowering into a spiral; beneath it there were hundreds of arms and hands and faces, looking up to the light, without voice or sound. The quick beats, the *douch douch douch*, the crowd. It was startling. So visually spectacular, it was designed to swallow you up, to abandon everything to the moment, to not think at all. The power of unity, all these people coming together. My very own community. My head was in the clouds. I found it; the very top. My heaven.

But after the ascent, comes the fall. It was suddenly very cold up there in the cloudless skies, without the press of bodies for warmth. The air conditioning had blades on the tips of its icy fingers. There was no escaping it, with no coat, boots or knee socks. I was wearing a pink boob tube. Not dressed for altitude.

After hours up there with no one to talk to, just me dancing alone behind my boyfriend and his work partner, both facing the projector screen with their backs to me, I was tired. I looked around at the platform, the cold steel of the equipment cases, the expanse of chipboard. There was space to lie down, but I was too wired to sleep. I slumped behind a speaker and closed my eyes, the night suddenly broken and bleeding.

I had been there so many times before. Checking out, sleep-walking, then drinking too much or taking too many drugs to try to feed this mental narcolepsy. Somewhere deep inside I must have felt the discomfort of always being on the periphery of someone else's more important life. Dragging behind. An inconvenient tag along. But it was also all that I knew. My boyfriend had a job to do. I was just hanging on to the back of his T-shirt.

One Thursday morning at 5 a.m. we loaded onto a tour bus from King's Cross to Glastonbury in pelting rain. I dozed on the narrow bed, and when I awoke watched transfixed through the back window slick wet with grey. There were rumours that the main stage was slipping down the hill. That weekend in various backstage fields, I moved from car to car to follow the line of cocaine. When the cocaine ran out, I popped pills, spun in circles to try to come up. I don't remember much of the bands we saw, but I do remember the ache of my thighs after repeatedly yanking my legs from mud. On the last morning, we all headed back to the tour bus, our eyes on our boots, staggering together but so far apart, a deadness in our heads and hearts, unable to speak – like the 'hollow men', stuffed men, with 'a headpiece filled with straw'.

Another time my boyfriend and I drove back from the Knebworth Festival after three nights on the go. Neither of us had slept. I kept slapping his face to keep him awake at the wheel. We swept by stragglers on the side of the road, past the grandeur of the stately home; a young man dirt black from head to toe screamed at the car, caught in some internal horror. This boy was in the dreamland of the dead, trapped 'in the twilight kingdom', the underworld. 'Rat's coat, crowskin, crossed staves.' We drove on past, as the last forgotten souls staggered from the grounds, and I looked over my shoulder to see the kid fall in the mud, calling out to some invisible friend. I'll never forget the terror on his face. Was his mind forever turned? Did he ever come back?

So many nights were doomed by drugs. How they strung me and my friends like puppets into a continual dance, in and out of the toilets. Keeping us alight, more invincible with each line. Until we hungrily ran a wet finger over the last trace of dust and drowned in the searing depression that followed. Four in the morning, back at home or at my friend's in Shoreditch, I would try to dampen the crash with a glass of wine, then in bed I would drift in and out of a frantic sleep of regret. We had shared these party moments in all their chemical euphoria so many times, and together, but so far apart we slumped into the nightmare of wired dreams. I would hear the birds start their chorus and watch the daylight seep into the room, trying to press my head into the pillow to dampen the thump of car doors as the neighbours went to work. The fug of my brain from too much alcohol, the dull throb in my nose from badly cut cocaine, the taste of cigarettes and stale wine in my throat. My lungs would hurt, my heart working overtime. The gravity of withdrawal made me useless, a dread high in my chest of how I would cope at work that day. My friend was there in the next room, sleepless too, cut up with the same self-persecution, yet neither of us would admit to it. We could not find the words. Getting up, our hands shaking over the kettle, we would try to recall the night before. When did we take the first line? We would laugh at how stupid we were to think it a good idea on a weeknight.

'Did you sleep?' I would ask her and catch sight of the edge in her face.

'A bit,' she would say, clattering into the teacups, spilling coffee grains all over the counter.

Sometimes after a weekend festival the hangover would last almost a week. My friends would ask – why do it if you can't handle the come down? But self-punishment was part of my mental landscape. I hated it but also welcomed it. It had dug its trenches deep. It held hands with the thrill of Friday coming around again, the wink and glitter of lights, the lure of the high. It stood at my side when I took the first line, and it clung to the tails of the euphoria, never far behind.

My dad once did a bad trip with his wife: sucked on a micro-dot and went skidding off to hell. They could not be in the same room together. Instead he lay alone in bed and closed his eyes against the wallpaper, now writhing with snakes. He felt the darkness fill him. In his mind, everything was gone. The nice Hampstead life with its posh porcelain and San Pellegrino on tap; swaggering cats, in and out, their tails fluffed up; patio doors open to the garden, all fresh and bright in the gentle sun. Seven hours in this nightmare, he said. He clung hold of the sheets, hurtling through his self-inflicted torture, fearing he would never make it back. How precarious it all seemed then: that textured life, his money, his many comforts. How easily he could lose it all. I wonder if this acid trip was a premonition.

Drugs had always hung around the sannyasins. After the implosion of Rajneeshpuram when the disciples scattered all over the world like fallout from a nail bomb, a lot of them took MDMA with them. First using it within therapeutic New Age community encounter groups, and later, breaking into the dance scene. In their semi-nomadic cycle, they would spend winter in Goa and then land in Ibiza for the summer taking jobs in hippy markets, nightclubs, New Age retreats, forming alternative Eastern-inspired communities. Ecstasy was already being used within the gay party scene, but it was believed to be the partying sannyasins of the late 1980s who introduced it to the mainstream dance scene throughout Europe. British DJs, discovering it in Ibiza, were thrilled, and took the vibe back to London. Shoom is now heralded as the club night that kicked off what was to become Loved Up rave culture that rocked through the 1990s. As Anthony D'Andrea discovered from his field work in Ibiza in the late 80s, 'the rave movement rapidly flowed from the underground to the mainstream, from Pune, to Oregon, to Ibiza, to London, and to the world. Within multiple flows of alternative subjects, objects and imaginaries across East and West, Osho sannyasins constituted a bridge between the 1970s New Age counterculture and the 1990s Techno rave movement.'

The ashram in India was still in operation, but there was a counterculture of sannyasins who didn't fit there anymore. These were the rebels who didn't abide by the house rules and found the commercialism with the ashram's expensive therapies hypocritical. But their thirst for transcendence most likely found expression on the dance floor, with the same familiar warmth of the crowd, that same communal trance, their own version of Bhagwan's buddhafield. Like the Rajneesh experience, it was not something that could be described or intellectualised. MDMA played on your senses, far from and beyond the tethering of language. Just as the sannyasin movement had offered a new, more permissive and transformative experience to my father and others of the wandering tribe in the late 1970s, rave culture and ecstasy, particularly, had a similar appeal in the late 80s and 90s.

My first ever experience with Class A drugs came via a sannyasin. I was twelve years old, the autumn after my dad had offered me ecstasy in Italy. I went with a friend to a sannyasin's place in Belsize Park. A red-washed living room with floaty silks and saris pinned to the walls, in an apartment on the top floor of one of the mansion houses on the Avenues. It was sunny outside, the afternoon; we must have been bunking off school. A woman drifted around in orange robes and her cigarettes kept burning out in an ashtray. She gave me and my friend a microdot. We left in excited chatter and hid behind a church to drop half each on our tongue. We walked through the streets and waited to come up; and then suddenly we both saw a man who looked like an egg sitting on a wall outside a school. Humpty Dumpty with a perfectly oval head, and trousers that sat on the curve of his egg body, no indent on the waist. An egg head, a painted-on tie, painted on trouser line and buttons in his fly, all in a garish purple. We stood and pointed and laughed and laughed, convinced he was real because we both saw him.

Many of the Great Dane's friends fried their brains on drugs. One of them holed up for months with his girlfriend in a council flat in King's Cross, existing on a diet of cocaine. Each morning they took a line for breakfast, and continued for lunch, and afternoon tea and dinner, until she collapsed in a corner. Another friend with a job in TV eased himself off years of heroin dependency by injecting methadone. My boyfriend and I would arrive with beers and sit in his bedsit among the scraps of paper, spent matches and discarded record sleeves, while he disappeared to the bathroom below. We would hear the sound of him crushing pills between the dub beats on the turntable, pounding them in a pestle and mortar. I had never seen pupils so small, eyes like pin pricks. I was fond of this friend. It tugged at my heart that he was trapped by his addiction – living in Kentish Town surrounded by the same people who supplied his drugs, a reminder each time he left his flat to go to work, on every corner as he walked to the tube station. He told me of a girl he had met, how they both danced a slow waltz around his living room, how they danced the two of them almost all through the night. A man who the Great Dane worked with, a sound engineer for big gigs and celebrity bands, took so much cocaine he woke up one morning to find his nasal cartilage on his pillow.

I lay back on a beanbag in my friend's lofty warehouse sometime before my twenty-first birthday. We were high up in the sky. Outside, the early light was expanding, but we had not slept. We were listening to Spiritualized. *All I want in life's a little bit of love to take the pain away, getting stronger every day.* We'd been in search of drugs for much of the night, and had sent her boyfriend out to Turnmills where he pushed through the crowds to find dealers twitching in dark corners. The effects of the pills we had taken were now fading to an agitated fuzz. 'Perhaps we're just bored with reality,' we agreed in our youthful naivety, our rebellion from the humdrum. But when I look back now, I see how I was running wildly from myself. In trying to annihilate that childish frightened voice, I was running off in all directions screaming, red lipstick on my teeth and my tights torn, my arms ecstatically flailing. I was doing what my dad had done. I was the runaway now.

Barthes writes of the passivity of the abyss, where we have no responsibility, 'the act [of dying] is not up to me.' I could lose myself to the blur of incompetence, a giggling, stupefied mess. I was blank-eyed and numb, a blanket over my head.

It was always the threat of love that called, like a seductive siren luring the voices from beneath the rocks. In the quiet moments in my boyfriend's flat, I would take myself to a solitary somewhere so I could listen to what the voices were saying. His bathroom was small and blue with a ginormous plastic fish on the wall that he had picked up from a film shoot. When I was in there it was like being in the depths of the sea, the voices echoing through the inside of a shell. I would run a bath, and sit in it until the water turned cold, and stare at my toes, the two parts of my mind at war – destructive words bubbling up from the depths of my unconscious, while that other self tried to catch them and to placate, to turn over and to understand. My internal saboteur waiting in the shadows, ready to jump at the slightest loving sigh or smile; to lash out when my defences were down; to destroy what was fluid, open, loving, before I could be destroyed. The more energy I gave this battle, the bigger it grew. *Get out get out get out*, the malevolent voices screamed, with guns and daggers. *Leave this thing. Walk out. You don't want it. It doesn't want you. Get out before he leaves you.*

But you love him, comes the rationale. *Look! You're going to be okay.*

I knew, but also didn't know, it was not real. It was so exhausting.

I know now that love is recognition. Finding that person who will affirm your feelings; to acknowledge and accept, to empathise. To listen. This is what helps you grow. Some of my friends had managed to find it, and I wanted it too, and yet the saboteur resurfaced every time I went near.

Eventually, tired out by the defensive anticipation of abandonment, I searched for a way to flee, to walk out. I gathered that if love was making me feel this way, then I had better destroy it. I cheated on my boyfriend with a dweebie guy I met at my twenty-first birthday party. He was Irish and pretty and his voice was like a song. I knew he was bad news, but I went with it anyway. We stood on the roof of my friend's warehouse flat, and watched the sun come up. I spent long nights in his council flat on Old Street drinking too much and listening to Radiohead.

The Great Dane was devastated. He trapped me in a room and shouted at me for four hours while playing his favourite tunes on the turntable. He refused to let me leave. I sat shaking in the corner, pushing out fake tears, begging him to forgive me like the girls do in sitcoms on the telly. Behind the hysterics I felt nothing. Maybe this was my way of dealing with my own shame. I had to flee myself, because I was capable of doing what my father did to us. I could walk away from a house I had just set alight, while its inhabitants were left there burning.

We were living together at the time in a one-bedroom flat in West London. My mum had come to visit one day when he was out, and I told her what I had done. She turned pale, and I knew what she was thinking. 'You worry me sometimes,' she said then, and has said to me since. 'There are parts of you I don't understand.' But sometimes we are driven to do the very thing we are most scared of. The fear it will happen to us creates a complex that sucks us in. We become the fly at the centre of the web we have woven. This man, this sweet protective man with the big heart, did not understand why I had pulled him to me so desperately, so scared of being left, only to do this to him. He told me that he had given himself entirely because I had asked him to, and then look at what I had done – the one thing I was most afraid would happen to me.

He wrote me a letter, but I am ashamed that I only skim read it. I wish I still had it. But I do remember him saying I was an injured bird, that my wings had been crushed, and he had wanted to love me back to health again.

Briefly, after fleeing, my mind cleared again. I was elated, cycling free. I threw myself into my job at *Time Out*. I had been lucky to land work checking listings the summer I had graduated, through a friend's mum who worked in the Around Town section of the magazine. I stayed here for the next ten years. Employees described it as a velvet-lined coffin. Once you were in, it felt like there was no better place to be, and so people generally didn't leave until they were pushed out. The Guides editorial department was on the second-from-top floor of its lofty industrial building on Tottenham Court Road, with its Jackson Pollock inspired multicoloured carpet and metal-framed windows that looked out over Senate House, the British Museum and Bloomsbury. I sat at my desk in the open-plan office and shadowed the kind editors, who gradually relieved me of my fact-checking duties by asking me to review a new shop that had just opened, or even a restaurant. As my writing got better, I was given a whole section to manage in the Shopping Guide, and then the fish section of the Restaurant Guide, all expenses paid. We socialised in the smoking room on the top floor, or sunbathed on the roof; after work each day we congregated in the Fitzrovia pubs, and I sobered up on my fast and dangerous cycle ride home.

Back on a beanbag in my friend's Shoreditch flat, we talked about cheating on men we might profess to love. We spoke of the excitement of the game. Of the thrill. The promise that this time it would be different, a more special kind of love. Was it the rush, a drug-like hit, the compulsion to do it again and again? I felt sick when we talked like this. Sick when her boyfriend returned with more drugs and we swallowed them with wine, as the bare frankness of daylight threatened to hit us between the eyes. Sick with myself and with the trail of poison as it bled through my veins. Then all was forgotten. Into the day we danced, our bodies like rags. In that space between life and death, we lost ourselves to the haze of the abyss.

In the last year of university, I had made a new friend, who came with an offering. Let's call her Astra. It was a glittery path that led me to a different clearing. She was so beautiful with high cheekbones, navy eyes and shiny brown hair, but she also had an edge. Her fake front tooth stained grey, a blight in an otherwise perfect face, replaced in childhood when she had knocked the original out in a public swimming pool. She dressed in wide-legged trousers and a waistcoat, leather court shoes with steel caps on their soles. She went clickety clickety click, and people looked up to watch her pass. Like a dancer on the stage, she had all the natural grace and charisma of a performer. She was from York and wore her accent with pride. I loved her hard vowels; the crassness of what came out of her pretty mouth; how easily she used the word 'cunt'.

Astra fast became a mirror of whom I could be. She was my lodestar. More strikingly pretty, and easier in her intelligence, yet her confidence was fragile and hard won. She tickled back to life the woman in me who had been in hiding. I cut off my wild locks of hair and got a boy's haircut in a moment of 'Why the fuck not?' and Astra got a job promotion. We ordered champagne at the Bug Bar.

It was that night that we met two men. One, sensible and unpretentious in his retro tan leather, while the other looked like he was visiting from some chilly Viking shore. Back at their flat – a box high in the Brixton sky – we shouted above the music. Joe up on his feet, while the Viking watched with arrogant detachment, an alien man, who sat against the wall smoking joint after joint, his blonde hair in tufts and bright blue eyes above high Scandinavian cheekbones. I noticed his fingers, coarsened from hard work on the oil rigs, his fingernails dented and stained black. He had come to visit from a distant harsher land. My David Bowie? My Starman? I hadn't learned anything. Regardless of having Astra at my side, I was still looking for an unknowable man to save me.

Joe adored Astra. With his eyes on her, she grew into her power. I wanted to be happy for her. I told myself, repeatedly. *She is your friend. You love her.* But her beauty and intelligence, her wit and ease, expanded before my eyes, faster than I could catch up, and in my failure to meet her I started to feel diminished. That freedom and ease had been mine, and now, like so many times before, I gave it away.

The Viking was an anomaly. He picked fights when we were out. Joe criticised him for his rebellion and inability to settle down. He was distracted. He was absent. His emotions were hard to read. I asked him to be with me exclusively, and he gave me evasive answers, housed inside philosophical riddles about the validity of commitment. *How can we possibly ever know what the future holds?* When I met him, he had boasted about having women in four cities. I tried to convince myself I was okay with it, but it sent me into a destructive spiral. My default position, to be loved less than I loved, was so familiar as was how sick it made me feel.

The Viking merely drifted into our love affair. There were no words of reassurance that levelled me up to being a conscious, sought-after choice, and I was too scared to question him: I wanted security, assurance, to be protected, to feel safe. The more detached he became, the more I felt the old fear returning. I knew it was doomed, but something was driving me forward. An inner guiding self that wanted to finally find that self-reliance that others take for granted, but had been whipped away from me at such a young age. I was on that train again, careering towards a brick wall, determined to re-enact the chaos of my past by placing myself once more at its centre. The two parts of me split, the most insistent in constant anxiety, trying to pre-empt danger and protect the little girl who did not deserve to be loved. The more my head spun, the more dust was kicked up in the drama of it all; the more an obscuring cloud grew. Did I keep standing in the firing line in the hope that one day I would become bullet-proof?

Things got worse before they could get better. I imagined that the Viking must see what I saw. That he must be in love with Astra, too. It was almost as if the very horror of such an idea brought it into plausible being. The more I imagined it, the deeper those imaginings embedded themselves in my psyche, and the truer they became. To me. For how can something felt so deeply, seen so vividly, believed so wholeheartedly, not be real?

There was alcohol mixed up in it too – copious amounts – glasses of wine in the Brixton high-rise, starting early, with the summer windows open and the buzz of St Matthew's Road, swirling through the air and tickling our expectant youthful faces. Every night was the same. More drink at the Crypt until the early hours. It should have been perfect, our foursome, but my jealousy got so corrosive that as I walked into a room where Astra and the Viking happened to be I was primed for the sudden silence, a quick springing apart, fine dust disturbed in the air. He had just kissed her. He had just told her that he loves her. Wretched, I shrank into the corner, a scrap of my former self, incapable of standing shoulder to shoulder with the person I most wanted to be aligned with. Astra and me: us against the world.

The moment everything turned quiet, the voices in my head lured me into their net, they trapped me in their vertiginous spiral, sucking me dry, making me immobile. I could not stand up. I could no longer laugh, or even smile. In photos of me taken at this time, I look startled, watching my anxiety like a horror film playing out from behind my eyes. All expression shut down. I couldn't even defend myself with speech.

My dad and his wife moved again in 1998. To the west coast of America this time, a redwood house built into the Marin Hills, just north of San Francisco and within easy reach of Mount Tamalpais and the unearthly Muir Woods. Success and a certain reputation publishing lightly spun books confected for the American market had come to my dad in his fifties and had awarded them both Green Cards, and sought-after US residency. Their house was beautiful, built on stilts with big windows looking out onto woods, with a tall heavy-beamed ceiling. It had platforms rather than rooms, like a grown-up tree house. Sunlight slanted clean through the trees' canopy, bright and then dark. The air was fresh, the neighbours wealthy. They appeared to be happy here, serving sweet California wine when I arrived from the airport, tired and dislocated after a long flight. I didn't go often, but I used my visits here as a kind of refuge. Half the week, I would drift through the fug of my jetlag, awake in the dead of night and hyper until lunch, slowly dropping by teatime, and then I would find rest. My stepmother would cook a nutritious early supper of omelette and salad, or stuffed aubergine, and feed me and Dad with green juice made with spinach and spirulina. I have a few photos of me looking happy when I visited around Christmas time, cosy in a new North Face coat that Dad bought me to protect me from the startling cold, my very own mobile feather duvet. I wore it until it split, and then I taped the split up and wore it some more.

Here, he and his wife made a lot of money, hundreds and thousands of dollars passed through their hands. They entertained the local bohemian literati interested in their stories, extraordinary enough without my father's inevitable embellishments. They served fine leafed tea from a silver teapot, and relaxed on George Smith sofas, covered in a cotton/linen mix, printed with a refined Gollut pattern – a faded version of French Empire toile de joie. Two luxuriant long-haired oriental cats stretched out on the mahogany furniture. A solid and heavy glass table. A bookshelf that shone. Large glasses of white wine: liquid sweetness in the Californian sun.

Money was behind everything. My stepmother liked to shop, and Dad went along with his credit card. They bought Armani; Prada; Chanel; Ralph Lauren. They shopped in Macy's. While she drifted around the aisles, he found an armchair, slumped shoulders, out of breath, sweat on his temples and the back of his hair; he stared into the middle distance and chewed the inside of his cheek. 'Are you all right?' I would ask, feeling bad that he had nothing to do. He would look up, surprised to see me there.

He also took me shopping: I tried on T-shirts and trousers, cardigans and shoes. He bought me J Crew, Nike, Calvin Klein. We ate out at expensive diners, passed the homeless in alleyways and pushing trolleys up steep San Franciscan hills, faces blackened with dirt and hard-baked wrinkles, skin reddened with sunburn, eyes squinting against the harsh light. The deprivation was far more extreme than anything I had seen in England. Dad would stop and give them $50 bills. On the way home, we would drop by Whole Foods to buy huge ripe organic vegetables and sushi, bottles of organic white wine.

Back at the house, I joined my stepmother and her friends in the great Redwood-beamed living room where they talked over tea. They gossiped about local men, those who were eligible, how much money they had. Dad and his wife exaggerated their European sophistication and traded on their premium English accents. But typically, my superior dad bad-mouthed the Americans behind their backs as arrogant, greedy and stupid while accepting their hospitality, admiration and dollars.

We visited Bolinas, a strange fog-bound coastal community further north, where we were invited to parties thrown by local writers and artists. We sat at an enormous round table, with up to twenty other guests: the food was macrobiotic and vegan, with a description of ingredients for each dish. Our first course, though, was enzyme tablets, a bottle given from left to right, swigged down with locally sourced mountain spring water. I had stood as commanded and held my arms out to hug each of them goodbye. 'Group hug,' they would say.

During one of these parties, Dad got up and unexpectedly left. I was in conversation with an artist who wore a paint-splattered smock, a paintbrush in his left breast pocket, who was telling me about his previous career as a banker in LA, and how he had given it all up to live full time in his holiday house in the hills. My father tugged on my jacket. 'We're leaving,' he said, heavy and morose, like an injured dog. His wife hadn't wanted to leave, but he stood outside sulking until she followed. In the car on the way home, he cursed those people. The artistic types. 'A bunch of idiots,' he said. 'Such stupid people.' He laughed in that awkward patronising way. 'Such bullshit.'

That Christmas visit, I stayed for New Year's Eve, and we three were invited to a friend's place, an apartment that overlooked Golden Gate Bridge. We went on to an exclusive club where we paid hundreds of dollars to eat a three-course meal and drink champagne. I have photographs of the three of us – my dad, his wife and me – together, with an unaccustomed lightness and freedom between us. Dad encouraged me onto the dance floor, and I was happy in his arms. He later told me he had been on drugs. He had been nipping to the toilet to take cocaine. I felt betrayed by this, that it was somehow wrong. That the unaccustomed amity between us was only synthetic. It was not unusual for my dad to search out intoxication. Despite barely bothering with drink when he lived with us, my mother T-total, as the slightest amount of alcohol made her dizzy, he had experimented those times in Italy. But I always had a sense that the drugs didn't sit comfortably with him. That he did them despite himself. He was always testing his limits, searching for something beyond the humdrum of the everyday, and he always woke up with regret. It is clear to me now, looking back, why it made me feel uncomfortable despite my own wayward drug-taking at the time. Parents are meant to be more sensible than their kids, straightforward and sorted out. It was unnerving to see him as much at sea as I had been.

From the outside, their life seemed good. Their books were selling and their company growing, they had money, a beautiful house and rich friends. But my brother and I soon learned of the rows that happened in this house. My stepmother admitted to Mum that it was during this period that Dad's drinking started getting out of hand. She was young and drawn to a more social outward-facing life, while my dad, never at ease with himself, was beginning to withdraw more from the world.

He had found solace in the warm shadows of the afternoon sun. He could hide in among the ancient giant trees. When I visited I liked to walk among the millionaires' tree houses built into the hillside, the cabins on stilts, the lush of shady green. Californian wine. Napa Valley restaurants. Such rich sweet nectar, like honey. It was a paradise of sorts, but there was a lot of sadness and artificiality here too, most evident in the stretched surgeoned faces in the cafés of Mill Valley and at Whole Foods.

My Viking and I went on a road trip to California, trekking, with all our holiday gear on our backs, through hot dusty National Parks, camping out in the wild. I was happiest when we went on adventures like these. He was a loner, at home in the mountains, brave and resourceful, a natural leader, and I had him all to myself.

We drove the Pacific Coast Highway from LA to San Francisco, stopping off at motels on the way. Our final stop was a visit for a few days with my dad. I was looking forward to introducing the two of them. But Dad was hostile and uncommunicative. He never felt comfortable with other men, and this one, taller than him, younger and lacking conciliatory charm, really raised his hackles. He served us burnt meat from the BBQ and made no effort at conversation. On our first evening, he told me he didn't like my boyfriend, and did not want him in his house. He asked me to tell him to leave. This astounded and embarrassed me. My friend may have been quiet, even detached, but he was in awe of my father and respectful of his place. He had done nothing to provoke this hostility.

I was furious. Was he jealous, a misguided possessiveness? A delayed paternal instinct? If so, it was too late. Or was it simply that he could not bear to have my gaze shift from him to another man? All my life I had been servile in my devotion and need of him, forgiving him everything. But now I stood apart, with another man in my orbit, a male energy I had chosen. My father, like a king of the jungle, felt compelled on some instinctive level to hang on to his dependants, the women and children in his tribe. When I confronted him about it – 'He's my boyfriend, why can't you be nice to him?' – heat rising in my chest, he retaliated. 'You're so like your mother,' he said. In likening me to the woman he had rejected for challenging him, he was threatening me with rejection too. If I became difficult, I would alienate him. If I stood my ground and opposed him, all would be lost. I knew that he was capable of cutting off entirely. A couple of times, when I had challenged him in a phone call, he hung up after telling me he never wanted to see me again.

Then there was the other side of him – those words calling again: *You are the only one who knows me*, his pathetic needy eyes. 'Don't say that sweetie. Don't be angry with me.' He knew it pained me to feel I had hurt him. But here in his house I questioned whether he used those words only to pull my strings, to keep me close, on his terms only. He had flung out this highfalutin idea that we were connected on some spiritual plane, and that no one, no boyfriend, nor friend, nor mother, nor rival, could come between us. I was so desperate for significance I had taken this literally. I was special to him. I should forgive him everything he had put us through. I had continued to give to him my devotion, my acceptance of his lies, shrugging at the promises never kept, ignoring the festering wound that does not close. But here, now, he revealed in the harshest light just how incapable he was of overcoming his overweening selfishness for one simple moment, of putting me first. And my boyfriend was my witness. Something had shifted. I had a deeper sense this time that my father was wrong.

Back in London, I took up running. I liked how strong it made me feel; that with optimum fitness I could escape into serenity. It was just me and my legs, driving me forward to some other place. I felt more in charge somehow. Running was also a way of sharing something with the Viking, who was strong and fit and liked the new curve of my body, and my confidence at signing up to run a marathon.

The New York marathon was in November. But before that, throughout September and October, he and I had another trip planned. We had taken time off work, to spend six weeks camping and trekking in the Peruvian mountains. Before that, even, was Joe's annual beach rave in the Gower Peninsula, August bank holiday weekend.

The night before we left for Wales, my mum came to say goodbye to us in our basement flat. She now lived in Bath, in a once derelict and beautiful Georgian house. I wouldn't be seeing her again until after Peru and after the marathon. She was tense, distracted. When I followed her out onto the front step, she hesitated, and, as if all her anxiety had flooded into my body I started shaking. 'What is it?' I asked, eyes wide, over-alert to everything.

'It's just so much,' she said, 'for your body to take.'

'I've been training–'

She held her hand on my arm, and her eyes turned serious, 'But you look so thin.'

Every day, I had been training. Going to the gym most lunch breaks, cycling to and from work and running around eight miles twice a week, with a longer run at the weekends. It was excessive, I knew. It had become a kind of obsession; but calculating the hours and totting up the calories felt like a good distraction from the warring voices in my head, and it was a way of growing in strength, of being physically more powerful. I liked the economy of my new body. The shapes it now made, the simplicity of sinew, bone and muscle. It had to be better than all those late nights, downing goblets of white wine. If I was training, mornings were everything. If I was running, it stopped my mind from knotting. I was anxious about the annual beach party Joe was holding. There would be booze, Astra, drugs; I didn't want to miss my weekend run.

'Mum, you should go,' I said, taking a step back and gripping hold of the door. 'You'll be driving home late.'

'Okay,' she said, nodding along with my sudden resolve.

'Okay?' I said taking another step back.

She sighed. 'I love you,' she said, and I laughed nervously.

'I love you too, Mum.'

Leaving our basement, she turned halfway up the stairs, and waved, just as I closed the door. I wanted to open it again and apologise for sending her away. I wanted to follow her to the car. If I slipped into the passenger seat, she might invite me back home with her. She would drive me out of London, along the M4, back to her magical house where she would warm up soup, made with rich chicken stock simmered overnight in the bottom oven of the AGA. Full and comfortable, I would fall into bed and give myself up to the best sleep of my life. Her rooms, those beds, her house like an eiderdown dream. I held tightly onto the handle of the door and knocked my forehead onto my knuckles. There was something in the way my mother had held on to that moment of saying goodbye that made me feel as if I was never going to see her again. I was to leave soon, to go so far away to another country, and then onto another even further away, running a race through hard hot streets I did not want to run. An image moved behind my eyes, a ghost of a thought; it was flimsy enough to dismiss as nothing at all, yet weighty somewhere deep inside me – a sudden fear that I was going to die.

★

In the van the next morning, I felt better, elevated, sitting high above the road, with the windows open. I put my face to the breeze. Everything packed in the back, his kayak, our wetsuits, bedding, cushions. He fiddled with the sound system, and lilting reggae rolled out, mellow through the cabin.

By the time we hit the motorway, he was on his third joint. Smoking while driving, his rangy hands on the steering wheel. I changed tapes, one of mine now, Stevie Wonder – *Don't you worry about a thiiiiinng*. I sang along and put my feet up on the dashboard.

'Your leg alright?' he asked, flashing a look at me.

'Uh-huh,' I said not wanting to make a thing of it. I ran my hand down the inside of my thigh to feel for the twitch of muscle. I had woken with another spasm in the night. The muscle in my thigh seized up, forcing me to sit bolt upright to ease the contraction. It had come from nowhere: I had not slipped nor pulled a muscle. It was almost as if I had conjured it out of nothing.

'It'll go away,' I said, digging my fingers in.

In the night I had ignored my body's insistence that I was merely human. My leg was not able to take the strain of this relentless training, the blood, muscle and bone. I ignored the thought that I was not as strong as I hoped. That I was not made of steel.

'You could still run this weekend if it feels better. Run along the coastal path,' he said.

'Yes, maybe.' I had that thought again, that it was all in my head, that I made it all up. The pain, the paranoia, the bad thoughts, the seething jealousy. Maybe I brought it on myself.

In the outskirts of Swansea, we searched for a supermarket sign. We had suggested that we buy the food for our small camp, enough for the four of us, for Astra and Joe. But the thought marked me like a Sharpie. I would not say it – 'What do you think we should get?' – that I could not bear for her name to surface between us.

We bought sausages and bacon and eggs and enough for two breakfasts and two dinners, thinking we would be at the pub or down on the beach most of the time. We cooked only breakfast last year, taking turns on two camp stoves, fried bacon, its grease eroding the white bread in our hands.

I found him in the alcohol aisle. 'Do you think Astra will want beer?' There it was, *her name*. He had said her name. It hit me. My heart twisted; my head fogged with adrenalin, the sharp bite of shame at being jealous of your best friend. It thrummed through my body like bad wine.

'I don't know.' I said the words as naturally as I could.

Then, of course back in the car, I lost the ease of the morning. Too self-conscious to sling my legs onto the dashboard in that casual way as before. I became creased and small, my chest tight, my breathing short, and I drowned in mean thoughts. *Why did you say that?* He does not normally ask. Never normally interested. *And yet here, you said*: 'Do you think *Astra* will want beer?'

When I saw her across the field, bright like the summer sun, she ran to me, and flung her arms around my neck. 'Thank God you're here. These people are driving me nuts.' She pulled a face, scrunching up her sun-freckled nose. So stunning. I rested my head on her shoulder and let her hold me. She smelt of shells and a fresh green scent like cucumber. My Astra. I felt the Welsh sea air on my skin, and in her arms my heart began to breathe again. It expanded. It beat a million tiny beats. *It is all in your mind.*

We lay on our backs in the sand dunes. Two pretty young things in vintage party dresses, various shades of pink and green. The Gower Peninsula. A hot August bank holiday. This was Joe's weekend, trudging through the sand with his sound system. It had started as an intimate party – just a few friends, but word had got around and the last two years had seen it grow into a kind of beach rave. The campers from our field would make their way a mile or so down the beach, following the music, Leftfield, Underworld.

All-day drinking. Some drugs. Once we had arrived and set up the tent, I had already snorted a line of coke – 'Give into it,' Astra had said, the glint of glitter on her cheekbone. The afternoon light glowed red in my poly-cotton cocoon, when I told myself I should let it all go. *You're uptight*, I had told myself. *It will take your mind off everything.* Like the running, the excessive training. It will take you away to someplace else.

They all emerged, a rainbow of summer colours, carrying bags of food, beer kegs and BBQs. Rugs and mats were thrown out onto the sand. Sausage-fat smoke greyed the bright evening light, and music started up: distorted beats of dub and reggae rising and falling as the sun burned orange and the air chilled. Colours softened to pastel blues, shell pink and yellow.

Astra got up on to her feet and began to dance, bouncy and light and on her toes. I stayed beside her to feel safe, but my hands hung awkwardly at my sides, and my legs dragged.

We had started too early. It was only eight o'clock. Eight o'clock and we were already on a come down.

I searched for my Viking and spotted him a way away on the mound of a sand dune, the last of the sun pinking his face. He was smoking and distant, his eyes on the horizon. 'You having a good time?' I asked looking up at him. He blew out a cloud of smoke but said nothing. Had he ignored me or not heard? I felt like a doll standing there, fragile and ready to break, shattering into tiny shards of porcelain.

Astra found some drugs – a pill, which she snapped in half. I considered not taking it, but only fleetingly. Not long enough to realise that if I said no, I might just sober up, and sit tight in the sand dune, with the safety of wisdom, and know that I could get my own high in the morning, jogging along the coastline while everyone was still partying.

I took a half, felt the hard edge of the pill caught in my throat, knocked back with the dregs of salivered beer. I waited for it to dissolve, to leech into my blood, watched the fire being lit, and strings of neon glowing like phosphorescence. More people were on their feet now, and the sound system rocking the end of the land, rolling and retreating like the sea. I waited for the fuzz – for my mind to blend with my body, that liquid ease – when all thoughts, all worries would lift. I waited, but it didn't come.

So, I left the party, and walked back to the campsite.

I crawled into the tent hoping to find release but found only myself – nothing else – just blackness, that enveloping silence, and my high shallow broken breath. I sat up in the confined space, the damp chill of the tent walls resting on my head, and realised I didn't have a torch. I searched my rucksack, but found it hard to focus, as if my mind and my hands had forgotten they were connected. No coherence between intention and action. I rummaged about, but put my hand into the same pocket, felt the same cloth, not deep enough, not thorough enough, with no real conviction. I searched and then forgot what I was doing. I gave up before starting all over again. I could not make sense of what was buried in this canvas, hidden in this bag, deep in my consciousness. I sat there in the darkness and wondered what to do. My head buzzed with static, too lazy now to catch a thought, too jazzy to sleep, or even to lie down and rest. The party is happening elsewhere. I am here on my own. I crawled back out.

In the campsite and car park there was just enough light to see, but as I ventured back onto the beach I hit black. No moon. No stars. No torch. It was so dark, so black, there was no shape, no movement, nothing. It was as if I had plucked my eyes out and blinded myself.

I tried to recall the path that led me here, and perhaps I walked along it for some distance. Perhaps I identified it beneath my feet for a time, but perhaps I also didn't. At some point I wandered off it. There was sand beneath me now. Cold sand. And my feet were sinking, finding it difficult to gain traction. I could hear the gentle crash and retreat of the sea to my left, and I guessed the sand dunes were to my right, but I also was not really aware of what I was thinking. Except my breath, persistent and demanding. My heart that started to stammer, *I'm scared*. The whoop and cry and music. I was still some distance away from the light.

How can it be so black? It is incomprehensible that something could be quite so impenetrable. Me, the city girl, so used to houses and cars and streetlights. But here, there was nothing, no trace, no outline, nowhere for my eyes to rest. It is still baffling to me, and I wonder if my brain was somehow playing a trick, to finally make me stop, but only by first taking me to the worst possible place of nightmare. Me alone, just a speck, staggering through infinite space. Would the blackness gently stop my hands and feet, and wrap its velvet arms around me? Instead it spat me out, with no consideration. I was just an ordinary being, lost on the beach that night. I was on my own, blinded, trying to find my way.

I thrust my feet forwards as I walked, as if they might have eyes, as if these legs, these athlete's legs that had been carrying me for all those miles of running, that had become trusty and strong, might have the power to lead tonight, to work hard for this addled brain. I sang to stay calm. The comfort of Stevie Wonder, again, *Don't you worry about a thing*, wavering with my broken breath.

But this time my body let me down. Suddenly one leg was caught but I was still moving until, like rubber on a slingshot, it sprung with tension. I fell forwards, and heard a pop. A simple sound, like a champagne cork being released from a bottle. I felt nothing when the bone snapped. I was unaware of where I landed or how, my consciousness split from the rest of me, everything distant and impersonal. I had no awareness of what stopped me in my tracks. In the complete darkness, I walked right into it, and it had gripped hold of my knee, locking my tibia, while the rest of me had propelled forward, my thigh taking all the weight. It was only days later in the hospital bed that I was to discover what had ensnared me: wire netting, thick like knotted metal, used to hold back the sand dunes, to stop them from collapsing.

'Shit.' I sat up and could suddenly see. As if a light had been switched on inside my head. I looked behind me at my leg – the one that had been held fast – now twisted and distorted beneath my colourful dress. It didn't look like it belonged to me, so I wriggled my toes to check.

Glancing at the expanse of sand and sea, I felt relieved to be able to see again. I was calm, profoundly indifferent, and utterly alone. I wondered, fleetingly, what might happen if no one found me, and thought to myself there are worse places to die. My leg was now useless; I couldn't get up on that foot. My femur was broken, and yet I felt nothing: no fear, no distress, no pain. I listened to the sound of the sea, its gentle susurration, and felt a cold breeze caress my skin. Perhaps I will bleed to death, I thought. Or die from the cold. A stupid girl in her party dress.

Then I saw a distant glow of rocking light, and two black figures attached, spindly creatures scaling the horizon, as if emerging from a post-apocalyptic desert. Their bodies grew into Giacometti shapes in the pulse and swing of their lanterns. The light expanded around them, filling up the sand, and the sky, the sea beyond. I found my voice then. 'Help,' I called, politely, towards the light. 'I think I've hurt myself.'

All flooded to gold, as they moved closer with simultaneous speed and slow motion. In my dissociated state there was no time. I drifted from my place there in the cold sand and watched it all from above: a young woman in a tangled pile of sand-dune wire, her psychedelic vintage dress smudged and torn, her eyes aglare.

That light. It illuminated the shock on their faces, swinging in and out.

'Can you get some help?'

'Oh, God,' they said. 'What have you done?'

I had a fleeting thought that they were useless, these young men, and that they will run away, and I will be left here to die. 'I need help,' I said.

'Yeah. Uh.'

But then a shifting of weight and air, a solid presence behind me and arms wrapped around my body. A soothing voice, which said: 'It's okay, I'm a doctor.'

I heard those words and let my body fall into that weight, let gravity take me, and I lay back in this woman's arms. I closed my eyes and finally let go. A doctor, I mustered, a doctor here on this beach, walking past at this time. The universe had decided to save me.

Drifting into half sleep, I wondered how different it would be if the sign had come earlier: before that first drink, that first line of coke, the second line, the ecstasy. Before the running. The marathon training. The starvation. The distracted boyfriend. Before the fractured voice that felt as if it was not heard, was never heard. My muteness, my fear and need. This small creature who thought she had got it right, but had missed the step, again. She kept doing that. The awkward arms and legs and the voices in her head.

Another doctor appeared and held my leg in traction – one miracle doctor at either end – and slowly faces appeared and disappeared, there and then gone, and another mini version of the party grew around me. 'One leg's shorter than the other,' one of them shouted.

I found it hard to keep afloat. The activity rolled on, talk and laughter, attempts to get help, faces in my face, demanding I stay awake – but I kept drifting, as if bobbing helplessly on a cold swell. I lost myself to the sand and the icy crack of air, star upon star upon star, the cold seeping from the ground and into my bones. I began to shake. Blankets and coats were tucked around my body. People were trying to help, but their faces were up close, empty black eyes and white strings of spittle, and shouting: talking over me, over that thin thread that kept slipping from my feeble grip. They shouted in my face. 'Stay awake!' 'Don't close your eyes. *Wooohoo!*' 'We don't want to lose you, *mate*.' Mate. Mate? Who the fuck are you calling mate?

My boyfriend was there, somewhere. I glimpsed his profile against the huge dome of the sky, lit bright by the tip of a cigarette, or a lighter or a lantern, glowing with ecstatic oblivion. Out there on the beach, I continued to drift away from the shifting light and dark, the star-studded world. *It is better* – a small voice from inside me tempted me with its song – *to be in the quiet of sleep.*

There was talk of a helicopter, of being airlifted to the hospital because the ambulance couldn't make it to the beach. There was talk of being stranded. I have no idea how long I was there, with my back in the sand, but it must have been hours. I watched the stars, which burned brightly, then died. It seemed like no time to me there beneath them on the ground, growing colder, the faces and voices growing more distant.

Finally, a vehicle approached across the sand, its white lights banging me awake, and a clatter and slam of doors. A Land Rover, and a few burly paramedics lumbering out. One of them took my hand. 'No pain relief for you, love,' he said, informed of the cocktail of narcotics I had taken.

They held the stretcher and told me that my leg would be secured into an inflated tube, and I wondered how I would get from here to there. I suddenly didn't want to move. Leave me here in the sand, in among the shell and broken bone, for the seagulls to find. *Please.* I stared up into the circle of them and must have looked scared, as one of them said: 'Don't worry. We'll need to lift you, but you can scream. It won't bother us.'

Which I did.

I heard the bones as they scraped against each other. I felt their looseness puncturing the periosteum, tearing at the connective tissue, my nerves firing. I felt the pain. It brought me back. It was a cruel pain, and it cut deep. I felt every unbearable second it took for them to lift me onto the stretcher, seconds that bled into a prolonged agonising scream. Everyone would have heard me. The families in the campsite, the two sci-fi men with their lanterns, all those people, drugged up, at the rave. They would turn as one towards the chilling sound. I had found my voice at last.

I was not to know my boyfriend, no longer my Viking, would resist getting into the ambulance with me, too concerned about missing the party. The next day, he visited the hospital and joked about how he could see my urine as it filled up the catheter bag; he pumped my bed with his foot, up and down, laughing oblivious of the hours of surgery I had endured. He visited me once before returning home, though I would stay in that bed for two weeks, too sick on morphine to sit up, and desperate to stop crying.

My mother drove each morning the four-hour round trip from Bath to sit at my bedside and read to me, while I vomited and cried and vomited again. I had such a bad reaction to the morphine she was scared I was going to die. She was so worried that she phoned my dad and asked him to come, to support us, but also to prove his love for me. But he didn't come. It did not suit him, so he batted it away. It was inconvenient, and he couldn't be bothered. 'She'll be fine,' he said dismissively. My mum didn't tell me any of this at the time. But none of it surprises me.

A man with learning difficulties who worked for the hospital brought me biscuits on the sly, and one day he showed me, proudly, that my story had made it into the local paper. 'Girl Breaks Leg at Beach Party', stranded in the Gower Peninsula. I was stranded, but then I had been saved by the everyday heroism of strangers.

The surgeon, working on a bank holiday weekend, had spent all day putting my leg back together again. I woke up halfway through the operation to hear them hammering a titanium rod down the centre of my femur in place of my bone marrow. How cool is that? I would finally have my robotic leg. I would finally be made of something stronger than bone. *Bang Bang Bang* I heard, and opened my eyes to strip lights and a blue shield. I remember crying out, 'I'm awake!' before a nurse looked at me with startled eyes and everything returned to black.

When I stopped vomiting and began to feel better, I spent my days chatting to a woman in a bed on the other side of the ward. I reassured her when she spoke about her anxieties over her daughter, unhappy in her marriage with two small children. 'Sometimes people just aren't right for each other,' I said. 'Maybe life would be better if they weren't together.'

We cancelled our trip to Peru. And I never made it to New York. I was very relieved about that. That, and the fact that I did not have to return to my boyfriend and our dark basement apartment for over a month to come. Instead, Mum came to collect me and took me to her home. She looked after me, then, as if I were a child again. Each morning, after waking, I hopped down the grand wooden staircase, and each evening I hauled myself up again, backwards, all my weight on my hands. Mum would run me a bath and help me into it, my leg withered beneath the light. Each week she drove me to the hospital where I sat on the edge of a bed and breathed hard, while the physio, who was sweet and kind, gently bounced my leg, to ease the knee, which had locked in shock, before lying me back down to help loosen the muscle in my groin that had contracted hard as rope. This accident left a large scar on my hip, far larger than the one I got from falling off my moped in Italy, and my mum cried when she saw it. She cried for the damage to her child's body, and the invisible pain that had provoked it. But I was proud of the scar. It was the visible sign of being broken and put back together. It spoke of recovery and of returning stronger. The surgeon told me that a callus of new bone would grow around the break and draw the fragments firmly together again. It would give my leg extra protection. I had been given another chance. I felt the split parts of me start to knit back together in that hospital bed. I became still again, for a time, centred, letting the world rotate around me.

The Scam

'Dad's coming to London.' My brother phoned me at work. It was 2003, about four years after my accident. 'Apparently he's being put up in the Connaught for free.'

I laughed, glanced about at my colleagues either side of me. 'By who? The bloody Russians?' I whispered down the phone. He had already emailed us with his excitement at this revelation. *You never guess what's happened! A long-lost relative died in a car accident and his lawyer got in touch as I'm the next surviving relative. An email. Can you believe it? Your clever Dad's going to finally make it!*

'And guess what,' my brother went on. 'He says the bloke who died and miraculously left him millions of dollars is called Saul Dunn.'

'But that's—'

'I know,' he laughed.

It was the pseudonym Dad had used for the science fiction novels he wrote in the 1970s, *Steeleye*, *The Evangelist* and *Cabal*.

'He says he knew him when they were kids – they're distant cousins, or something.'

'Really?' I believed it for a minute. Could imagine a story: *We had some dealings. Saul and me, running around in our nappies at our grandparents' house in Bracknell.* I felt slightly sick: 'Do you really think?'

'You don't believe him, do you?' my brother said, shocked.

No. It was ridiculous, but I also couldn't quite believe that *he* believed it – how could anyone?

I changed tack: 'Does Mum know?'

'I guess she doesn't know he's staying at the Connaught.' Ben's tone said it all.

'He *always* stays at expensive hotels.'

'But this is slightly different–'

'It must be *thousands*,' I whispered.

During Dad and his wife's successful years they often blasted tons of money on expensive hotels. Charlotte Street Hotel was their favourite. Dad was extravagant. Took us to Harrods where he would order champagne in the food hall and buy us things – guilt money, we called it. I would glide through the sleek corridors, fingering Miu Miu handbags, Mulberry, Girbaud. He liked to spend money, often on credit. But the Connaught? It was off the scale.

'But what if it's *true*?' I said.

He laughed. 'Is it *ever* true?'

I let the tension go, fell against the back of my chair. My brother was good at pulling me back from the brink.

'Yeah,' I laughed. 'What's he like?'

'I've got to go,' he said, as I heard his new baby's cries rising in the background.

'Are you going to see him?' I asked quickly, over his toddler daughter shouting.

'The Connaught must have an insane minibar,' he said, before hanging up.

I didn't really think of it over the next few weeks. I went back to my life, my job at *Time Out*, writing and editing their city guides. I was turning thirty that year, looking to the future with a steady gaze. I had met a man who made me happy. After work I returned to him in his Stoke Newington flat, or met at a local pub with our friends. After the Viking who wasn't, I had vowed not to waste any more time with wasters, manipulators, drunks. I was in a good place. There was no need to look back.

My father had lived in the States for the past six or so years, and I was well used to his absence. He was in Bolinas now, the seaside town that I had found so oppressive when I had visited him the Christmas before, after his wife had left. We shared emails and I sensed he was a bit lost since she had gone, but he had a new girlfriend, the butcher from across the way. Our communication was always punctuated by Monty Python style-humour, silly jokes and riddles; an excuse to say hello, small gestures to bridge the distance between us, a reminder that we were both still there. I had no sense that there was anything wrong.

The first time I saw him in his opulent hotel suite, he was standing behind the bar, holding a smudged crystal glass of brown liquid; there was an empty bottle of Jack Daniels on the counter beside him and a collection of half-drunk cans of coke, but I was mostly struck by the distance in his eyes, and how much his hands shook. The suite was the size of a small house with a living room, bathroom and bedroom attached, a walk-in wardrobe, and a kitchen, but it was the bar that shone brightly. It appeared to swell in the middle of the room, holding my father captive; I guess he felt safe behind its circling arms. He was beaten. Pale, puffy and edgy, as if he was already slipping away. 'Dad, let's go for a walk,' I suggested gently.

'A walk?' he said, like a tired old clown. 'But I might miss them.'

He had been there for three days already, waiting. This was the day the Russians were finally coming. But nothing felt real. There was something obscene about this place, this velvet asylum, as if the whole story of wealth had to be stitched from such cushioning fabric in order to protect its privileged from the harshness of outside. Only here my father was kept prisoner by the promise of something phantasmal.

The chilled air-con was too insistent. It slapped my face, and dried my mouth, causing my throat to contract. It smothered my senses, stretching a film across my ears. The room was soundless like a padded cell. You could barely hear yourself walk across the carpet. Any movement of traffic or children banished behind triple glazed glass; the light from the sun and its warmth, deadened by gauzy net. It suited my father fine. He wanted his privacy, to be left alone to watch TV, drink, pace and dream of money. He might have been in that room for a thousand years, compelled by the same circular thought, calling room service for snacks to eat on the bed, dropping crumbs from his scones and leaving sticky marks from the jam, careless because someone else would clean up after him. He had told himself that someone was even going to foot the bill.

'The park is out there,' I said heading for the door. 'We don't have to go far.'

'But they're coming,' he said, his breath short with anxiety and the sheer effort of moving. 'The Russians.'

'The fresh air will do you good.'

In Hyde Park, we walked to the fountains, the circular wall where tourists took photos while their children reached over the side to grasp at pennies, deceptively magnified. The sky was overcast, and the air felt cold. I wanted to fill the silence but did not want to talk about the reason he was here, although it hung between us like bad breath. What if I tell him something of my life? He never asked, but I always tried, although my voice dulled somewhere deep in my throat. 'Dad, he asked me to marry him.'

'Who?'

'The man I told you about, when I was in the States. I showed you a picture.'

'Oh, that funny-looking man,' he said, laughing to himself.

I flinched but didn't defend him. 'We're getting married, he asked me.'

'And *what*?' Dad stopped and looked over at me.

'I said yes.'

He chuckled to himself as if he were in on a joke that I didn't yet understand. 'You sure about that?'

'He's a good man,' I said. 'He's a sweet man.' In my mind

another voice started to emerge – this one was clearer, stronger, it grew into its height, a beautiful woman in command, dressed in a tight figure-hugging jumpsuit with spikes in her heels. She spoke firmly into my ear, she whispered. *'Not like him.'*

'Bloody marriage,' Dad muttered. He sighed. 'I guess you'll want children, like your brother. You'll get all stressed. Your brother barely comes to see me. Thinks he's above all that, family man.' As if it were a crime.

I did want children, just as I wanted a good husband, someone I could rely on and who would stand by those he loved. I was fed up with that constant sense of unease, the tug and pull that nothing is quite what it seems. I had learned to stand back and see it for what it was. But more than anything, I wanted my children to have a good dad. I had burst into tears when I saw my brother in the hospital with his firstborn, blown away by the rush of love I felt for my niece but also by how completely he offered his love to his daughter. In the hospital corridor I said to my mum: 'Did you see the way he looked at her?' The simple love between father and daughter, unadulterated, as it should be. She had all of him. It was never like that between me and my dad.

I had met my future husband at a Halloween party. I was dressed up in a black satin top with small witch's peaks stitched into the shoulders, a slash of red lipstick. My hair was long, highlighted blonde. I had noticed him across the dance floor, soft-eyed above a Hoxton beard. He was gentle and kind, and set his heart on me. He told me a few weeks later that he was convinced I had been sent to him from the stars, and he had been sent to that party to meet me. He ran a small design agency with offices on Exmouth Market, which was expanding, and I admired his consistency and clarity of vision; that he was hard working. I felt safe when I was with him. On our first date, we sat opposite each other on a tiny table in the midst of a buzzing pub, and I showed him the contents of my handbag, tipping my lipstick, blusher, vials of different coloured glitter, old tissues, receipts, pens, mini notepads – all my rubbish displayed on the table between us. He nodded and smiled affectionately. He put his hand out to me and I took it. Suddenly everything felt easy.

Stop causing trouble, I said to myself. Keep the drama and wild romance for your writing. During this time, I had a dream. It was of a small blonde girl, and a large white bed. I decided that the blonde girl was me, a part of me, as if she lived in my heart. But in the dream, she crawled from within me, out through my jumper and hopped into my purse, helping me close the clasp over her mischievous head. 'Keep it locked shut,' she said, peering through the tiny gap, her eyes in the light, glinting like diamonds. 'Don't you dare let me out.' I tucked her into my handbag and followed this kind man's lead.

Sometimes, when I had a bath, I allowed myself to wish – what did I wish for? A book and a baby. In those soft midnight moments, I let myself believe that it really was possible.

'What if I said you don't need to do it?' Dad said, stopping at a bench and hovering over it as if he wanted to sit down. He looked at me with unfocused eyes. 'You don't need to get married. You don't need anyone to look after you.' He must have seen the surprise on my face, because he smiled for the first time. 'You see, I can still read your mind.' It made me jolt. I did not want him doing this to me anymore.

'Maybe I *want* someone to look after me,' I challenged him.

He turned to me with water in his eyes. 'Your dad's going to help you out. There'll be enough for you to buy a house.'

'But I love him, Dad,' I said. When I had been in California that last Christmas, and so new in our relationship, I had felt bereft without him.

'Love. Hmm. I'm offering you the world.'

'That's nice Dad,' I said flatly, too used to his big empty gestures.

'Believe me,' he said, and his bloodshot gaze bumped into and away from me. He looked so small suddenly, so vulnerable.

A stream of sunlight blasted through the fountain and covered the world in crystals, and I thought: What if?

'How much?' I asked without looking at him.

'Maybe a million?'

But I was tired of it. I saw an image of my dad, returning to visit us all those years ago. I must have been six or seven. He was back from Pune, or New York State, or perhaps it was later and he had been in Oregon. He had given up everything for Bhagwan by that point. In a borrowed car, he drove me and my brother along Regent's Crescent and pointed to one of the grand Victorian stucco houses and told us that a man he knew had given it to him, 'as if it were a biscuit' he threw from over his shoulder. Grinning, we gazed out of the window at the imposing houses, like extravagantly decorated cakes, imagining skidding down the curved stairs, and flying in our socks along the marble shined floors. I believed him then, as children do, but I was not a child anymore.

'But Dad–'

'They're paying for the suite,' he added defensively. 'Why would they pay for my flight here and the room – a thousand a night – if they aren't serious?'

'They are paying for your room at the Connaught, so they can give you money?'

'It's my money. A long-lost relative. He died. An accident. His family too. They traced him. To me. My cousin. Haha! Can you believe it? I knew he'd do good. No next of kin. Repatriate. Millions.'

Why would barristers, trying to trace a next of kin, pay thousands of pounds to put you up in one of the smartest hotels in London, in order to give you money that is your right? *Dad! You're deluded!* – I wanted to scream. But I didn't. Dad the clown, the trickster, the narcissist who would turn nasty if you reflected his behaviour back at him. It was easier to go along with it.

★

Back at the hotel, my father changed his shirt. The walk had made him sweat. I sat down as he poured himself another drink. 'You can go now,' he said from the safety of the bar again. 'You've been so sweet, my daughter. But you can leave me alone now.' I knew why he wanted me to go, so he could drink and be anxious, obsessional, paranoid, delusional, on his own. There was a business card on the table; it had a name and a telephone number on it. *Russian*. I had a fleeting and frightening thought: if my father disappears. If they take him. I bent it between my fingers and put it in my pocket.

'I want to come with you,' I said over my shoulder.

'No, sweetie.'

My back was to him as he padded across the room. He had mentioned money, money he needed to give them in order to be given something in return. Lawyer's fees, administration. 'Not much,' he had said.

I was aware of him at the safe, punching the keys. Its little swing door opening on its hinges. I thought about turning around to face him, to burst his bubble of subterfuge. I heard him take the cash out and stuff it – wads of it – into a plastic bag. My heart beat fast, my body filled with the heat of panic.

'I'm coming with you,' I said, but I only half stood up.

'You're not,' he said and put on his coat. I clutched the card in my pocket.

He took the money and in a swift moment he left the room. A blast of air escaped just before he closed the door.

I remained beneath the elaborate corniced ceiling, held tight by the Victorian upholstered chair, as if I were circled by briars. Was I just as deluded: too desperate to cling to that balloon that went up and on to a better life, to a new normal of marshmallow clouds and clear blue? Did I just not see what was happening? I was still drinking a lot then. Moving from pub to pub through Fitzrovia after work. Long, drawn-out social weekends. It was what we did; what my friends and I had been doing all through our teens, our twenties. We didn't think of ourselves as having drink problems, just as I didn't think of my dad as an alcoholic. I had no idea that the drink might have seeped deep into his psyche, distorting the world around him, accentuating his desperately grandiose and artificial sense of self.

I imagine him clinging to the handrail, and wonder if he felt lucky for a moment as he told himself the story that got twisted somewhere in its telling, or if he attempted to walk with dignity. Perhaps he forced a smile when he saw the men who stood straight-backed in the lobby, as he fought with himself not to turn and run, the bag of cash stuffed on the inside of his jacket. His last chance to save himself.

I did stand up. I have no memory of how I got to the top of the stairs that overlooked the hotel lobby, but in my mind's eye I see the slick and shine of the dark mahogany, broad and gloating. Dad hovers on the bottom stair, his hand a sweaty mess from the firmness of his grip, as if he is about to plunge into deep water. He then takes his final step onto the slippery stone. Did he look back and see me? All three men are standing, but I see one in particular, neatly dressed in a starched blue shirt. He is young and slim, his hair the colour of sand. I must have felt such fright, my heart pushing into my throat. Yet I did nothing. I imagine my father wiping his palms on his cashmere trousers before shaking their hands and apologising. I imagine he feels sick when he gives them the money. But he is compelled by something greater than himself, let's call it hope, or a final reckoning, that here at last he will get his dues, something for nothing.

I do not remember what happened after that. How I got back to the room, and what Dad said when he joined me, whether I questioned him again. I imagine I put on my coat and swiftly left, rushing back to normal, my safe and simple life. Desperate to escape my own shame at not turning as he took out the money, of not stopping him. On some level I wonder if I knew then that I had failed him. He had walked towards his death down those dark stairs and I had let him.

★

My father boarded the flight out of there, empty handed, $50,000 down. He went back to his seaside house in the back end of California and hid, seeking solace among his bottles. It was easier to lose himself to alcohol than to admit the self-loathing he must have felt at getting it so wrong. Such corrosive shame intensifying the overwhelming desire to deaden it again.

And what of my inaction? I look back now and see that I too was consumed by a need that was beyond me, like so many women at the beginning of their thirties. In the throes of the promise of romance and stability – 'the grand ambition of romantic love', as Esther Perel names it – with the firm belief that marriage would save me. The pagoda of roses that stood perfectly in the glow of the sun, opening to reveal a path where my new husband and I could walk together, hand in hand into eternity. My emotional life had been such a mess up until now and at last I could put all that turmoil behind me.

The Giveaway

His timing was impeccable. My father's slow and painful journey towards death took a decisive turn during the run-up to my wedding. I had finally escaped from his grasp is how I saw it, met a man who was good for me, who blessed me with his simplicity, and the promise of a normal, contented life. I was no longer in thrall to my father and the insidious repercussions of his self-centredness. This is how I understood it in 2005; this is what I believed.

In my teens and early twenties my indenture to a self-harming subjugation to a series of men who were inappropriately older, emotionally dominant or absent, was now over. My husband broke form. Ours was not a threatening relationship of sudden shots and retaliative fire. I had hoped in linking my path to his that I had finally grown into myself and become stronger and better equipped. How different this man would be, in his treatment of our future children and of me.

How convenient, then, that the man I had spent a lifetime in need of, trapped as I was in the repetitive, debilitating mantra 'I am loved less than I love', reached out just as I was attempting to plant my tentative feet into tender new soil. Dad had offered to help pay for the wedding. We had planned to have it at my mum's house in Bath, and though it was going to be big, swelled with our friends and families, with all my mum's siblings and my cousins, it was homemade too. But I was not aware at the time that he was struggling to find any money to help. The Russian scam, the magical solution to end the tedium of his work, which would free him from having to ingratiate himself to those 'publisher arseholes', that failed to give him the good life he felt he deserved, had broken him. But, at the time, none of us had any idea how bad things were. Yet, even as I write these words now, I wonder if we could not see it, or if we simply chose not to.

He had been in London for work less than a year before and I was shocked at how bad he looked. He was hunched and overweight, the skin on his legs unusually pale. He was nervy, sweat clumping up his hair. He had started a dental procedure to acquire a mouth full of implants, long-awaited after the terrible dentistry he had endured at the hands of a sannyasin dentist in Pune – 'it's going to cost me tens of thousands of dollars,' he had said proudly, only it was complicated by his oversensitive gag reflex. His throat would contract in defence each time the dentist tried to put anything in his mouth. His teeth were pulled out one by one, but it was too difficult to secure the new ones in their place.

It was upsetting to be with him. He was distracted and unfocused, and kept speaking with an irritating flamboyance, repeating himself, talking in circles as if he were grasping at scraps of memory, so coloured by the stories he had been telling himself over so many years that even he could not disentangle the truth. He spoke incessantly about his lost wife, clutching his mobile phone in the hope she would call. We sat together on the train to Bath, and he spoke on and on desperately inflating their love, trying to demonstrate their closeness through objects she had chosen to buy him: 'Now what about this signet ring,' he said showing me an ebony-faced ring on his little finger. 'It's an antique. It cost thousands.' He tried to take it off, but his finger was too swollen. 'Every time we came to London, she bought me something special. She would go shopping in the morning and come back with a big bag of surprises.' He measured it with his hands, as big as a metre, no a metre squared. 'It was this big,' he said with the wonder of a child, lisping now through the gaps in his teeth.

He told me about the novel he had written about her, *Promise of Dawn*. The ghost of her. In the novel the character of my father is lonely without his wife, and her ghost gives him a special kiss on the forehead which transforms him, brings a simpler state, a little like meditation; she teaches him how to be present, to stop the yearning that takes him everywhere but here, this place, right now. She heals his restlessness.

He slept in a bed that I made nice for him in Mum's top-floor bedroom, and yet he left the covers in a mess and walked through his twisted towel in his shoes. He was blind to the nuanced light in the trees, the tender breeze as it whistled through the sash windows, seeing only the phone as it flashed with his absent wife's name and number. He was lost to the now, in idle thoughts about what he wanted to buy her in the Antiques Arcade.

I must have turned away from the discomfort of it all, because later, in the run-up to the wedding (and I still find it difficult to admit to this), I would not let up about the money he had promised. In the most literal way conceivable, I was holding him to account. But we were all playing the same old tune: he had exaggerated the truth of what he could afford for fear of letting us down, and had kept us hanging on, and he'd only admitted he could not afford to help when it was too late. By which time we had sent out the fancy invites, maxed out on the number of guests, bought the dress, hired my friend as a caterer, and ordered the roses – all on money we and my mum had scrabbled together. My uncle paid for the champagne.

For years Dad had lived the life of a millionaire, regardless of his fluctuating freelancer's bank balance. All those expensive hotels and designer clothes. This image, of how he and his wife chose only the best for themselves, shopping in Harrods, frittering excessive amounts of money on a cashmere cardigan or a thousand-pound coat because they didn't pack enough warm clothes, was still in my mind when I pestered him with emails. But there was another dynamic too. We were used to being let down. Just this one time I wanted him to come through. But my fear that he would not keep his promise made me all the more persistent. We had been listening to this song for decades. The money will come, he would say. You just have to be patient.

In fact, he never paid our mum maintenance when we were children; no standing order – so dull, so predictable, so lacking in gratitude and drama. Instead he made grandiose gestures, buying me a pair of shiny orange high-heeled shoes (when we needed school shoes) and buying my brother a leather bomber jacket (which he never wore). When we were older, we became accustomed to promises of sweet gifts in our bank accounts, promises that were repeated over months. The dependence went both ways. In our hopeful expectation, we were hooked in, glued to the end of the phone or incessantly on email, checking in – *Dad, have you sent it yet?* We wanted the money, but mostly it was an excuse for us to make contact, to have something to talk about; sadly, he liked to have us there, dangling, for it also disempowered us. We carried on like this for years, until one day I was struck by how premeditated his tricks were. In a fancy London hotel suite, I overheard him phoning the bank to transfer £50 he had promised me for months, only to hear him misread the sort code. It dawned on me that this was his technique: when the money still did not arrive, he could put hand to heart and say, in all honesty: 'I transferred it, sweetie, only the bank sent it to the wrong account!' These were the kind of lies that we had to navigate. Cold and slippery, designed solely for him to escape blame.

So, I persisted. I was so tired of the lying, the stalling, the resistance, of all the promises not kept. I was trying to forge a new life, no longer looking back. I was angry. I climbed onto my flimsy pedestal and felt justified in shaking a fist at him and yelling. I continued to ask for what he had promised he would give. He was my father. It was my wedding. It was my right. I even had a romantic notion of him giving me away. But then, I had never belonged to him in any conventional sense. He had not supported me and nurtured me to maturity, preparing me for the day when he could step back from being my 'daddy', my number one. What I did not realise in my defensive determination to cut the ties was the toxicity of our relationship, and how trapped inside it I still was.

When I look back now at emails we exchanged during this period, I can see how I pushed him. But I can also see something else: his desperation and fear, that he was on the edge, about to lose everything. *'Please, please my darling daughter, understand the following without doubt.'* He said all the things I wanted to hear: *'You are my dearest child and loved by me in the deepest part of my heart; I will find the money for you as sure as night is dark and day is light; I will be there in Bath when the wedding happens and love you and give you away as the best father can.'* But then he loses it, flagrantly, writing in capitals: *'THERE IS NO DOUBT THAT ALL THIS IS TRUE. IF YOU DO NOT BELIEVE IT, IT HAS NOTHING TO DO WITH ME.'* And then the sannyasin avoidance trick kicks in: *'What else can I say? I cannot change your doubts – I can only fulfil my promise. I cannot change the future until it happens when the present will be true.'* In effect, he blamed me for my fear that once again he would let me down. *'PLEASE GOD STOP MAKING IT ALL SO DIFFICULT!'* he shouted through email.

I saw his defence of himself as pathological. I was flying high towards my new life, and in my attempt to draw a line under the past and move on I was determined to make him stop and listen. I wanted him to unlock the gate and let me through into my future. I wanted to be given permission to walk away.

Since moving to New York, his wife had distanced herself from us and we were no longer close. The two of us no longer like sisters. She had initially gone there to create space in her relationship with Dad, to work out how she felt. But when he quickly moved in the local butcher, had her sleep in their bed among all his wife's beautiful things, she was profoundly shocked. He clearly did not want to live alone, and he had grasped at the first woman who was available. In New York, his wife went to an event as part of my mother's book tour for her biography of Queen Elizabeth and Mary Queen of Scots and they had a sorrowful meeting over coffee at my mum's hotel. They both knew what it was like to have loved such a vulnerable and maddening man. Perhaps his wife should not have been surprised. My father was a master of avoidance, a ravenous maw of need. He could barely live with himself when she was around, so how could he be alone? She had already decided on her path to freedom and self-determination. By the time of my wedding she was married again and pregnant with her first child.

During the run-up to my wedding, Dad's emails got worse. He was either ranting at the injustice of the pressure we were putting him under, or he was boasting about how much he was worth and his indomitable health. '*Please note you guys that your dad is made of tough stuff and is not going to deteriorate in any form or for any reason either in the near future or the distant! . . . He plans and is told that he will live into is 90s . . . and that he will by then, and well before, being living back in he old land of the UK. He will be owner of a 2 million dollar property and more. Please don't worry – all will be well. I just learned – and was made an offer for this gorgeous house – $1.4 million – almost three times the purchase value – projected forward this means that by his death and will – 2035 – be worth approximately $26 million!!!!!!!!!!*'

The typos are his own.

He fell over outside the store and hurt his leg. He smashed a treasured antique lamp that had survived his many travels. He blacked out while driving. He had been prescribed sleeping pills, he told us, and they were causing him all sorts of problems. He was drinking while taking them. Then the butcher sent me a message saying she was concerned about him. Another email arrived a few weeks before my wedding:

well you might be too late for any kind of sanity.........this man is
on pills and alcohol 24-7 and yes I am a friend but YOU are his
FAMILY I advise you to do something about it.......get together as
a family and deal with it sweetie

I was angry at her tone, but also, I realise now, wired with guilt
– we were his family, and yet it was not that straightforward.
He had made it almost impossible for us to help him. When we
confronted him about his drinking, he said there was nothing to
worry about. It was still hard to believe a stranger's word over
his, even in light of all those ridiculous lies. Dad would be with
us for the wedding, so I would see him for myself. I was busy. I
had a major event to organise. I saw the butcher's plea as a sign of
the American propensity to pathologise everything. You drink
therefore you are an alcoholic. I put it down to over-reaction
and carried on.

But then the phone calls got worse. Late at night, he phoned
me, sometimes incoherent other times pleading. A week before
my wedding, I went for a fake tan on the Roman Road, was told
to go to bed in it then shower it off the next day. 'Don't wash
your hands,' the tanning lady said. 'Your face. Nothing!' That
night, my father phoned. He was crying, inconsolably. He told
me many things. He said he was sorry about everything. For
being an idiot, he said. He felt ashamed. He felt scared. He said:
I love you. 'I love you so much,' he said, and I sat cross-legged in
the centre of the bed and sobbed at hearing his desperation – the
sound of his heart breaking in his voice, a glimpse of his truth? A
chink of light? He sobbed with me, together we cried.

When I put down the phone I was hot and stuffed up from
crying. I went to the bathroom and looked in the mirror, and
there were white streaks cut through my cheeks where the tears
had washed away the brown. However hard I tried to scrub them
off they wouldn't go. Faded tear marks stained onto my face on my
wedding day; if you looked closely enough you could see them.

★

The pills and alcohol were messing with his mind, but we might have stopped and thought more about why he was self-medicating. Of course, his wife was gone, and he missed her terribly. He had tried to fill the void by moving the first available woman into the house, who also appeared to have a drink problem. None of this helped.

Perhaps, underlying it all, was an existential questioning; my father's fear of his ordinariness, a subterranean terror that he might be made of common lead rather than gold, and then of the rarest kind. He had reached middle age, a natural time of crisis, when everything that has happened before is thrown into question. Jung suggests that the second part of a person's life can be the time to reach one's potential, for personal growth and individuation, a drawing together of disparate parts, and a chance to experiment with those aspects of a personality previously ignored: the sportsman becomes the scholar; the extrovert goes back to college. Classically, it is a time to stop and become more reflective; what now that you have the right job, the right house, and your children are launched? But my father had not bothered himself with anything so mundane, did not care about building a sturdy foundation for a more soul-filled second half of life.

In reality, he did it all the wrong way round. By the time he might have been drawn back to his family and a more contented period of slowing down, he had nothing left to give and had no interest in what we could offer.

He had spent his entire life in flight, running so far from what was expected of him that he simply did not know how to stop. Even when he ran out of fuel he kept on running. In the end, he dropped off the edge of the world, his feet barely treading the air as he fell.

On top of it all, I was slipping from his grasp, the last woman in his life whom he had any hold over. However much I challenged him, he could always rely on me to be the admiring mirror that sustained him, the one that reflected him back at twice his natural size. If the spell that had bound me to him broke, like all the others, would he have to finally face himself alone?

I laugh at this now, because I was going nowhere. On the verge of marriage, I was desperate to finally grow up, and yet I was still bound up in my father's fantasy. I was still bewitched from his first poisonous kiss that night I was born. I desired to be consumed, as Kathryn Harrison wrote in *The Kiss*. But love to me meant rejection, and along with rejection came passion – the power my father still had to make me weak. Such a misplaced romanticism.

At the last moment my father booked his flight and came to the wedding. That morning, he arrived dishevelled, and shuffled solemnly around my mother's house, which was soft with scent from the armfuls of old-fashioned garden roses and alive with pre-wedding fuss. He obviously didn't want to be there. He made comments to my brother about how all this, this place, this house that our mum had financed independently, and devoted so many years to, could have been his. Was he really laying claim to a life rebuilt from the ashes he had left? My brother laughed it off. We were so used to his delusions.

But that morning, before my wedding, my brother also tried to keep our father away from me.

When Dad caught a glimpse of me in my dress, tears welled up in his eyes. As I saw him cry, I cried too, and worried that my makeup would run. I took a deep breath and smiled through the tears, smiled when the camera clicked. I am hunched in these photos. His weight on my back. Burdened, in my beautiful dress.

At the Assembly Rooms in Bath, I drifted down the aisle in my dress of lace and net, white as a ghost and my face veiled, my father's lumpen body beside me, his eyes on the floor. In photos he looks scarily like Boris Karloff's monster in Frankenstein. He walked with me but was not really there. I shook beside him, anxious that I would not make it, my independence from him and my departure on this new adventure, my chance of being loved, of being 'normal'. He passed my hand to the man who was to be my husband, but he barely acknowledged us, head down, feet shuffling back to the support of the chair. He did not really give me away, and I was not ready to let him go. He sat next to my mother and her husband in the first row but could not last the short ceremony. He got up halfway through and walked out.

At the celebration, my father always appeared to be alone. He parked himself at one of the tables set up in the garden, heavy and slow; people sat with him and tried to engage but when he failed to respond they drifted away. I moved around the lawn, holding my dress tail, my heels sinking into the soft earth, laughing about the shock of the weather after a night of barely sleeping, sitting in the kitchen with my mum at four in the morning watching through the window the threads of rain. For months we had been deliberating over whether or not to have a marquee and my mum said we didn't need it. 'We will all cram into the house if need be.' Her pioneering can-do nature was contagious and so often right. But I knew, when the rains stopped, that luck was on our side. I would catch a glimpse at my father now and again, hoping to see that he was making an effort to talk, an anxious knot in my stomach tightening. As a deflection, I would offer my glass for a top-up of champagne. When I looked again, his seat was empty. I searched for him. 'Where's Dad?' He had gone, back to the hotel, slipping out without saying goodbye. I felt nothing but sad relief.

When the sun finally broke through the thick cloud, a warm pink glow, we got our photographs, shapes of lace lit like fire, a bright flame of gold, reflections in the tall Georgian windows. In that moment I drifted with a new lightness. I am not hunched in these photos, but standing upright, my features open.

It had been different at my brother's wedding half a decade before. My father had his wife still; his mother was there too, and his sister had come from America. I was single then, no boyfriend, and had stood by his side, as a kind of protector when he was reunited after so many years with my mother's family who had once loved him so much. One by one, they had taken his hand or hugged him. Even my grandfather, who had bailed us out when we almost lost the house. But this time, at my wedding, I was the centre of the show, and there was no time to put my father first. Reflecting back, I see that this probably suited him fine. It freed him to return to his hotel in Bath, to close the door against the demands of an increasingly inhospitable world, and climb onto the bed, take off his socks and fold them into a ball, throw them into the corner, press keys on the remote control and top up his glass.

We had great fun dancing that night, me and all my friends under the canopy of the great Oriental Plane tree, and the next day my father flew back to California. The day after that my new husband and I left for Croatia to begin our honeymoon.

While we were away, we got a phone call. My dad had fallen down the stairs and had broken several vertebrae in his neck. He had ended up in intensive care. The doctors had pumped his stomach because there were so many drugs and so much alcohol mixed up in there. His now ex-wife had flown from New York to be with him, and she called on my brother and me. She, like the butcher, was angry at us for not doing more. *He needs you. You are his children. You owe him that.* My brother with two children and a wife on their family holiday. Me, with my new husband and the fragile makings of a new start.

Our mother defended us with a letter. She had been supportive for so long. She was fond of his second wife, but she loved us intensely and was fed up with our dad's dominance in everyone's lives. I see her as an eagle soaring above, scanning the ground, waiting for the right moment. Convinced our father would have held back certain truths from his second wife to suit his own heroic view of himself, she felt the need to clarify the situation. 'The past informs the present,' she wrote at the start of her letter to his ex-wife, and these words reverberated like the sound of a cymbal.

He had left his children all those years ago. No communication for months on end. He barely knew how bad it was because he never asked. No maintenance. No financial help. But worse was his total lack of interest in his children's daily lives, their schoolwork, friends, hopes and fears. He was always as far away as possible from them.

She spoke of how lucky he had been, despite all this provocation, to have his two ex-wives still at his side, and his children who had never stopped loving him. '*My children have had a mostly absent father, self-centred and unreliable in his promises, while charming with his occasional presence: they now have to cope, far too soon, with a father whose self-inflicted wounds demand they fly more than halfway round the world on borrowed money, ignoring their responsibilities to their own fledgling families in the process.*' She went on to say that my dad had become increasingly inaccessible and self-obsessed and, it seemed now, lethally oblivious to the harm his drinking was doing. '*I think perhaps we have all been too indulgent and tentative in our treatment of him and now have to be more clear-sighted and honest to help to get him to face up to reality after a lifetime of evasion and self-delusion.*' She signed the letter with the following. '*Any understandable anger you may feel does not belong at my children's door.*'

But of course we went. How could we not? We were faced at last with the shocking truth – our dad was in the last stages of alcoholism. If he didn't go into a rehabilitation programme, he was going to die.

While a part of me didn't want to leave the comfortable life I was trying desperately to create, another part was secretly pleased. My father was where I wanted him, alone, at last. I could slip into the gap his wife had left and do what she had failed to do. I would save him. I am now struck by Ted Hughes's translation of Ovid's *Metamorphoses* and the myth of Myrrha, whose incestuous love for her father caused her to transform into a tree that exudes the precious sap through a wound in her bark. This is symbolic of her tears. I did not share these feelings for my father, but like Myrrha, I had a blind obsession, a wilful paralysis. Myrrha's father, unaware of his daughter's feelings, asks her what kind of man she wants her husband to be. She answers, 'One like you.' In the depth of my heart, this was my secret.

When all the lights were out and my mind was ready for sleep, a small voice asked: *Will he finally love me? Will he see how important I am? Can I make him need me?*

I saw my father cry only a handful of times. The day he left us for good, after his escape to India, after he had returned and my mum had refused to share him with his Dutch girlfriend. We four had stood in the yellow-lit hallway at home, darkness outside. My brother and I were crying because we knew that this was the last time. He would never come home again. I was afraid, also, that he would be in danger out there on the road with tears fogging his eyes. That he would crash his car and die.

He cried that last week in Bolinas. At the doctor's, and then when my brother and I would arrive at his house at 5 a.m. just to catch a moment of sobriety before the drinking started again – he leaned up on the crumpled sofa where he slept, gripped his head and sobbed into his hands, desperate with weakness, stripped of all will by the force of his addiction.

I saw him cry in between these two book-end moments at his mother's deathbed, in 2001, just six years before he himself died. She was white and ethereal, like an angel. She shone in the hospice bed. She looked so like a child. She held his hand, and he clapped the other hand over his face, and his big body barked with the pain. My beloved dad.

And he cried that time he visited me a year before my wedding so soon after the scam, when together we went to see my mum in Bath, and he stayed the night. The day before he flew back to the States, to Bolinas and his clapboard house, he stood in my mother's doorway, diminished. I wonder now if he was feeling the weight of returning to his house alone, his wife no longer there, because his face was lopsided with sadness. I cannot recall why he had made this trip, came all that way to see us; it was out of character for him to visit alone. I wonder now if in this moment he was attempting to ask for our help. But when I sat in the light of the window, staring up at him, my star of a dad, I was struck by the tears and how small he suddenly appeared, knocked sideways, floored by how sad he looked. A sorrow bubbled up from deep within me, like blood from a knife wound straight to the heart. I had no control over the tears that flooded out of me. Water down my cheeks, over my chin, across my collarbone. Water drenching my shirt, rushing down my sleeves, and into my socks. 'What is it?' he asked, backing into the wall for balance. 'Stop it, will you? Why do you always do this to me?' Was it my fear for his loneliness, my need to protect him, my inability to do that one simple thing? My knowledge, somewhere deep inside, of where he was heading? That corner of the self that knows only truth. Knowing, but not letting myself know, where this was all going to end.

Once, in Bolinas, I watched a girl dance in the corner of Smiley's, the bar next door to where my dad lived. In my memory it is sunset, a long, drawn-out afternoon of heat and shadows. She is beautiful and her skin is brown, and she moves before a full-length mirror. Her hair is pinned back to reveal thin shoulders and the minute shifts of muscle and bone. The butcher had told me that the girl had been a child actress, and then she went mad. On the surface, she had appeared to have everything, fame, wealth and beauty, and then she lost it all. She set up home in her car. The girl still dances in my mind, to soft country music, all fiddle and slap. She is not aware of anyone watching. She closes her eyes and lets the music carry her to oblivion. I notice her bare feet, and their vulnerability, so delicate and dirty. They are feet that have trudged over nettles up on the stony hills, trampling on old wire fences and brambles, making paths through broken glass and abandoned syringes; they are feet that now feel nothing. 'She stole from your dad,' the butcher had told me. 'He took her in and gave her money and then she broke into the house.'

There were others in the town who he helped. He gave money to the local legend, Tree House John, who lived between trailers and commercial garages, and was ripped off by a load of meth addicts who regularly plied him with booze to steal his social security. Dad helped a friend of the butcher who lived on the shaded side of town, and came over to feast on Dad's food and wine. He looked after the butcher, too, gave her a home and let her drive his SUV. He also left her his credit card each time he went to the dentist to have his teeth pulled out, and she dined out on his money with her friends at the local dim sum.

My dad was drawn to people who were in need, and perhaps this was part of his attraction to this bizarre place. Here he could be the mad king of the ship of fools, the captain of this motley crew, in their muddled search for paradise.

But he had a softness in his heart. I am reminded of his empathy when he was a child, curious at seeing the disfigurement on his dad's uncle's face. I think of the boy at boarding school fearful for all those other little boys. This same boy grew into a man who felt most at home in a clapboard house in a dead-end seaside town attracting the crazed and lost. I am reminded of an old drunk who followed me onto the bus in London and when I saw my father in him, he gave me a maverick wink. 'You think you know me,' it said. I think of the many faces of my dad.

I return to Jung's theory of midlife and the calling to something more restorative like a clear bright light in the distance. He considered it a time when the ego should give way to the universal, so that a person might 'contemplate the deeper significance of human existence'. My father had not been afraid of change – it was admirable how easily he'd transformed his life in his thirties, how he had been able to give up his attachment to the comfort of family and home, and all that was known, in order to embrace what he believed to be a kind of spiritualism, a potential remedy for his soul in those early days. How willing he was to move forward. And yet here, in those last years in Bolinas, he'd got stuck. When middle age should have brought with it its own unique momentum, my father had manoeuvred himself into deadlock.

That lanky boy again, with the blonde blanket of hair, the big blue eyes and the forlorn expression. What was his dream? What did he hope for his life? Did not my father owe him more than this?

Addiction

On my dad's bookshelf in the living room of his house in Bolinas there was a line of brown plastic bottles, and he knew exactly how many pills were in each: sleeping pills, antidepressants, something to numb the pain, something to dampen his urge for alcohol. My brother and I had abandoned our lives and rushed to his rescue. Every day he drew our attention to those pills: how few were left, and how anxious he was about running out. Endocet; Vicodin; Diazepam. So much stronger than anything he would be prescribed in the UK.

'Hey, you've come to visit your old dad!' he'd said when my brother and I arrived with our suitcases at his gate. 'You came all the way from England? For a holiday?' He stood up with difficulty from a chair on his porch, colourless and tortured. I glanced at my brother. *He didn't know we were coming.* I muttered under my breath, 'We should have reminded him when we were at the airport.' But we had been so shocked at the sudden plans once Dad had returned from hospital. He needed looking after and refused to wear his neck brace; his ex-wife was pinning her hopes on us getting him onto a rehabilitation programme. We were stunned by the sudden wrench away from our lives, and anxious about what we would find.

My brother strode forward through the gate, taking stock of our father. 'Come on,' he said, ushering me to follow him. Dad was shrunken and feeble, in an oversized T-shirt. His hair was overgrown and greasy. He shuffled through the screen door and we followed him into the house. The living room was dark and smelt of stale booze, empty bottles lying on the floor, tangled sheets he'd slept on for what looked like weeks, half on and half off the sofa.

'Dad,' I said dropping my bag. 'Let's open the curtains.'

That first day, we drove him to the Family Medical Center to get more pills, despite it being less than five minutes away. We had to, because he could barely walk. I held onto him as he stumbled from the car on trembling legs. Wired with too little sleep, I had too many questions, but I could barely look up from my feet. When I caught a glimpse of him, tears stung my eyes. He was only fifty-nine, yet he looked like death. It had been just one month since Dad was at my wedding, but he had aged a thousand years.

In the waiting room, we avoided the receptionists and their phoney smiles. I sat beside him, putting a reassuring hand on his withered knee while he stared into the near distance. He was not there. My dad was not there. Just a numb drained face, toothless, gums that ground round and round, chewing what was left of his lips. This man seated next to me but miles off inside his own vacancy smelt of urine and booze, of unclean clothes from days of sleeping in the same tracksuit. He had become the man who you make an arc to avoid when coming across him lying drunk on the street.

The women at reception kept staring at us, openly displaying their contempt. I drew closer to my dad, and muttered words of reassurance. I wanted to shout at them. *Fuck off. Look the other way.* I wanted to stand up and accuse this supposedly inclusive small-town community of spitting my father out. *Take it away for your gossip*, I wanted to say. Luckily Dad had no idea what was going on.

When the doctor called us in, our dad sat on the examining couch, which was pumped up so high that his six-foot-man legs dangled beneath him like a child's. He cried. So many tears came out of him, and I wondered if he was crying for the state of his life, but he was crying for his ex-wife. His big hand rubbed the tears from his eyes: 'I miss her,' he said. 'I love her.' The doctor stood in the corner of the room and nodded, made notes on his clipboard and prescribed him more antidepressants. My brother and I, stupefied in the bright fluorescent light, said nothing.

'I need to sleep,' my dad said when we got back to the house. He was sitting awkwardly on a sofa that had collapsed beneath his weight. His tracksuit bottoms were caught up on his calf, exposing the shocking white of his skin. I straightened the covers for him, plumped the cushions.

He watched TV. He drank. He dozed. He made phone calls, repeatedly, to his ex-wife in New York, his energy returning again. 'Honey, the kids are giving me a hard time. They're telling me I'm drinking. I'm not drinking.' I tidied away the bottle that he helped himself to as he lay back on the sofa, the phone held to his ear, a stupid smile on his face. I heard her twitter some sweet words as I walked into the kitchen. There were plates marked with the crust of days-old food. Nothing in the fridge. Vats of cranberry juice on the kitchen table felt inappropriately pink.

When I went back into the living room, my dad was redialling her number. Tutting to himself when she didn't answer. He picked up a different phone – my dad, the trickster – as if a different handset might catch her out. There were three phones, all portable, in various states of charge. Redial. Redial. Redial. 'Everyone's against me. Nobody is listening.'

'The pills,' he said. 'Do I have enough pills?'

My brother and I were too scared to fall asleep, that first night, terrified of what might happen if we let our vigil slip. Our dad had mumbled and groaned in the kitchen as he'd attempted earlier to make us dinner, and brandished a large knife. When he had finally sat down, he was too drunk, and we too upset, to eat anything. As my brother and I, no longer kids, but lying together for safety and comfort in the spare bed, listened to him crashing about downstairs, and to those other drunks out on the street, ejected from Smiley's at closing time, our eyes stretched wide in a house that no longer felt like his. We turned to each other in the near darkness, focusing in on the features we knew, our reassurance, and my brother said, 'I can't sleep here.' He suggested we find a motel.

Each day we visited our father, and each night we moved to different accommodation. In one motel, we slept together in synthetic sheets in a floral bed; in the next we pushed the mattresses side by side, so we could hear each other breathing. We bought massive bags of crisps from the 7-Eleven and drank sugary fizzy drinks. Comfort food. We watched telly and smoked cigarettes. Each morning, jet-lagged, we woke at four.

After sleeping, Dad would be more lucid. There were no lights on in the house, but he left the door unlocked. We would watch him from the doorway, sleeping on the sofa in the stink of old wine, the moving images from the TV reflected on his faded body. We cleared empty bottles and washed dishes, emptied the fridge of old food. Dad's cat, Hope, meowed at our feet, but there was nothing to feed her. She curled her long tail around our legs.

He sat up on his makeshift bed and squinted through the dark when we came in. When he saw us, he cried. That big body, that big reduced body, that hand that now clapped itself over his eyes, the same hand I loved to hold as a child, when I could wrap my palm around just one finger. 'I'm sorry,' he said, crying into this hand. 'I feel so ashamed.'

I made him scrambled egg. Egg was all that was in the fridge. It was all that he would eat. 'It'll help your insides,' I said, imagining it literally binding all that slop inside him. He had hiccups that would go on for hours.

He sat beneath the glow of the table light and spooned it into his mouth, staring blankly into space, egg on his chin, egg on his cheek. I asked if he wanted tea? Coffee? Toast? 'Oh, lovey, you're so nice to me. You've always been so nice to me. You know how to look after me.'

I turned from the sink and offered him more egg. 'I could make you an omelette?' I said brightly, but he was lost to himself again and didn't answer. He was sleepwalking, caught in a day-time nightmare of his own making. There was nothing going on behind his eyes.

My brother would swing from sympathy and sweetness – his eldest child and the son, the boy he had always been so proud of – to anger and a fierce protectiveness of me. Later that day, in the corridor, when our dad had gone back to drinking, he whispered: 'All that bullshit. Saying you're good at this and that – Don't fall for it –'

'He needs help,' I interrupted.

'No,' he said. 'He knows if he says all of that you'll want to stay and help him. He wants you to look after him. That's the only reason he's saying it.'

It did not matter. The embers of my protective love for my father had been stirred into flame. How could he cope on his own? There was no one there to make sure he was eating, or to get him to wash himself and check that he cleaned his clothes. No one there to stop him from drinking.

You know me, my daughter. You're the only person in the world who understands me.

As each day bled into the next, our life back in London grew more distant. My husband's voice on the phone was too light, and his words were too removed. I had no patience for the delay and crackle.

'How is it going?'

'It's difficult,' I said.

'Are you okay?'

I couldn't begin to articulate the horror of what had become of my father, and perhaps a part of me did not want to. But even if I had tried, I could feel the thousands of miles between us, the mass and unfathomable depths of the Atlantic Ocean. Our lives together had only just begun and yet a grenade had landed between us. The man who I had been devoted to all these years was fading into dereliction, and my heart was still with his. It was beyond words: just a deeply powerful, personal sense of protectiveness for my father, for our love, for all that was private between us. I had almost escaped him when, in one desperate last throw, he had reached out and asked me to take his hand. To do so would mean I had to retreat from the possibility of anything else, of my own life, my new marriage. Like a clam, I clamped shut. I did not know what to say to the man who loved me on the other side of the world. 'It's difficult to talk about it,' I told my husband, and so didn't.

'Are you there?' he asked into the silence.

'Yes, I'm here.'

'I thought I'd lost you.'

As the sun rose, my brother and I sat together on the porch and smoked cigarettes while Dad lurched about, in and out of the swing door. 'You're smoking,' he said, and laughed. 'Such a horrible habit. I had no problem giving it up. I smoked and smoked, and then one day I decided I didn't need to anymore. That day I stopped, and I never picked up a cigarette again. You see?' he said hovering at the door. 'Your dad doesn't have a problem. It's you with the problem.' He pointed to me, his legs unsteady. 'If you don't give up that evil weed it will kill you.' Then his face crumpled, and he clasped his hands together and said, 'Why are you smoking?'

'It's nothing compared to what you're doing,' I said, astounded at his deflection. 'Don't shift the blame to us.'

'What do you mean?' he asked, swaying there in the doorway. 'What does that mean?' He seemed genuinely confused. 'I don't smoke!'

'Stop pretending,' I said stubbing out my cigarette. I clenched my jaw, fire in my head.

'What sweetie, what is it? What's wrong?'

'You're drinking already.'

'I don't drink.' But he had a big wet drip down his T-shirt. 'I don't drink,' he said as he started his dance back to the living room, swigging from the bottle he kept at the top of the book-shelf, or maybe it was the one out back, by the bins.

'Just going out with the rubbish,' he'd say with a jubilant bounce in his step, and a barely filled bag in his hand.

'Just going in to check my emails.' There was another bottle in his study.

He left money in an envelope by the front gate. For Tree House John, he said. 'He's a drunk,' he added, with derision. 'He needs money for alcohol,' as if it were a weakness he was able to acknowledge in another but not in himself. But then we spotted the man, with his layers of dirt-black clothes and overgrown hair, returning to leave a plastic bag of wine by the gate. I imagined Dad texting him, squinting at the small letters on his Nokia phone, 'My bloody kids are here. They won't leave me alone.'

We were shocked by the depth of our father's self-deception. At this time, we were completely unschooled in addiction or its therapies. We confronted him about his drinking, speaking plainly to his face, and adamantly he told us that it was not true. Our mission on coming here was to encourage him into rehab, and yet we could not even get him to admit to drinking alcohol. Denial may be a defence mechanism to protect the alcoholic from their blind dependence on something that is destroying their lives, but it is a cognitive failure, too. Fixed denial, like my dad's, could be the result of a neurological inability to grasp the truth. In other words, his brain was addled, the neurons weren't firing properly, he was suffering from structural and ir-reparable brain damage from the amount of alcohol he had been imbibing, together with his nutritional deprivation, not eating and unable to hold anything down. His liver was damaged. He had wet brain.

It was all spinning on an axis. A house of cards ready to fall. It was a nightmare week. The madness in his sudden jubilant mood as he grinned inanely and clapped his hands, his shocking white feet in broken slippers. 'Right, sweeties. You're here for a holiday. We could go into town. We could go to the zoo. Shall we take a trip?' He broke off, went into the garden, came back into the kitchen and then ducked into his study and out again, a fresh wet stain on his T-shirt.

The only time we went anywhere with our father that week was to Berkeley to visit his healer. Dad was insistent that we mustn't be late. 'This guy is a saviour,' he told us. 'A Chinese mystic. The only man who can heal me.' It was a long way: about fifty miles along the motorway, and my brother drove Dad's massive four-by-four, despite the car pulling to the left, and brakes that didn't quite work. On the way, we stopped to pick up his dry cleaning, which was months overdue: a huge collection of designer jackets and shirts, all immaculately ironed, which Dad attempted to pay for with three rejected cards. The bill was a couple of hundred dollars, which my brother finally paid, and carefully folded the shirts into the boot of the car. When we looked around, our father was gone. The car park around us was empty. 'Where is he?' I asked, thinking for a moment he had given up on us.

'He's probably gone for a drink,' my brother said wearily.

We sat in the car and waited for him, and soon he returned, burping strawberry Hooch which he'd found in some local bar. He spent the entire rest of the journey asleep, his body, reduced and childlike, sliding around on the massive leather passenger seat. When we finally reached Berkeley, the healer sent Dad away, saying he'd got the wrong day, so we despondently took the motorway back again.

Back at the house I made him food, but he refused to eat. I saw him peel off his tracksuit bottoms and leave them in a pile on the floor with a sloppy shit in the middle. He did not pause to acknowledge what he had done, was not ashamed. He walked off and left his soiled tracksuit on the floor as if he were a toddler, not yet developmentally capable of controlling his bodily functions.

I cleaned his shit from the corners of the bathroom, smeared all over the toilet seat, the banister and along the corridor. Once I started looking, I found it everywhere. I zapped corners with disinfectant, picked up dust and hair, rubbed dirt from the bath. I swept, washed dishes, cooked, cleared away the empty bottles. I sat through our awkward silences, cried when he cried, and when he started drinking and denying, drinking and denying, I shouted at him: 'You're a liar,' I said, because that is what he was.

We tried to care for our father each day, while he led us on this merry-go-round of horror. My brother went through the pile of paperwork on his desk and had long conversations with the bank. He tried to assess what was coming in and what was owed. Dad's accounts were a mess, and there were so many bills left unopened. Warning letters. Reds.

Back at the motel, I read a book on alcoholism. For the first time I learned that alcohol is a poison, a chemical called ethanol, which is a solvent, to fuel cars. We had long phone calls with his sister, who had been through AA herself, and believed that alcoholism is a disease, that Dad was born with this propensity. She told me that addiction flourished in their mum's family. It was an insider joke that their grandfather could drink sixteen pints at lunchtime, but the repercussions of his addiction reverberated like a drumbeat through the generations. Aged just four, their mother was left alone to look after her two younger brothers while her own mother went out in search of her husband to retrieve him from the pub. Scared by the wind, the little girl fled the house and wandered into a nearby wood and got lost. It took an age for her to be found. She was left abandoned and on her own, frozen with fear in the dark and cold, with the trees whipped by the wind and moaning. There were monsters in the shadows. This anxiety followed my grandmother into adult life and exacerbated her volatile nature, leaving her in the darkness of the irrational. Her fear of the wind never left her.

According to Dad's sister, their own grandmother was tough and controlling, but she was also the caretaker of an alcoholic husband, a man who was not capable of looking after himself. In Al-anon circles this type of controlling nature of family members of alcoholics is characterised as the four Ms – Managing, Manipulation, Mothering and Martyrdom – a shorthand for taking on too much in the fear that without you nothing would get done at all. My grandmother absorbed this from her own mother and then repeated it in her relationships, overly alert to any possibility that her husband might go down the same road of chaos she had experienced as a child, watchful and reproving in her anxiety to put a stop to it before it had even begun.

There was addiction too in the family of my dad's father. Both his uncles owned a successful pharmacy in Cranford where they wrote themselves prescriptions for every kind of upper and downer, and kicked off each day with whisky in their tea. His alcoholic aunt later lived on the seafront in Bognor Regis and harassed her brother, my grandfather, with threatening letters that she would walk into the sea. She drank herself to death, the story goes, and left all her money to a cats' home. My grandfather was an insomniac and used Scotch to get himself to sleep at night. Later, in retirement, he turned to sleeping pills, mixing them with his heart pills and antidepressants in a deadly cocktail.

Like so many other families in their generation, my father's parents had a drinks cabinet on display, full of colourful bottles, paper umbrellas, long twirly glass cocktail sticks, and coloured plastic mixers topped by seductive women in swimsuits. As a teenager, my aunt stole alcohol from the bottles and filled them up with water.

Perhaps Dad didn't stand a chance.

Now, after years of reading and a period of teaching a group of recovering addicts, I believe my father was born with a

predisposition that his environment made worse. He was forever trying to break the bounds of his limitations, and alcohol
became another way for him to expand his world. But it was not
the most successful of his ploys for transcendence. If my father
was the *puer*, the eternal child, then this was his most destructive
regression. To be alcoholic is to check out of everyday tasks,
to pass on life. It is to push people away and choose alcohol
above anything else. My father wanted to be lulled back to the
liquid warmth of his mother, away from the chaos of his life,
where he didn't need to think about anything except sucking on
a bottle.

During that week in Bolinas, Dad threw us out of his house
for challenging his drinking. We could not understand how this
man before us, roaring drunk and surrounded by the evidence,
could continue to deny it. His madness began to infect us. 'Are
we making this up?' The three of us stood on the step, between
the porch and white gate that separated the house from the street,
and all those drunks at Smiley's. My father stood with his back to
the house, my brother and I one step closer to escape. My brother
was shouting, while I cried. He was shouting at his Dad, my
brother six-foot-five, and my father a weak old man.

'Look at what you're doing to her,' my dad said, trying to
deflect my brother's anger, using me as his armour. He squinted
to try to focus, his hands on his knees to steady himself.

'No, Dad,' my brother shouted back, doubling in size. 'It's not
me who's doing this. It's you.' He let all the years of frustration
and pain fire up his words, and he shouted at our father that he
had never faced up to anything. That he had spent a lifetime
running away, blaming Mum, blaming us, blaming anything
and everybody, all to avoid stopping, pausing, listening. 'Look at
yourself!' he shouted. 'Look at what you're doing!'

'Son,' he pleaded. 'Don't say that.'

But look at what a mess he was in.

We left. We walked away from our father and escaped in our
car, out of the drive, out of that town, away from the judging

eyes. My brother with his hands on the wheel blindly taking the roads that led out of nowhere. He said nothing, until he swerved up onto the side of the street and turned to me. 'It's a nightmare,' he said. 'It's useless. We've got to leave. We've got to go. We're not doing any good here,' his face red with pain. But I was so far from leaving.

My brother tried to convince me that it was not our dad in that house in that washed-up seaside town. Our dad had already gone. He had left us all those years ago. Standing on the curb in Hampstead, the three of us, when he told us he had a new name, a new identity, that he was no longer our father. We had not believed him then. We had clung on in our need. Now my brother was trying to cut that final thread and take stock of what our father had set in motion all those years before. 'He is not our dad', he said. The booze had slipped up from behind him like a serpent and had stolen the scraps of what was left.

My brother had rung my mum from Bolinas, she tells me now, and had tried to describe what it had felt like to be there, with him, our dad, drunk and raving in the next room. 'It is like the scariest horror film,' he'd whispered down the phone, 'where you're struggling with a monster, but suddenly you get a glimpse of the person, the real person that you know and love, and it is the most painful and terrible thing.' He had paused, and she let him go on. 'But I know, mum, that it is not real. It is only a ghost of that love. The real love is not there anymore.' This is what my brother felt, but I didn't, not yet.

He turned to me in the car. 'I'm going to book the next flight,' he said. 'You're coming with me.'

I shook my head. 'You can leave me here,' I said.

I would stay and look after him.

Back at home some months later, I spoke to a psychologist friend. When I told her I was frightened of the grieving, she said she believed that I was grieving already and perhaps I had been for most of my life. She also said that he will put out his hand and he will pull you down with him. My aunt had said the same. She had warned me not to be that person who loves uncritically, keeping the place clean, keeping him fed enough, and comfortable enough to continue drinking. I knew all this, and yet I was still prepared to stay. I wonder now if it was easier that way. I had done what was expected of me, and I had stepped into adulthood, but I didn't know if I wanted it. If I continued to love my father with such intensity, I could remain that troubled child and avoid truly loving someone else.

That night our father tried to track us down by phone. He had been ringing the local hotels and had finally got ours. 'Are my children there?' he shouted at the receptionist. 'They're my children. What do you mean they don't want to talk to me?'

The next day, we went back to him, early to try to catch him at his least incoherent.

At first, his local acquaintances feigned concern. Then they started swiping his books, CDs and clothes; someone even took his camera. The house was slowly dismantled around him. The only valuable things they didn't take were what he wore: an ancient Roman signet ring, on his little finger, and his incredibly expensive watch. We quickly realised the reality: Dad was beyond bankruptcy, and his mortgage payments were in arrears. His dependence on alcohol had robbed him of his faculties, his ability to work, his reserves for paying bills. There was nothing left.

We attempted to keep it together, tried to make him understand that he needed help. We grabbed at the fraying thread of his early-morning guilt, but he was lost to us the moment the alcohol entered his bloodstream. My brother held onto the belief that he still had a choice in whether or not he took that first drink, but I feared it was too late. He was so ill and totally incapable of rational thought, which made him incredibly vulnerable.

The next time my brother and I discussed leaving, he challenged me again: 'Don't you see what he's doing? He's never taken responsibility for anything. We're not helping him.' But how could we let our anger at the past affect our care for him now? What if this was our final chance to save him?

My brother quietly reminded me of my husband back in London, my new life, and the chance to create a family of my own. He wanted me to find a way to finally reject our father.

But Dad made it easy for me in the end. He asked us to leave before I could tell him that I wanted to stay. He rejected me again, and in the process he saved me.

We arrived at his house that last day, and he was showered and dressed, his hair combed, the radio on and curtains open. 'I got a leaflet for AA.' My brother and I looked at each other. 'There's this amazing guy who's offered to be my guardian. He's been through it all. He's one of the top guys, and he's taken me under his wing. You've done so much for your dad, Sweeties. You can both go now.' His hand shook as he pushed a strand of wet hair from his forehead.

I asked him, 'Are you sure?' I looked closely into his eyes. 'Dad, I can look after you.'

'You're so sweet to me,' he said again. 'My daughter. But I'm going to get better!'

My brother and I spent the afternoon in San Francisco, where we bought clothes and trainers from Macy's. We made jokes and laughed, attempting to shrug the weight from our shoulders, and yet we didn't believe our own lightness. We knew it was a ruse, a cunning plan of Dad's to make us leave. He was not going to recover. He would never stick with AA. There was no special guardian who would help him give up the booze. He would soon find reasons to look down on all those 'stupid self-obsessed' people. A part of me was relieved that we had been given permission to leave, but the realisation that he did not really need me, not even when he was dying, was heartbreaking. He wanted us to go, so he could be left alone with his drink. Drink was his love now. It was his comfort, his medicine.

We had wondered if he'd caught glimpses of the nightmare of his life and what he had become during those early mornings, when we gently roused him from sleep, after his blood had been filtered a little of poison – even if just a few hours before the steady drip of alcohol contaminated it again. Had he seen clearly in those moments when we stood at the door above his make-shift bed, when he held his head in his hands with shame? Or was it just too painful for him to look?

'I'm tired,' he'd say. It was his mantra. 'So tired.'

I hugged him goodbye. 'Make sure this isn't the last time I see you,' I said, trying to look into his eyes.

I never did see him again.

Weeks later, after we'd gone, our dad was to be caught breaking into the Coast Café in Bolinas in the middle of the night trying to steal booze. He had stumbled through the dark to the opposite side of the road, had smashed a window and set off the alarm, and the police had been called. He had run out of drink and the shops were closed, so the rational next step in his addict's mind was to break in and take what he so desperately needed. The fact that he would never get away with it was irrelevant, the need was now, the result of his actions was no consequence, his rational mind was shot. The police felt sorry for him and let him go with a warning.

'I'm all right. Just calm down. I'm all right,' he had said that week with tears in his eyes, trying to defend himself when we confronted him. 'I am not drinking.' Shouting. 'I AM NOT DRINKING!' We were to have emails like this – hundreds of them. The months before he lost everything and was deported back to the UK. In his emails he begged us for money so he could pay his bills, which we wired via Western Union. My brother sent him hundreds of dollars, all of which was pissed away on booze, this thing he now needed more than water. We sent him money until we could not send it any longer. And the emails turned nasty: *'Fuck off,'* he wrote, venom spilling from his fingertips. *'This is bullshit. I am neither an alcoholic nor any of your fantasy notions – please get out of this theme.'* He told us that his house, his two-million-dollar house, would be left to his ex-wife *'and nothing to you two . . . Successful people, to hell with you.'* He railed. But his house had been mortgaged up to the hilt before the bank then took it away.

Within the year, I was pregnant with my first child. My brother took over the day-to-day management of our father's self-destruction. He had conversations with banks in California, in the UK, and those offshore in Switzerland and Jersey; he dealt with the hire purchase on cars that had gone unpaid, the hospital in San Francisco and the bills that were piling up in the absence of medical insurance. When I asked if I could help, he reassured me that there was no need, he had it under control. So I embraced my chance to create new life, and revitalise my own. I put my hand into my husband's. In those precious months, I felt renewed, empowered, grateful to be given the chance of making us a family. As our baby grew inside me, I focused my energies inwards and looked outwards only to our future.

I wanted to give birth to our baby in water, at home. Water was a gentle transition into a world that no longer felt predictable or safe, and home was controllable. A doctor friend advised us to write a birth plan, but also to be prepared that it might not happen the way we wanted. 'Your baby will have her own agenda. It's up to her in the end.' But into this sea of calm I was working so hard to create, my father was dipping in daily, phoning me in various states of distress, rattling my carefully constructed cage, my hard-won equanimity. I wanted – needed – to be in control. My mother was anxious that I consider all the options, but she stressed continuity of care was what mattered most. When she knew my plan, she suggested she contribute half of the cost of an independent midwife. I said I wanted her to be there.

In our flat our midwife arrived and sat for our introductory session in our leather armchair, spring sun flooding in through the window, turning her blonde hair white. She was calm and authoritative, and I fought my urge to rest my head on her breast.

On the other side of the world, my father had a seizure. He ended up in intensive care. He went through detox and after returning home he had another seizure and was hospitalised all over again. His ex-wife was still ringing him daily and keeping us informed. The hospital report states that he had switched from Jack Daniels to wine and that he was drinking five or six bottles a day.

Over the period of a week or so, when he had gone quiet on us, his ex-wife flew out to him, only to find him lying in his shit on the floor. He had not moved for days, it seemed, other than to throw his credit cards onto the porch so the locals could buy him more booze. She managed to get him into the bath but couldn't get him out again, and so had to call on a police officer from the street. The officer asked my dad what date it was, and he said 1930. We guess he'd experienced a series of mini strokes. From the hospital, at the advice of the doctors, he still refused to go into a rehabilitation programme. He also refused to stay in the hospital and allow them to monitor his alcohol withdrawal. The doctors had no power to hold him against his will. The hospital signed off his release papers with the following: 'Chronic alcoholism with evidence of multiple system injury including brain injury with seizure disorder, liver injury with elevated liver function and social dysfunction due to alcoholism.'

There was no one to go home to. The butcher had left long ago, and another woman, who my dad at some point had taken in, had since been picked up by the police and incarcerated for some undisclosed reason. His ex-wife, in her desperation, sent us brochures for expensive hotels and a private rehabilitation centre, which the doctors advised us against until Dad was prepared to take the situation seriously. 'There's no point in paying crazy prices if your dad still refuses to go.'

I was angry. I told my dad I did not believe him when he said he was not drinking, and he turned nasty. 'Why don't you just go off and have your baby,' he said before hanging up the phone. He then called back the next morning and told me a story. His ex-wife had landed a fantastic publishing deal with Taschen, he said. 'They're going to publish all our books. We're going to make loads of money,' he went on. 'I felt like we had hope again. Then Hope went missing.' I pressed the phone closer to my ear to listen. 'I don't know how it happened, maybe someone left the door open, but Hope left and was nowhere to be found. And I was really sad about this, because I had grown quite attached to Hope and I didn't want to lose her.' It sounded so bizarre, like Dad was existing in some alternative reality, until I realised he was talking about his cat. 'Then, just now, she returned. Twenty-four hours later Hope came back.' He said with a smile in his voice.

'Ah, that's good Dad,' I said, not sure how he wanted me to react.

'I thought you might be interested in the symbolism of that story for your novel–' Dad said.

Then he talked about love and how it is the only thing that keeps him going, his love of those people who are closest to him, and how he loves me, and I am the centre of his world – *my wonderful daughter.* So proud of you, he said, tears breaking through his voice. It made me cry, even though I had been here before. 'I should go now,' he said suddenly, with me crying and spluttering down the phone. 'I'll be churning you up with all this talk.' He hung up the phone, leaving me a mess on the floor. My father had two heads. The monster and the child. The monster and the trickster. The monster and the fucker. The sins of my father. A Master Manipulator.

Throughout my pregnancy, he called me every day, the sharp ring of the phone cutting through our marshmallow world. Sometimes I cried and sometimes I held the receiver away from my ear. But I always picked up. He never asked about my pregnancy, and I never told him. I was going through the motions, showing I still loved him, but a part of me was hardening off, guarding myself and my family. Instinctively I kept that energy locked inside, for the baby, for our new life. It was needed for all the challenges to come. It was easier, somehow, to cut off emotionally from my father in order to care for this new child growing inside me than it had been to care solely for myself.

But like a curse on my happiness, we had a surprise visit from a wicked witch from my past. During a midwife visit we were presented with a list of our local antenatal teachers, and one name sprang off the page. The same name of the woman who had been my mother's antenatal teacher and friend when she was pregnant with me. My heart jumped into my throat, blood to my cheeks. This woman was now presented to us as our local childbirth support thirty years later. Placing my hand on my belly and feeling the fragile new heartbeat of my unborn baby, I felt the gravity of the betrayal by her and my father. She had betrayed my mother at a time when she was most vulnerable. But worse than that, she had broken the sisterly bond between them, that women look out for women.

I held the list in my hand and glanced at my husband. With this tender new baby growing inside me, I felt all the usual intensity of passion and protectiveness, yet a new feeling had bolted to the surface. One that felt deeply personal and private. It was a surprising and overwhelming fury.

She was a shadow in my father's eyes the first time he looked at me, the night I came into the world, and she was here again when I was facing the biggest challenge of my life, giving birth to my first baby and entering motherhood, grasping resolutely at happiness and stability. Her betrayal was unforgiveable.

A few years later, my midwife, who had become a friend, invited me to a screening of a documentary she had taken part in while working in a birthing centre in India, and it happened to be at this woman's house. I considered my life was stable enough to go. Travelling there, I imagined I might even be brave enough to confront her, but when she answered the door I was surprised at my shock of vertigo. She was small and pinched and didn't recognise me, so I reminded her of my mother's name, when she blushed, rather flustered, and invited me in. The corridor of the house appeared dark and long, and it wavered with my sudden broken breath. There were guests in the living room, flashes of colour and crashes of sound, but she led me to the basement. I touched the walls as I followed her, trying to steady myself, to push them back, their undulating form. Down the stairs I came into a dark kitchen, and my head filled with a sudden fury, a train crash of old pain. All I heard was my heart, surprising in its fierceness, its ache and cry.

She must have been anxious because she would not stop talking. She mentioned my mother's name to her husband who sat at the kitchen table. 'Do you remember?' He nodded and stared, his face caught in a thought, a little too long. I stood there, unable to speak. I might have nodded to her questions, my voice might have been heard, but to me it was as small as a bird's.

Returning home, I phoned my mum and cried, not just because of the ghosts of the past that seeing this woman had called forth, but all the different sadnesses that had happened since, the mistakes made and words that had got caught in my throat, so much unexpressed, and how my father's ghosts kept following me, so alive still in the present. How a key would turn in my brain, and deep down I still blamed myself for everything. Then a week or so later, Mum did the most unexpected thing. She wrote to this woman. Her letter began that I had recently turned forty and it had made her think of my birth all those years ago. She wrote she had been grateful to her for being a good friend, for being her mentor and childbirth support. My mother wrote, *I was so touched when you thought to clean my kitchen while I was in hospital giving birth to my beautiful daughter.* But she mostly wanted to tell her that she knew about her affair with her husband. That he had told her some years later. *I want you to know that I know*, she wrote. She added that I had returned from her house

in distress and that it had made her realise that she had to confront this herself and not leave me to cope with a grief that was
not mine.

My mother needed to take the burden from me, but she also
knew how secrets and silence disempower, and she needed to
take back her power.

At the beginning of October 2006, less than a month after
my daughter was born, my father arrived in England in a wheelchair. We had been told he was in need of hospital care. My
brother and mum and her sister, who was a nurse, met him at the
airport and took him to a cottage hospital in Devon. I stayed at
home with my tiny daughter.

Six months later he was dead.

A sweet young policeman came to my mother's door in Bath
to give us the news.

A week after our father died, my brother sat in the morning
light of my mother's sitting room with Dad's bag open on his
lap, and his broken slippers at his feet. I stood in the doorway,
one foot in and one foot out. There were notebooks in the bag,
poems, diary entries, an unfinished manuscript for his second
novel and his proposal for *Dousing the Flame*.

In one of the inside pockets there was a mobile phone. My
brother switched it on, surprised to find it still had power. He
put our Dad's voicemail on speakerphone, so we could hear his
voice: *I'm sorry I can't get to the phone. Please leave a message.* There
were eight new messages that hadn't been listened to. They were
from his ex-wife. 'Hello, my darling,' she said in a broken voice.
She paused. My brother looked over at me. 'I just wanted to hear
you,' she said. 'I want to tell you that I miss you. That I love you.'
She had phoned him after he had died, repeatedly, to listen to his
voice. To hear it again and again.

My father would not have wanted his ashes to be blown into
the sea off Felpham Beach in Bognor Regis. He hated the place

where his parents grew old and more neurotic, its muted parochialism, the smell of death wafting through the hedge-lined dead-end streets. He had avoided visiting, resisting any reminders of his mundane foundations, but also of what awaits us all. But where else could we throw his ashes? Italy was long ago, a time when he was in the grip of a guru who distorted his views. Islington? He had left us there. And America had killed him. This is what my brother and I believed. So we scattered them at Felpham Beach regardless. Still too shocked to think of him; too stunned by the sudden whip of his self-destruction. So hurt, still, and so angry. We stood down from the concrete concourse where, as children, we had walked so many times with his parents, mostly without him. And we threw his ashes into the sea. The ashes blew at us and they covered my sleeve. I glanced back at my brother and together we laughed.

In the quiet of years since passed, I now wonder whether he would have been happier with his ashes in the sky above Hampstead Heath, where he had walked his dogs. In the slow hours reading back the personal writings he wrote, I see how much he loved Tuscany. Its tall swaying cypress trees, and the morning sun flooding into the villa from all sides blurring the edges of his uncertainty.

In *Promise of Dawn*, the novel my father wrote four years before he died, he models himself on his main character, Gideon, and his ex-wife on Nicki, Gideon's wife, who despite being dead, watches him like a guardian angel. They communicate in another dimension, somewhere between life and death. Together again, they travel back to Italy: *'The contrasts in Tuscany are blazing hot summer and Arctic winter, iron and gold, tired and passionate, deep day and lightening-night. The spring is awakening, the fall poetic; there is silence in the air of the mornings.'* I am touched by his nostalgia for this slow, undemanding and sensuous place.

'When you die you will pass through that veil, and we will be together again in the same body, as one . . . there are no different realms, only the same realm – one world, one universe, one place.'

When my father, in his imagination, is in Italy with his wife, he searches out the peace – simple and undisturbed: *'We felt small there, and alone, a good feeling in a way, for we could indulge our appetite for one another's talk sitting on the bed. I forgot my fantasies, my fears, sometimes, and then we were happy.'*

The Return

Each year we go to the same place in Cornwall. A private estate with a collection of coves and houses along the coastline. In the summer we camp, and for the past four years we have also stayed over New Year, in a small, thatched cottage with an open fire. We go as a family, me, my two children, and now my partner too. On occasion, before the end of my marriage, I visited alone. I thought up an idea for a novel here one autumn, and then returned the following winter to write it. Over the years, this particular place in the furthest western tip of the country has become a kind of spiritual home. It has witnessed important turning points in my life and has helped me find a way back to myself.

I visited alone in February in the aftershock of the 2014 storms. I stayed in a house perched on a lonely headland that looked out on the sea. The only source of heat was a woodburning stove, and there was intermittent electricity from a small wind-mill that clattered and swayed outside the bedroom window. It was brutal that winter: even having a wash was a chore, just a dribble of a cold-water shower in the toilet cubicle and a hot-water ceramic bath exposed to the elements outside. Thrown up as a wartime lookout and barely upgraded since, the house moaned in the wind and cracks in the windows let the water in. That first night, I could barely sleep for the wind that shook the house, pummelling the windows. At times it felt as if the house and I might be picked up and thrown into the sea. I heard voices through the stairs, chattering through my head, from the pitch-black outside, and the mud track that led to a vertiginous drop. I buried my face in my pillow, pulled up the duvet. I was still married then, but deeply unhappy. Had I been looking to punish myself for failing to make things work, I could not have chosen a better place; but this was more a visceral need to strip back to the bone, to see what I was made of beneath, whether shell or stone.

There is a circular walk which skirts the few houses dotted along the cliff-line, and stutters further down to the low-lying clusters of rocks that reach out to sea. You can take the well-trodden path along the top, or the one down below, less used, that curves against the dark rock, like a dragon's tail at rest. I like the risk of this path, how at times it goes right to the edge of the precipice, with a hard, black drop beneath to waves that suck and thrash the jagged outcrop. There are rabbit holes, and dips that trick your feet. The drop is precipitous.

That year, I stood there in my raincoat and mittens, the wind stinging my eyes, and marvelled at my precariousness. Like Myrrha 'torn between her fear of death and the fatigue of living', I knew not what to hope for. What if I was taken for a moment by an impulse so great that I jumped? There was nothing to stop the momentum of rolling down the grassy hill, faster and faster, over the edge, smashing onto the rocks beneath, to be sucked away by the raging sea. There is always the potential for surprise here, even when it is calm. The sea winks with its diamond shards of light and its deceptive regularity, and the sun and wind can be blinding. The dragon might wake up, his massive tail holding the tension of millennia lifting and slamming and cracking the rocks beneath. Or what if, like Myrrha, I was frozen in time, transformed into a wind-shocked tree? 'The earth enclosed her legs; roots slanted outward from her toes; supported by those roots, a tall trunk rose.' I braced my legs that winter and felt the earth yield beneath my boots.

In the calm and still of the morning chill, I ran the outdoor hot-water bath and lay beneath the birds circling up and above, my skin as white as the sky, and in one desperate breath I held the sweet air deep in my lungs. For years I had longed for something elusive and unreal, bound by the fantasy of the ideal, suffering from the inevitable rejection, and my guilt. I had hidden all my true feelings from my good husband, self-persecution followed by withdrawal. We were both sick to the bones with the distance that had grown between us, and I could no longer tolerate that same oscillating pattern from childhood. An energy that was up there in the high quiver of the clouds, not down here in the bass notes of my heart, where it mattered. I felt it like an illness in my body and was so scared it would kill me if I did not walk away.

During the dark months when my husband and I started to disentangle our lives, I found myself ringing around local drug and alcohol recovery services, offering my time voluntarily to teach creative writing. I had no idea why this felt like the right time to do it – it was not rational when the weight had shifted so immeasurably towards me having to stand on my own for the first time since becoming a mother, needing to find new ways to earn a living. But there was something driving me towards it, something that I had no real control over. When it all fell into place so easily, it felt fortuitous. What followed was a transformative nine months, with Arts Council funding behind me, which culminated in a nationwide callout and an anthology of recovery stories, *A Wild and Precious Life*, by those who had been in the group as well as other emerging writers. In the end it was life changing for so many, and for me.

I had been warned by my supervisor at the recovery service that the biggest challenge of teaching a group recovering from addiction was retention, because of the chaos that so often surrounded them. I worked hard to keep my hopes in check, but we had a solid group of six or more who turned up each week. They came to the centre to see their key workers and therapists but also to take part in abstinence programmes. For some, it was the first time they had faced a life without alcohol or drugs. This meant different things to different people. Some were eager to write about their pasts; others simply sat there and cried, rivers of liquid pouring out of them like a dam had been opened, years of defences broken down. I learned that alcohol and drugs are inhibitors, and often their absence brings catharsis, a surrender to the repressed pain perhaps, but also a reawakening, and a chance to start again, and to build a life with more solid foundations.

I led a number of group exercises, in order for the confident writers to support those less so, and together we produced art. In one particular exercise we wrote about our keys, what they locked up, or unlocked, the keyrings we kept and why, what they meant to us in our daily lives.

One of my students, Susie, wrote this: _Blue stone keyring. Swimming Hackney Lido_ _Boy kick splashing in my face with wondrous smile. A little dive under plastic line-rope and up with hair sleek, back swimming and happy kicking. Aeroplane up there in the blue. Where are you going? Oh, take me with you. Girl gliding by, her elegant neck moving like a poem._

Many in the group saw the symbolism of a key leading them to somewhere new, but protecting them, too. Inevitably the writing also brought us home.

I was particularly struck by Susie. The first time I met her was when my supervisor and I were recruiting and we took part in the weekly choir. She stood tall, her hair long down her back, and sang with such passion and commitment, her eyes closed, and it moved me that she was so present in the moment of singing, ready to give herself to its transcendent power. She was not remotely self-conscious, more lost to a private bliss. She was keen to join the writing group, and after a few sessions came with her notebooks, placing them on the table in front of her, pages of black scrawl, writing after writing, a lot of it crossed out, on scraps of paper that had little order. My image of this notebook now is of her cradling it in her arms, as if it were a very precious part of her. When she read out in class, both my supervisor and I were in awe of her talent. She had the ability to get straight to the heart of what mattered to her – her warm and loving upbringing in a big rambling town house with many siblings; her fragile mother; her friendship with an Indian boy at school; the devastation of her beloved brother's suicide. She held the room with her husky voice and pacing, keeping us enthralled by the surprising words that only she could have found, that only she could have made work. This was talent like I had never known.

But she had spent most of her life dependent on either heroin or alcohol, almost forty years of addiction. She told me about the first time she injected. She had been a talented actress, and had just started drama school, excited to have discovered how good she was, but also frightened of failing, and she was grieving her brother's recent suicide. She decided one day to go to a man's house whom she knew could get hold of heroin and she asked to try it. It was as simple and as shocking as that. She was hooked from that first time, and then when she tried to give it up years later, she transferred her addiction to drink. Her health was not good, but she came to most classes; if she ever missed a session it was because she had a doctor's appointment, and she would tell me in advance. I was struck by her commitment to recovery: aged sixty, her health compromised, no job, no children; but she still had a large and supportive family and felt so lucky to have them. This was enough of a reason for her to get well again. I knew how difficult it was for her. For all her curiosity, vitality and charisma, she carried the ghost of her addicted self like a heavy, weather-worn coat.

During my time teaching there, I often asked myself why – why was I doing it? I knew I wanted to understand addiction better. I wanted to know why I had been so powerless to make a change to my dad's life. I realise now that it was also important for me to see what recovery looked like, that it was possible when my father had so spectacularly failed.

Susie helped me. I brought many texts to the classroom and she was particularly interested in *A Trip to Echo Spring: Why Writers Drink*, in which Olivia Laing threads a kind of biography of six literary legends – Raymond Carver, John Cheever, Ernest Hemingway, Tennessee Williams, John Berryman and F. Scott Fitzgerald – and studies their relationship to drinking. Laing is careful not to fall for the trope of the glamorous drinking and writing lifestyle, balancing it with its chaotic reality, its private tragedy and the mess it brought to these men's lives, the fights, the illness, the catastrophic early deaths. Discussing the book in class, Susie was interested in the question of whether I thought alcohol was not helpful after all to creativity? I suggested that because these men were particularly talented, they could get away with it when they were young, but alcohol is a poison and consuming any toxin over a long period of time would inevitably take its toll. Drink might act as a stabiliser to the intensity of feeling, but you could also equally say it helped you disappear from the world, ducking out, as my father had so often done. It took the edge off feeling and therefore compromised the finest perceptions. I spoke of the need for clarity, that writing well in my opinion meant facing up to things with courage, thinking clearly and deeply, while allowing oneself the ability to fall into reverie and yet also being alert to all the meaningful associations made. I wondered if drinking, for most of us, obscured this.

I reflected on what alcohol does to me, how it blurs the lens, how I had noticed not so long ago that when I had a glass of wine before watching a film it prevented me from fully engaging, from fully feeling, from being fully present in my life – open to the signs, the opportunities for both beauty and for pain.

One day, Susie came to class and told me of her revelation that she wrote better sober than drunk – it was the first time she had realised this by diving into that big-paged notebook and reading back her words from different periods in her life and comparing them. After one of our classes she had found herself on a bench in London Fields gripped by a sudden flooding need to put words on the page, and so many words at that; but better, still, she had a strong sense that what she had written was good. This was a new feeling for her. A deep engagement with her craft, which had given her a rush of adrenalin, a buzz like no other. I knew, then, why I had felt compelled to come here. If I could make a difference to one person's life it was worth it, and it had already healed something in me.

I remember my father saying to me with his typical arrogance that he didn't bother reading fiction, even though he had spent most of his adult life writing 'the next bestseller' but having great difficulty trying to find a publisher for it. He declared that his reason for not reading other writers was because so many of them were shit. But it was my father's words that were evasive. It was he who hid behind pretentious poetics. The trickster. The fraud. My mother always said he was insubstantial somehow, it was so hard to get to the core of him, to what he really felt about anything, 'like biting on a pillow'. I had been so disappointed that the one time he had the chance to write something truthful, in his memoir on being an alcoholic, he had ventriloquised himself through the puppet of another person's life.

My brother kept the Mulberry bag, and I kept what was in it. Dad's plastic folder of writing, which he referred to in those last months of his life. I had looked in this folder many times, but for some reason I had failed to see everything that was in it. I took out an envelope and turned it upside down, and a few things fell out: order stubs from the B&B where he stayed, *vodka, chicken nuggets and chips*; his driving licence; and his Green Card. There was also a comb with wisps still of his hair. I looked again at his proposal for *Dousing the Flame*. I read it more closely this time. To give him credit, he had admitted to using the diary of an-other man, and he was honest about not differentiating between the two voices, that he wanted their stories to blend into one. I wonder, though, on reflection, whether this was simply because he didn't have enough to write about on his own account, as he resisted so resolutely investigating his personal plight, and was uncomfortable with the focus being solely on him – especially if it was less than adulatory. It was obvious to me which of the entries belonged to my father and I was relieved to find they were honest.

Bolinas, March 3rd 2004
It's been a long time since I felt myself. I was ready to put my thoughts down, but alas not now. Barking, Barking, barking, soon to be sober – one fine day uncanny – photo poem sad. On reflection I did cook one of my fave dishes – spinach, lamb, garlic, honey, onion, olive oil and trusty pots [potatoes] – 8.02pm woops (cut my hand)

Ilfracombe, October 16th 2006
Expecting the worst and getting the best. Distrust – all my life I never trusted the ones I was closest to, because I didn't trust myself – I am 'bad' beneath it all, beneath the surface, and obsessive about it, so every event that doesn't live up to my expectations brings fear, even if the outcome is positive EVERY BLOODY TIME!!

Today is windy and threatening rain, but looks OK. Waiting for A's parcel with swiss chocolate and a little money and of course it doesn't come – the watched pot again, still only simmers. Who is teaching me this? When this comes I can go back to the library and buy myself a packet of chocolate digestives – NOT FUCK-ING VODKA!! One addiction – my work, was interrupted by another, alcohol, like a busy road of madness, vehicles colliding.

November 4th 2006
There's a window in my dry house room which is perpetually open wide and scares me as it represents the final fall. It is like an outside version of the inner cataclysm. I keep away from it with the curtain closed at all times, but it is surrounded by bad

dreams and nightmares. I will get out of this place but not by the second floor window!! Keep it simple, wash hair, body clean, neck and back pain quelled, telephone will work soon and I can talk through these insanities in moments to come.

What if my father was right, and I was the only person who really knew him? While I had secretly hoped it to be true, I also guarded myself with my belief that Dad said it because it was something I wanted to hear. His earliest lesson at his doting mother's knee: *tell her what she wants to hear and she will be happy and love me.* It was his way of binding people to him. But what if I did know him better than anyone else? In a previous incarnation of this book I named it *Starman*, because I was convinced by the end of writing it that I had been given the gift to know my father – the only one to see the Starman in him, what Shakespeare called the 'glassy essence', that elusive diamond that twinkles in all of us like a jewel, to be glimpsed if we look closely enough. The authentic, empathetic self. Perhaps his failure to be the father I needed him to be was simply because he could not abandon the seven-year-old self. My father had to put his arms around his tiny trembling shoulders, because no one else would.

But then I realised I was not seeing clearly enough, had never really until now. Thinking of him in epic mythological terms trapped me still in his thrall, as I had been my entire life. The thought that he was innocent, powerless, and that he had behaved the way he did only because bad things had happened to him. My father, the pathetic fool, the victim of everyone else's expectations. He had been misunderstood all his life and here I was contorting myself and my own truth to finally excuse him. It was what he wanted, after all.

But what of all those opportunities to make a change? As my mother had put it in her letter to his second wife, he had two intelligent women stand by him his entire life, he had his children who would have done anything for him, and once upon a time he also had friends, and a home, and a career, and money, and success. Yet it was never enough. He never chose us, even when he was dying. My mother invited him for Christmas to meet my daughter, his latest grandchild, but he would not come. And yet I still looked up to him, my North Star, with light sparkling in my eyes.

But my father was not a Starman. One night in a fitful sleep two words bubbled up from my consciousness: Bad Dad. I woke up asking myself, how does a man drop so rapidly from such heights? Starman was what he wanted. Bad Dad is what he was. The realisation of this sat solemnly in my stomach. My parent is a bad person is not an easy thought, because where does that leave me?

When I was a child, I liked to press my face to my father's belly, which was round and firm. I fell into a trance in his arms, into the realm of sleep without sleeping. I was enchanted and comforted. He rocked me, and I returned to the safety of the cradle. We still dance together. When I listen to David Bowie's 'Starman' in the car, I let myself indulge. In my mind we are dancing, laughing, holding each other close. He is in my heart in these moments, and it is still a comfort for me to enter into this fantasy. Who could blame me? At my father's cremation, a part of me had gone with him. I slipped into his pocket, and lay with him, feeling the heat, a slight white part of me, in among the bone, skin and hair. I blew out of the chimney with the dust and the ash and hovered there, the two of us caught on a breeze. *There's a starman waiting in the sky.* I searched him out, because I needed him, but I also wanted that search.

Perhaps my brother was right that the only way to stop the pain is to cut off and walk away. But there are lots of different ways of looking at it, and I am still not sure if any one of them is right. What I do know is that being the daughter of a liar has made me honest; I know how important it is to wipe the smear from the glass. When I am asked a question, I hesitate because I want to find the right words. When I write I want to be ac-curate; I want to capture the specificity of experience. I want to live and love honestly and with all my heart open. But I also want to engage with those people who are different from me, because I want to be challenged and I want to understand what sometimes feels inexplicable. Is this the gift my father gave me? I am the only person to understand him not in order to forgive him, but in order to forgive myself for trying. I stand straight and blow the dust of his earthly remains from my arm, those bits of incinerated skin and bone that clung on when we tried to throw his ashes into the sea.

That coat still hangs in my wardrobe, its sleeve rubbing on all the other sleeves, or maybe I washed it and every last grain of him out of the fibre of my being.

Now my partner joins me in Cornwall, and together we walk the narrow path towards Cudden Point, beneath a ceiling of laburnum, thrown from blinding light to sudden shade. We walk in single file because we have to. There are spots of light through the foliage, moving circles across the sun-baked mud underfoot, flashing through my eyes. There is no sound but the steady pad of our feet as they move through this circular cavern, and the swoosh of foliage against a knee or arm. The wind is someplace else. That tempestuous world has become obscured by the canopy of thorn and bush; we can't even hear the sea. He clasps his hands behind his back as he walks and wiggles his fingers for me to touch them.

At the gate we stop, and the world opens up, surprising in its beauty, every time, grey and shimmering. A cargo boat is hazy on the horizon, and St Michael's Mount sits proud and handsome like a floating castle. In the field before us rabbits dart across the spongey grass and duck into hiding.

Further on we walk, and over the hills and mounds the view expands until it is on all sides. Nothing but sea and sky and the craggy end of the land. The evening sun is insistent, spilling its magic on the world, releasing scents of sleepy camomile. We continue along the circular path, with the dragon at our back, and the sun sheds the last of its warmth. Tall shadows form and the barbarism returns in its moving giant silhouette. At a promontory, with no one in sight, we find the last of the sun and we snatch it for a honey-scented hug.

The grass has turned pale yellow to sand, the heather more lilac than grape. It has been a long and forgiving summer. Later we will swim deep, bobbing in our wetsuits; we'll look up to the cottage that sits perched in a bed of sea grass like feathers, where we dream of holidaying in future years. The pockmarked rock, and slices of granite through slate, feels cool and weather-worn beneath our stone-hardened feet as we pad back up the path.

We will do this walk again. Together, the two of us, and sometimes four, but I will also do it alone. I will take my time, reduced by its magnificence; my mind lost to my senses, entwined and yet flowing; what I see out here merged with what I feel. I will be free from everything. A woman at the window of the little house that looks out at the sea, at the slice of gold through the horizon. She has a notebook in her hand, and a candle is lit once the view turns charcoal. A woman in the hot-water bath, beneath an infinite sky, watching the swifts and swallows as they form circles up there in the light. Alone, just her, the rock and the sea, which continues to shift, its colour changing, jade to silver to grey. The sun glows gold in that moment like a benediction, and she feels her aloneness, but no fear. Not anyone's wife, not anyone's mother, not anyone's daughter.

I will slip out on the ridge of the hillside and I will cry again at the precipitous drop, at my instinct, both for light and for dark, and the certainty and precariousness of all that.

Sources

Literary influences

A Lover's Discourse, Fragments, Roland Barthes, translated by Richard Howard, published by Hill and Wang, a division of Farrar, Strauss and Giroux, 1978

Four Quartets, T.S. Eliot, published by Faber & Faber, 2001

My Life in Orange, Tim Guest, published by Granta, 2004

Tales from Ovid, Ted Hughes, published by Faber & Faber, 1997

The Common Reader, Virginia Woolf, published by Vintage Classics, 2003

The Complete Poems and Plays of T.S. Eliot, published by Faber and Faber, 1969

The Illustrated Strafford Shakespeare, published by Chancellor Press, 1982

The Kiss, Kathryn Harrison, published by Fourth Estate, 1997

The Patrick Melrose Novels, Edward St Aubyn, published by Picador, 2004

The Tempest, edited by Virginia Mason Vaughan and Alden T. Vaughan, published by Bloomsbury, The Arden Shakespeare, 1999

Psychoanalysis, trauma and addiction

Boarding School Syndrome, Joy Schaverien, published by Routledge, 2015

How to Read Freud, Josh Cohen, published by Granta, 2005

In the Realm of the Hungry Ghosts: Close Encounters with Addiction, Gabor Maté M.D, published by Vintage Canada, 2012

Learning from Experience, Wilfred R. Bion, published by Routledge, 1984

Memories, Dreams, Reflections, C.G Jung, Fontana Press, published by Harper Collins, 1995

The Body Keeps the Score: Mind, Brain and Body in the Transformation of Trauma, Bessel van der Kolk, published by Penguin, 2015

The Confusion of Tongues: A Return to Sandor Ferenczi, Miguel Gutierrez-Pelaez, published by Routledge, 2018

The Interpretation of Dreams, Sigmund Freud, published by Wordsworth Editions, 1997

The State of Affairs: Rethinking Infidelity, Esther Perel, published by Harper Collins, 2017

The Trauma of Birth, Otto Rank, published by Kegan Paul, Trench, Trubner and Co., Ltd. 1929

Traumatic Narcissism, Relational Systems of Subjugation, Daniel Shaw, published by Routledge, 2014

Spiritualism

Life of Osho, Sam, published by Sannyas, 1997

Love, Freedom, Aloneness, The Koan of Relationships, Osho, St Martin's Griffin, New York, 2001

Sex Matters, From Sex to Superconsciousness, Osho, published by St Martin's Griffin, New York, 2002

The Bhagavad Gita, by Swami Chidbhavananda, published by the Secretary, Sri Ramakrishna Tapovanam, Tirupparaitturai, Tiruchirappalli Dist., Tamil Nadu, 1982

The Man Who Wanted to Meet God: Myths and Stories That Explain the Inexplicable by Shantanand Saraswati, published by Bell Tower, 1996

The Orange Book, The Meditation Techniques of Bhagwan Shree

Rajneesh, published by Ma Anand Sheela, Rajneesh Foundation International, Rajneeshpuram, Oregon, 1980

'The Spiritual Economy of Nightclubs and Raves: Osho Sannyasins As Party Promoters in Ibiza and Pune/Goa', by Anthony D'Andrea, *Culture and Religion*, volume 7, 2006

Film and audio

Child of the Commune (*Communekind*), a film by Maroesja Perizonius, 2004

This Jungian Life, with Deborah Stewart, Lisa Marchiano and Joseph Lee, https://thisjungianlife.com/

Wild Wild Country, Netflix documentary series, directed by Maclain Way and Chapman Way, 2018

Acknowledgements

This book has been a long journey for me, and I was so lucky to land two people who believed in it with such conviction. Thank you to my agent Cathryn Summerhayes for being so clear in your vision, and my editor Jenny Lord, whose perceptive and sensitive editing has astounded me.

Particular gratitude to Julia Bell, Gillian Stern and Marina Benjamin who have helped me craft this memoir at various stages and have been champions of the book. Also to first readers Isabel, Nova, Jess, Robin; and mostly my mother, Jane, for your keen eye and generosity in sharing your history and stories.

Thank you to the Royal Society of Authors for a hardship grant, which allowed me to continue writing through the pandemic.

Thank you to Gulab, Maroesja, Deva and Kristen for conversations about Bhagwan and his movement. I am also grateful to Lisa Marchiano for your help in guiding me to certain texts, and for hours of inspiring podcasts with Deborah Stewart and Joseph Lee, *This Jungian Life*.

Love and gratitude to my mother and brother for supporting me in writing this book, and for staying steady when emotions were running high! My children, Dora and Arlo, for your love and patience. Thank you also to Caroline for taking the time to revisit childhood memories, however difficult. Also to the two Nicks, Nick Ostler for your intellectual interventions and to Nick Steel for your continued support and belief in me. Zoe, of course, for your constancy and calm, and for holding the fort with London Lit Lab when the writing took over. And finally, I could not have written this book without Robin at my side; thank you for our amazing conversations and literary inspiration, and for being the reason I had to re-enter this story so I could finally set it free.

About the Author

Lily Dunn is a writer, teacher and lecturer in creative writing and narrative non-fiction at Bath Spa University. She is the author of one novel, *Shadowing the Sun*, and co-editor with Zoe Gilbert of *A Wild and Precious Life*, an anthology of recovery stories.